The Economics of
Public Issues

Eighteenth Edition

Roger LeRoy Miller
Research Professor of Economics
University of Texas–Arlington

Daniel K. Benjamin
Clemson University, South Carolina and
PERC, Bozeman, Montana

Douglass C. North
Washington University
St. Louis, Missouri

P9-CSE-505

PEARSON

Boston Columbus Indianapolis New York San Francisco Upper Saddle River
Amsterdam CapeTown Dubai London Madrid Milan Munich Paris Montreal Toronto
Delhi Mexico City Sao Paulo Sydney Hong Kong Seoul Singapore Taipei Tokyo

Editor in Chief: Donna Battista
Executive Editor: David Alexander
Sr. Editorial Project Manager: Carolyn Terbush
Editorial Assistant: Patrick Henning
Director of Marketing: Maggie Moylan
Marketing Manager: Lori DeShazo
Marketing Assistant: Kim Lovato
Managing Editor: Jeff Holcomb
Sr. Production Project Manager: Kathryn Dinovo

Sr. Manufacturing Buyer: Carol Melville
Art Director: Jayne Conte
Cover Art: Fotolia
Full-Service Project Management: Cenveo®
    Publisher Services/Nesbitt Graphics
Printer/Binder: Edwards Brothers Malloy
    Jackson Road
Cover Printer: Lehigh-Phoenix Color/Hagerstown
Text Font: Times LT Std

Credits and acknowledgments borrowed from other sources and reproduced, with permission, in this textbook appear on the appropriate page within text.

Library of Congress Cataloging-in-Publication Data
Miller, Roger LeRoy.
  The economics of public issues / Roger LeRoy Miller, Research Professor of Economics University of Texas, Arlington, Daniel K. Benjamin, Clemson University, South Carolina and PERC, Bozeman, Montana, Douglass C. North, Washington University St. Louis, Missouri. — Eighteenth edition.
      pages cm. — (The Pearson series in economics)
  Includes bibliographical references and index.
  ISBN 978-0-13-302293-3
  1. Economics. 2. Industrial policy. 3. Economic policy. I. Benjamin, Daniel K.
II. North, Douglass Cecil. III. Title.
  HB171.M544 2013
  330.973'0932—dc23

                                                           2013019068

10 9 8 7 6 5 4 3

ISBN-10: 0-13-302293-5
ISBN-13: 978-0-13-302293-3

To Bob Glaser,

Who continues to amaze me with his

thoughtful political and economic comments.

—R.L.M.

To Henry Benjamin Barks,

Long-awaited addition to the crew,

may you always have a star to steer by.

—D.K.B.

CONTENTS

SUGGESTIONS FOR USE

At the request of our readers, we include the following table to help you incorporate the chapters of this book into your syllabus. Depending on the breadth of your course, you may also want to consult the companion paperback, *The Economics of Macro Issues,* 6th edition, which features macroeconomic topics and a similar table in its preface.

Economics Topics	Recommended Chapters in The Economics of Public Issues, 18th Edition
Introduction to Economics	6, 8, 9, 22
Opportunity Costs and Scarcity	1, 2, 7, 8, 12, 20, 25, 26, 27, 28, 31
Demand and Supply	6, 8, 10, 11,
Demand and Supply Applications	7, 8, 9, 10, 12, 13
The Public Sector and Public Choice	1, 2, 6, 7, 8, 9, 10, 12, 13, 18, 19, 23, 26, 27
Taxes, Transfers, and Public Spending	12, 15, 19, 20, 22, 23, 24, 27
Consumer Behavior	2, 3, 4, 5, 18, 19, 20, 21, 25, 27, 28
Elasticity of Demand and Supply	2, 3, 6, 8, 9, 10, 22, 27
Rents, Profits, and the Financial Environment of Business	10, 14, 15, 16, 17, 18, 19, 23
Firm Production and Cost	1, 2, 3, 10, 11, 13, 20, 22, 27, 28
Perfect Competition	22
Monopoly	16, 17, 19
Monopolistic Competition	3
Oligopoly	3, 17
Regulation and Antitrust	1, 3, 10, 13, 20, 26, 27
Unions and the Labor Market	11, 13, 14, 17, 31
Income, Poverty, and Health Care	4, 8, 24
Environmental Economics	5, 7, 9, 20, 21, 25, 26, 27, 28
International Trade	5, 7, 14, 29, 30, 31
International Finance	29, 30, 31

PREFACE

As economists, we see economic issues all around us every day of every year. Not everyone agrees with economists, though. Many contemporary public issues appear to be inherently noneconomic. In this book, we attempt to show readers that most public issues have at least a core of basic economics inside them. To be sure, you will find controversy in the pages that follow. Noneconomists tend to react in, well, a noneconomic way. In our view, the one guiding feature that ties all of the issues in this new edition together is that they illustrate the power of economics in explaining the world around us. We also believe that the way in which we illustrate the application of economic science can be entertaining.

NEW TO THIS EDITION

One of the hardest problems we face in each edition is which new chapters to add. What we have done is to select topics that possess a sense of immediacy and that will hopefully be of the most interest for our readers. The new issues include the following:

- Surf Gangs (lessons from surfers on property rights and economic efficiency)
- All Fracked Up (how a boom in natural gas exploration is making us richer *and* greener)
- Over $1 Trillion in College Debt, and Rising (but for many young people, borrowing to go to college is still the right thing to do)
- The Deception of Green Energy (the unsustainability of wind farms, solar panels, and electric cars)
- Save a Turtle, Kill a Person (why bans on plastic bags waste resources, harm the environment, and threaten human lives)
- The Economics of the Big Mac (lessons we can learn from the ultimate burger)

CONTINUED USE OF END-OF-CHAPTER QUESTIONS

The response to our end-of-chapter questions has been so favorable that we have continued using them, revising them, and adding them to the new chapters. The range of difficulty remains wide, but we always include questions about the basics of the material covered in each chapter.

GLOSSARY, SELECTED READINGS, AND WEB LINKS

We have continued our previous use of a Glossary and list of Selected Readings at the back of the book. Within each chapter, the glossary terms are set in boldface the first time they are used. Of course, the selected readings only scratch the surface of the literature from which we have drawn our materials for preparation of this edition.

AS USUAL, A COMPLETE REVISION OF ALL OTHER CHAPTERS

We pride ourselves in making this book as current and relevant as possible. Therefore, you will notice many updates in chapters remaining from the previous edition as well as larger changes whenever necessary.

As before, we have maintained seven parts, ranging from foundations, supply and demand, to labor markets, property rights, and globalization.

INSTRUCTOR'S MANUAL

Every instructor will want to access the *Instructor's Manual* that accompanies *The Economics of Public Issues*. It is available online to all adopters of the book. In writing this manual, we have tried to incorporate the very best of the teaching aids that we use when we teach from *The Economics of Public Issues*. For each chapter, the features of this manual are:

- A synopsis that cuts to the core of the economic issues involved in the chapter.
- A concise exposition of the "behind the scenes" economic foundations of the text. In almost all situations, this exposition is supplemented with one or more diagrams that we have found to be particularly useful as teaching tools.
- Answers to the Discussion Questions posed at the end of the chapter, answers that further develop the basic economic analysis of the chapter, and almost always suggest new avenues of discussion.

SPECIAL THANKS AND ACKNOWLEDGMENTS

Several chapters in this edition draw on the "Tangents" column that Benjamin writes for *PERC Reports*. We are grateful to the Property and

Environment Research Center (PERC) for permission to use that material. Special thanks go to Cyril Morong of San Antonio College for his unstinting willingness to propose new topics and new readings for existing topics. In addition, many other users of the last edition of this book, as well as several extremely diligent and thoughtful reviewers, offered suggestions for the current edition. Those professors who participated in this review are Jim Marsis, Salve Regina University; Morris Coats, Nicholls State University; Nancy Short, Duke University; Robert Miller, American River College–Los Rios; John McArthur, Wofford College; Daniel D. Kuester, Kansas State University; Tomi Ovaska, Youngstown State University; Cyril Morong, San Antonio College; David Flint, Texas A&M University; Ronnie Liggett, University of Texas–Arlington.

We also thank David Alexander, Noel Seibert, and Carolyn Terbush for shepherding the project, Sue Jasin for her expert manuscript preparation, and Robbie Benjamin, whose editorial skills once again have improved the final product. All errors remain, of course, solely our own.

R.L.M.
D.K.B.
D.C.N.

PART ONE

The Foundations of Economic Analysis

Introduction

Our world is one of **scarcity**. We want more than we have. The reason is simple. Although we live in a world of limited **resources,** we have unlimited wants. This does not mean we all live and breathe solely to drive the fastest cars or wear the latest clothes. It means that we all want the right to make decisions about how resources are used—even if what we want to do with those resources is to feed starving children in developing nations.

Given the existence of scarcity, we must make choices. We cannot have more of everything, so to get more of some things, we must give up other things. Economists express this simple idea by saying that we face **trade-offs.** For example, a student who wants higher grades generally must devote more time to studying and less time to, say, watching movies. The trade-off in this instance is between grades and entertainment.

DEATH BY BUREAUCRAT

The concept of a trade-off is one of the basic principles you must grasp to understand the economics of public issues. We illustrate the simplicity of these principles with Chapter 1, which examines a behind-the-scenes trade-off made every day on our behalf by the U.S. Food and Drug Administration (FDA). This federal government agency is charged with ensuring that new prescription medicines are both safe and effective. In carrying out its duties, the FDA requires pharmaceutical companies to subject proposed new drugs to extensive testing. Additional testing improves the chances that a drug will be both safe and effective, but it also slows the approval of new drugs, thus depriving some individuals of the ability to use such drugs to treat their illnesses.

The drug approval process undoubtedly reduces pain and suffering for some people, and even saves the lives of others because it lowers the chances that an unsafe or ineffective drug will reach the market. Yet because the process also slows the rate at which drugs reach the market (and may even prevent some safe and effective drugs from ever being introduced), the pain and suffering of other individuals are increased. Indeed, some people die as a result. This, then, is the terrible trade-off we face in Chapter 1: Who shall live and who shall die?

SUPERSIZE IT

In a world of scarcity, incentives play a key role in understanding behavior. In Chapter 2, we see that even subtle changes in incentives can have profound effects. Obesity is rising in the United States, chiefly as a result of three separate economic forces at work. First, wages paid in sedentary occupations have risen relative to those in physically demanding jobs, inducing people to spend more of their time exercising their brains at work, rather than their muscles. An even more important factor, however, is that the entry of women into the workforce has increased the demand for prepackaged prepared foods—which have been gladly supplied by producers. Such foods have sharply reduced the **full cost** of eating (especially the full cost of snacks), and so increased the amount of food consumed.

Finally, a variety of public policy changes have raised the full cost of consuming cigarettes over the last twenty years or so. This in turn has induced people to substitute from cigarettes to food. On balance, the health effects of this last development likely have been positive. Nevertheless, because expanding waistlines today will almost surely generate adverse health effects in the future, we can expect obesity to be a widely debated public issue in the years to come.

FLYING THE FRIENDLY SKIES

All public issues compel us to face the question of how to make the best choices. Economists argue that doing so requires the use of what we call **marginal analysis.** The term *marginal* in this context means "incremental" or "additional." All choices involve costs and benefits—we give up something for anything we get. As we engage in more of any activity (eating, studying, or sleeping, for example), the **marginal benefits** of that activity eventually decline: The *additional* benefits associated with an *additional* unit of the activity get lower. In contrast, the **marginal**

costs of an activity eventually rise as we engage in more and more of it. The best choices are made when we equate the marginal benefits and marginal costs of the activity. That is, we try to determine whether engaging in any more of a given activity would produce additional costs that exceed the additional benefits.

In Chapter 3 we apply the principles of marginal analysis to the issue of airline safety. How safe is it to travel at 600 miles per hour seven miles above the ground? How safe should it be? The answers to these and other questions can be explored using marginal analysis. One of the conclusions we reach is that perfect safety is simply not in the cards. Every time you step into an airplane (or even the street), there is some risk that your journey will end unhappily. As disconcerting as this might sound at first, we think you will find after reading this chapter that once the costs and benefits are taken into account, you would have it no other way.

The Mystery of Wealth

Every choice we make entails a **cost:** In a world of scarcity, something must be given up to obtain anything of value. Costs, combined with the benefits of our choices, comprise the **incentives** that ultimately inform and guide our decisions. That these decisions—and thus the incentives—have real and lasting consequences is nowhere more evident than in Chapter 4. Here we seek to answer a simple but profound question: Why are the citizens of some nations rich while the inhabitants of others are poor? Your initial answer might be "because of differences in the **natural resource endowments** of the nations." It is true that ample endowments of energy, timber, and fertile land all help raise wealth. But it turns out that natural resources are only a very small part of the answer.

Far more important in determining the wealth of the citizenry are the fundamental political and legal **institutions** of a nation. Institutions such as political stability, secure private property rights, and legal systems based on the **rule of law** create the incentives that encourage people to make long-term investments in improving land and in all forms of **physical** and **human capital.** These investments raise the **capital stock,** which in turn provides for more growth long into the future. The cumulative effects of this growth over time eventually yield much higher standards of living—they make us rich. Thus, incentives, comprising both costs and benefits, turn out to be an integral component of the foundations of economic analysis, as well as the foundations of society.

SURF GANGS

Economic principles manifest themselves not only on the land and in the air, but also at sea—as we illustrate with an examination of California surfers and Maine lobstermen. The incentives to use—or misuse—a resource are importantly driven by whether access to that resource is **closed access** or **open access.** When access to a resource is open, as it is with surf breaks in California and most fisheries around the world, no one may legally be excluded from the resource. The result is **overexploitation** of the resource. With popular surfing spots, surfers tend to crowd into them so that the resulting experience for all is miserable, sometimes even dangerously so. With Maine lobsters, the open access has threatened the lobster population with overfishing.

In response to this overexploitation, private citizens have taken the lead in closing access to the resources in question. In California, so-called surf gangs (groups of local surfers) adopt and enforce rules regarding who may surf and when they are allowed to do it. Congestion on the waves is reduced and the overall surfing experience is dramatically improved. In Maine, lobster gangs (groups of local commercial lobstermen) have formed to prevent outside fishermen from overexploiting the most productive fishing grounds.

Perhaps the greatest beneficiary of the lobster gangs has been the population of Maine lobsters, which has reached record highs, largely because of the closed access enforced by the local fishermen. Indeed, on balance, even though some people lose when access is closed (those surfers and commercial fishermen who are excluded), limiting access to congested or overexploited resources has been shown to improve the well-being of the vast majority of individuals, and increase human wealth, in the broadest sense of that term. In a world of scarcity, this is a fact that simply cannot be avoided.

CHAPTER 1

Death by Bureaucrat

How would you rather die? From a lethal reaction to a drug prescribed by your doctor? Or because your doctor failed to prescribe a drug that would have saved your life? If this choice sounds like one you would rather not make, consider this: Employees of the Food and Drug Administration (FDA) make that decision on behalf of millions of Americans many times each year. More precisely, FDA bureaucrats decide whether or not new medicines (prescription drugs) should be allowed to go on sale in the United States. If the FDA rules against a drug, physicians in America may not legally prescribe it, even if thousands of lives are being saved by the drug each year in other countries.

A BRIEF HISTORY OF THE FDA

The FDA's authority to make such decisions dates back to the passage of the Food and Drug Safety Act of 1906. The law required that medicines be correctly labeled as to their contents and that they not contain any substances harmful to consumers' health. Due to this legislation, Dr. Hostatter's Stomach Bitters and Kickapoo Indian Sagwa, along with numerous rum-laden concoctions, cocaine-based potions, and supposed anticancer remedies disappeared from druggists' shelves. The law was expanded in 1938 with the passage of the Food, Drug, and Cosmetic Act, which forced manufacturers to demonstrate the safety of new drugs before being allowed to offer them for sale. (This law was prompted by the deaths of 107 people who had taken Elixir Sulfanilamide, an antibiotic that had been errantly mixed with poisonous diethylene glycol, a chemical cousin of antifreeze.)

The next step in U.S. drug regulation came after a spate of severe birth defects among infants whose mothers during pregnancy had taken a sleep aid known as thalidomide. When these birth defects first became apparent, the drug was already widely used in Europe and Canada, and the FDA was nearing approval for its use in America. In fact, about 2.5 million thalidomide tablets were already in the hands of U.S. physicians as samples. The FDA ordered all of the samples destroyed and prohibited the sale of the drug in the United States. This incident led to the 1962 Kefauver–Harris Amendments to the 1938 Food, Drug, and Cosmetic Act, radically altering the drug-approval process in the United States.

THE IMPACT OF THE 1962 AMENDMENTS

Before the 1962 amendments, the FDA was expected to approve a new drug application within 180 days, unless the application failed to show that the drug was safe. The 1962 amendments added a "proof of efficacy" requirement and also removed the time constraint on the FDA. The FDA has free rein to determine how much and what type of evidence it will demand before approving a drug for sale, and thus may take as long as it pleases before either granting or refusing approval.

The 1962 amendments drastically increased the costs of introducing a new drug and markedly slowed the approval process. Before 1962, for example, the average time between filing and approval of a new drug application was seven months. By 1967, it was thirty months; and by the late 1970s, it had risen to eight to ten years. The protracted approval process involves costly testing by the drug companies—$800 million or more for each new drug—and delays the receipt of any potential revenue from new drugs. Both the delays and the higher costs reduced the expected profitability of new drugs, so fewer new drugs have been brought onto the market.

Debate continues over how much FDA regulation is needed to ensure that drugs are both safe and efficacious, but there is little doubt that the 1962 amendments resulted in a U.S. "drug lag." On average, drugs take far longer to reach the market in the United States than they do in Europe. Admittedly, it takes time to ensure that patients benefit from, rather than are harmed by, new drugs, but regulation-induced drug lag can itself be life-threatening. Dr. George Hitchings, a winner of the Nobel Prize in Medicine, estimated that the five-year lag in introducing Septra (an antibiotic) to the United States killed 80,000 people in this country. Similarly, the introduction of a class of drugs called beta blockers (used to treat heart attack victims and people with high blood pressure) was delayed nearly a decade in

America relative to Europe. According to several researchers, the lag in the FDA approval of these drugs cost the lives of at least 250,000 Americans.

TERRIBLE TRADE-OFF

In effect, the law requires FDA bureaucrats to make what is truly a terrible trade-off. Lives are saved because unsafe or ineffective drugs are kept off the market, but the regulatory process delays (or even prevents) the introduction of some safe and efficacious drugs, thereby costing lives. Let us now take a more systematic look at this trade-off.

Every time a new drug is introduced, there is a chance that it should not have been—either because it has adverse side effects that outweigh the therapeutic benefits (it is not safe) or because it really does little to help the individuals who take it (it is not effective). When such a drug is introduced, we say that a **Type I error** has been committed. Since 1962, the incidence of Type I error—the thalidomide possibility—has been reduced by the added testing required by the FDA. But other people have been the victims of what is called **Type II error.** Their cost is the pain, suffering, and death that occur because the 1962 amendments have prevented or delayed the introduction of safe, efficacious drugs. Type II error—as with Septra or beta blockers—occurs when a drug *should* be introduced but is held back by FDA regulation.

Over the past thirty years, outcries over the harm caused by the drug lag have sometimes induced the agency to shorten the testing period when the costs of Type I error are small relative to the damages due to Type II error—as with terminally ill patients. One famous example involved azidothymidine (AZT), which emerged as a possible treatment for AIDS. Gay men, among whom AIDS was most prevalent at the time, took the lead in pressuring the FDA to approve the drug quickly, and the FDA responded accordingly, giving it the OK after only eighteen months of testing. Similarly, Taxol, an important new drug used to treat breast cancer, received expedited review by the FDA because of pressure applied by women in whose families there was a history of breast cancer.

The FDA now has a formal program in which it seeks to expedite testing for drugs that seem to offer great promise for alleviating death or suffering. Nevertheless, although the average approval time for new drugs has shortened considerably, it still takes roughly ten times as long for a new drug to be approved as it did before the 1962 amendments.

LESSONS FROM THE FDA STORY

What can we learn from the FDA regulation of new drugs that will guide us in thinking about other public issues of our time? There are several key principles:

1. *There is no free lunch.* Every choice, and thus every policy, entails a **cost**—something must be given up. In a world of **scarcity,** we cannot have more of everything; so to get more of some things, we must give up other things. Although FDA review of drugs saves lives by preventing the introduction of unsafe or ineffective drugs, the cost is billions of dollars of added expenses, plus delayed availability of safe and efficacious drugs, resulting in the deaths of hundreds of thousands of people.

2. *The cost of an action is the alternative that is sacrificed.* Economists often express costs (and benefits) in dollars because this is a simple means of accounting for and measuring them. That does not mean that costs have to be monetary, nor does it mean that economics is incapable of analyzing costs and benefits that are quite human. The costs that led to the 1938 and 1962 amendments were the very visible deaths caused by sulfanilamide and the terrible birth defects due to thalidomide. Subsequent revisions to the FDA process for reviewing drugs, as with AZT and Taxol, have been in response to the adverse health effects caused by the regulation-induced drug lag.

3. *The relevant costs and benefits are the marginal (incremental) ones.* The relevant question is not whether safety is good or bad; it is instead how much safety we want—which can only be answered by looking at the added (marginal) benefits of more safety compared to the added (marginal) costs. One possible response to the sulfanilamide poisonings or thalidomide was to have outlawed new drugs altogether. That would guarantee that no more people would be harmed by new drugs. But surely this "solution" would not be sensible, because the marginal cost (more Type II errors) would exceed the marginal benefit (fewer Type I errors).

4. *People respond to incentives.* And this is true whether we are talking about consumers, suppliers, or government bureaucrats. Here the incentive to amend the law in 1938 and 1962 was the very visible death and disfigurement of individuals. The eventual FDA decision to speed up the review process was prompted by intense lobbying by individuals who believed (correctly, as it turned out) that they might be benefited by drugs not yet approved.

5. *Things aren't always as they seem.* Many analyses of the effects of government policies take an approach that does not fully recognize the actions that people would otherwise have taken. Thus, official pronouncements about the effects of policies routinely misrepresent their impact—not because there is necessarily any attempt to deceive but because it is often difficult to know what would have happened otherwise. Pharmaceutical manufacturers, for example, have strong incentives to avoid introducing drugs that are unsafe or ineffective because the companies are subject to loss of reputation and to lawsuits. For similar reasons, physicians have strong incentives to avoid prescribing such drugs for their patients. Even without FDA regulation, there would thus be extensive testing of new drugs before their introduction. Hence, it is incorrect to ascribe the generally safe and effective nature of modern drugs entirely to FDA protection. The flip side, however, is that the drug development process is inherently long, complicated, and costly. Even without FDA oversight, some people would die waiting for new drugs because self-interested manufacturers would insist on some testing and cautious physicians would proceed slowly in prescribing new drugs.

The people who work at the FDA (and members of Congress) are publicly castigated when they "allow" a Type I error to occur—especially when it is a drug that kills people. Thus, FDA bureaucrats have a strong incentive to avoid such errors. But when testing delays cause a Type II error, as with Septra, it is almost impossible to point to specific people who died because the drug was delayed. As a result, officials at the FDA are rarely attacked directly for such delays. Because the costs of Type II errors are much more difficult to discern than the costs of Type I errors, many observers believe that there is an inherent bias at the FDA in favor of being "safe rather than sorry"— in other words, excessive testing.

6. *Policies always have unintended consequences, and as a result, their net benefits are almost always less than anticipated.* In the case of government regulations, balancing incremental costs and benefits (see principle 3) fails to make good headlines. Instead, what gets politicians reelected and regulators promoted are *absolute* notions such as safety (and motherhood and apple pie). Thus, if a little safety is good, more must be better, so why not simply mandate that drug testing "guarantee" that everyone is free of risk from dangerous drugs? Eventually, the reality of principle 3 sinks in, but in this instance not before the drug lag had killed many people.

As is often true with important public issues, our story has one more interesting twist. Thalidomide is back on the market. In 1998, the

FDA approved its use in treating Hansen's disease (leprosy), and in 2006, the FDA gave physicians the OK to use it in treating bone marrow cancer. In each instance, there are strong protections to prevent pregnant women from taking the drug. And so perhaps the very drug that brought us the deadly drug lag will turn out to be a lifesaver for a new generation of patients.

DISCUSSION QUESTIONS

1. Why don't individuals simply force the FDA to do what is best for consumers of prescription drugs?

2. Why don't the employees at the FDA accurately balance the marginal benefits to drug consumers against the marginal costs to those consumers?

3. Does the structure of the drug industry have any bearing on the types of errors that drug firms are likely to make? That is, would a drug industry made up of numerous highly competitive firms be more or less likely to introduce unsafe drugs than an industry consisting of a few large firms?

4. How could the incentives facing the people at the FDA be changed to reduce the incidence of Type II errors? (*Hint:* Is it possible to compare the FDA approval process with the drug-approval process in other nations?)

5. What would be the advantages and disadvantages of a regulatory system in which, rather than having the FDA permit or prohibit new drugs, the FDA merely published its opinions about the safety and efficacy of drugs and then allowed physicians to make their own decisions about whether or not to prescribe the drugs for their patients?

6. Suppose, for simplicity, that Type I and Type II errors resulted in deaths only. Keeping in mind that too little caution produces Type I errors and too much caution produces Type II errors, what would be the best mix of Type I and Type II errors?

CHAPTER 2

Supersize It

At least one major fast food company has urged customers to "Supersize It." Americans seem to have been taking the message to heart, putting on pounds at a record pace. In the 1960s, the average American man weighed 166 pounds. Today he tips the scales at about 194 pounds. Over the same span, the average American woman put on almost as much weight, rising to 165 pounds from her previous 140 pounds. The weight gains have been largest among people who were heavier to begin with, so obesity in America has more than doubled over this period. Over 30 percent of Americans now have a body mass index (BMI, a measure of weight relative to height) in excess of 30, the level at which doctors say a person passes from overweight to obese.[1] What explains these developments? Not surprisingly, economic analysis has a lot to say on this question. In fact, some fairly simple changes in demand and supply explain why waistlines in America and elsewhere in the world have been expanding so quickly.

WEIGHT IN THE TWENTIETH CENTURY

Actually, Americans put on weight throughout all of the twentieth century, largely due to two factors. First, wages in sedentary occupations (those relying on brains rather than brawn) rose relative to those

---

1 Using the English measurement system, BMI equals 704.5 multiplied by weight in pounds and then divided by the square of height in inches. BMIs in the range 20–25 are considered healthy. Below 20 is thin, 25–30 is overweight, and 30 and above is obese—the range in which significant adverse health effects (ranging from diabetes to heart disease) begin to show up. Someone who is 5′6″ and weighs over 185 pounds is officially obese, as is true for someone who stands 6′0″ and weighs more than 220 pounds.

in active occupations. People responded by leaving jobs in manufacturing and agriculture and starting work in service and management jobs. This reduced their calorie expenditures on the job and helped push up average weights. Second, the relative price of food declined during the twentieth century. As predicted by the **law of demand,** this induced people to eat more, increasing their caloric intake and their body weights. Between about 1900 and 1960, the weight of the average male rose 16 pounds, with similar but slightly smaller gains for the average female.

These weight gains during the first part of the twentieth century were probably healthful. Many Americans at the beginning of the twentieth century were actually malnourished, and the added poundage led to better health outcomes for them. The excess weight we added during the last half century is an entirely different matter. By the 1960s, average BMI in the United States was already at the high end of the healthy range of 20–25, so the extra pounds since then have pushed us into the unhealthful categories of overweight and even obese.

WHY THE WEIGHT GAINS?

How can we explain this surge in poundage? There are three key components. First, as mentioned above, levels of physical activity have declined, although not nearly as much as many popular commentators would have us believe. The big move from active to sedentary employments took place before 1970, so it cannot explain the weight gains since then. Still, caloric energy expenditures by both men and women in the United States have been falling. Americans are spending less time at work and on household chores, and more time watching TV, looking at computer monitors, and engaging in social networking. Overall, per capita caloric energy expenditures have dropped a bit more than 25 percent since the 1960s. This is only a small part of the story, however. Indeed, it can explain only a few of the pounds Americans have added over the past few decades. The rest comes from higher caloric intake.

By far the most important reason for this added caloric intake appears to be a change in the way food is prepared. Due to major developments in food processing technology, the **time cost** involved in preparing meals has fallen dramatically. This has reduced the **full cost** (money plus time cost) of food, leading to the consumption of significantly more calories. The result has been expanding waistlines.

Changes in Food Preparation

In the 1960s, food was prepared in the home by family members and eaten there. Since then, there have been numerous technological innovations in food processing, including:

- Vacuum packing
- Flash freezing
- Improved preservatives and flavorings
- The microwave

Much food preparation now is done outside the home by manufacturers who specialize in that activity and then sell the packaged, prepared food to the consumer to be eaten at home. Thus, over the past 40 years, the amount of time spent on food preparation and cleanup in the home has fallen in half. In addition, outside the home, convenient, tasty prepackaged foods are now merely a few steps away in a vending machine, rather than being 10–20 minutes away in the nearest store. On both counts, the full cost of consuming food has declined, and people are consuming more calories. Moreover, they are doing it not by eating more calories at each meal, but rather by eating more "meals" (actually snacks) during the day. Caloric intake during the traditional meals of breakfast, lunch, and dinner has remained nearly constant at about 1,800 per day for men and 1,400 per day for women. But both sexes have nearly doubled their intake of calories from snacks, and thus total per capita daily intake has risen significantly.

Those Extra Calories

A few questions remain. First, are the additional calories that Americans are consuming each day—the equivalent of a soft drink or a few cookies—really enough to account for the poundage we have been accumulating? The answer is "yes." An extra 150 calories per day for men of average weight and activity levels will eventually lead to 11 pounds of excess waistline baggage. For women, the same 150 calories per day would eventually add an extra 13 pounds. (The weight gain from these extra calories eventually levels off, because as people get heavier they burn more calories just doing the things they usually do.)

The second question is: What started the revolution in food processing that made these extra calories cheaper? Although the answer to this is not completely settled, the most likely source may be found in the workforce decisions of women. In the 1960s, women began entering the workforce in unprecedented numbers. Indeed, the **labor force participation rate** of women nearly doubled between 1960 and 2000. Moreover, women have moved into occupations and professions, such as medicine, law, and the upper ranks of business, in which annual earnings are much higher than in the earlier traditional fields of female employment, such as teaching and nursing. Thus, the **opportunity cost** of women's time has been rising, in turn increasing the demand for labor-saving conveniences, such as prepared foods. The food industry has responded just as economic analysis would predict.

DOES CHEAP FOOD MAKE US WORSE OFF?

A third question being asked by some people is: Are Americans really better off due to the lower cost of food? Ordinarily, economists would argue that a technological improvement that lowered the costs of a good definitely would improve the lot of consumers. In the present situation, however, the adverse health effects of the extra calories are starting to become significant. Obesity is implicated in diabetes, heart disease, strokes, depression, and some cancers, and the number of people who are disabled due to obesity-related injuries or other health problems is rising sharply. It is estimated that over $200 billion per year is now spent on obesity-related health problems—about 10 percent of our total health care spending. Ominously, the costs of obesity-related health care are expected to *triple* over the next 15 years or so.

As the poundage has piled up across the country, so too have the sales of diet books, as well as the rates of expensive bariatric surgery (in which the stomach is reduced in size to cut caloric intake and absorption). All in all, some analysts have suggested, maybe the lower cost of food has made people *worse* off, by inducing them to do something that they would rather not do—put on weight. This might be particularly true for people who are said to have little self-control over the amount they eat. There may be something to this argument, but it's also true that people who live in cold weather climates, such as Montana, the Dakotas, and Minnesota, routinely complain about the weather in the winter. People in such climes also spend far more than the average person on clothes to offset the adverse effects of the cold weather. Surely we would not want to argue that such people are worse off for having chosen to live where they do, rather than in warmer locales. Similarly, in the case of people who are said to lack control over the amount they eat, just who is it that shall decide—and enforce—their caloric intake?

The Role of Smoking

There is one final point to our story, one that illustrates that even the best of intentions sometimes yield adverse unintended consequences. Over the same period that Americans have been packing on the pounds, the taxes on cigarettes have risen sharply, even while the number of places where it is lawful to smoke has shrunk significantly. On both counts, the full cost of smoking (price per pack, plus the hassle) has been rising, and one consequence is that smoking has declined in the United States. It is well known that people have a tendency to eat more when they stop smoking, and this very fact seems to be showing up in the national statistics on excess poundage.

Where the full costs of smoking have risen the greatest, so too has the incidence of obesity. In effect, people are being induced to substitute eating for smoking. Despite the adverse health effects of the resulting weight gains, the *net* health trade-offs here are likely positive, given the highly lethal effects of smoking. Still, this development reminds us that although people's behavior can easily be understood by examining the incentives they face, sometimes it is difficult to determine ahead of time what the full range of incentives will be.

Discussion Questions

1. Calculate your own BMI, based on the formula in footnote 1, but keep it Top Secret. For comparison purposes, consider the following data for approximate average height and weight of major college football players, by position:

Position	Height (Inches)	Weight (Pounds)
Quarterback	75	220
Running back	71	215
Wide receiver	73	195

   Is the average player at any of these positions officially obese? What factors other than just weight and height might be important in assessing the "healthy" BMI for an individual?

2. Many insurance companies now impose a surcharge (in effect, a higher premium) for people who use tobacco products. What effect on tobacco usage do you predict such surcharges to have? What would be the expected effect of an insurance surcharge for people who are obese?

3. Over the past 25 years, many state and local governments have (i) sharply raised cigarette taxes and (ii) sharply limited the number of places where people may smoke. Both policy changes have helped reduce the amount of cigarette smoking in the United States. If these same governments decided that they wished to reduce obesity, how might they go about doing so?

4. The technological changes in food preparation seem to have had the greatest effect on the time costs of a "meal," rather than affecting the time cost of consuming extra calories during any given meal. What does economics predict about what we should observe has happened to the number of meals consumed each day, relative to the number of calories consumed per meal?

5. The change in food preparation technologies over the past 40 years caused the biggest reduction in time costs for married women. What does economics predict should have happened to the weight of married women relative to other people?

6. During the twentieth century, the cost of the automobile fell drastically, leading to a dramatic rise in the number of miles driven. All this driving led to automobile accidents, which now kill more than 30,000 people each year and maim hundreds of thousands more. Is it possible that the fall in the price of the automobile actually made Americans worse off? How much would your answer depend on whether those fatalities were among the people driving the cars as opposed to innocent bystanders, such as pedestrians and children? (*Hint:* Look at the chapters in Part Six.)

CHAPTER 3

Flying the Friendly Skies?

Most of us hop into our car with little thought for our personal safety, beyond perhaps the act of putting on seat belts. Yet even though travel on scheduled, commercial airlines is safer than driving to work or to the grocery store, many people approach air travel with a sense of foreboding, if not downright fear.

If we were to think carefully about the wisdom of traveling 600 miles per hour in an aluminum tube 7 miles above the earth, several questions might come to mind. How safe is this? How safe should it be? Because the people who operate airlines are not in it for fun, does their interest in making a buck ignore our interest in making it home in one piece? Is some form of government regulation the only way to ensure safety in the skies?

THE ECONOMICS OF SAFETY

The science of economics begins with one simple principle: We live in a world of **scarcity,** which implies that to get more of any good, we must sacrifice some of other goods. This is just as true of safety as it is of pizzas or haircuts or works of art. Safety confers benefits (we live longer and more enjoyably), but achieving it also entails **costs** (we must give up something to obtain that safety).

As the degree of safety rises, the total benefits of safety rise, but the marginal (or incremental) benefits of additional safety decline. Consider a simple example: Adding exit doors to an airplane increases the number of people who can escape in the event of an emergency evacuation. Nevertheless, each *additional* door adds less in safety benefits than the previous one. If the fourth door enables, say, an extra ten people to escape, the fifth may enable only an extra six to escape. (If this sounds implausible, imagine having a door for each person. The last door added will enable at most one more person to escape.) So we say that the marginal (or incremental) benefit of safety declines as the amount of safety increases.

Let's look now at the other side of the equation. As the amount of safety increases, both the total and the marginal (incremental) costs of providing safety rise. Having a fuel gauge on the plane's instrument panel clearly enhances safety because it reduces the chance that the plane will run out of fuel while in flight.[1] It is always possible that a fuel gauge will malfunction, so having a backup fuel gauge also adds to safety. Because having two gauges is more costly than having just one, the total costs of safety rise as safety increases. It is also clear, however, that while the cost of the second gauge is (at least) as great as the cost of the first, the second gauge has a smaller positive impact on safety. Thus, the cost per unit of additional (incremental) safety is higher for the second fuel gauge than for the first.

How Safe Is Safe Enough?

How much safety should we have? For an economist, the answer to such a question is generally expressed in terms of **marginal benefits** and **marginal costs.** The economically *efficient* level of safety occurs when the marginal cost of increasing safety just equals the marginal benefit of that increased safety. Put somewhat differently, if the marginal benefits of adding (or keeping) a safety feature exceed the marginal costs of doing so, the feature is worthwhile. If the added benefits of a safety device do *not* exceed the added costs, we should refrain from installing the device. Note there are two related issues here: How safe should we *be*, and how should we *achieve* that level of safety?

Both of these issues took on added urgency on the morning of September 11, 2001, when terrorists hijacked and crashed four U.S. commercial jetliners. This episode revealed that air travel was far less safe than previously believed. Immediately, it was clear that we should devote additional resources to airline safety. What was not clear was how *much* additional resources should be thus devoted and precisely *what* changes should be made. For example, almost everyone agreed that more careful screening of passengers and baggage at airports would produce important safety benefits. But how should we achieve this?

---

1 Notice that we say "reduces" rather than "eliminates." In 1978, a United Airlines pilot preoccupied with a malfunctioning landing gear evidently failed to pay sufficient attention to his cockpit gauges. When the plane was forced to crash-land after running out of fuel, eight people died.

Should carry-on bags be prohibited or just examined more carefully? How thoroughly should checked luggage be screened for bombs? Even now, our answers to these questions are evolving as we learn more about the extent of the threat and the costs of alternative responses to it. Nevertheless, throughout the process, economic principles can help us make the most sensible decisions.

In general, the efficient level of safety will not be perfect safety because perfection is simply too costly to achieve. For example, to be absolutely certain that no one is ever killed or injured in an airplane crash, we would have to prevent all travel in airplanes—an unrealistic and impracticable prospect. This means that if we wish to enjoy the advantages of flying, we must be willing to accept *some* risk—a conclusion that each of us implicitly accepts every time we step aboard an airplane.

THE IMPORTANCE OF CIRCUMSTANCES

Changes in circumstances can alter the efficient level of safety. For example, if a technological change reduces the costs of bomb-scanning equipment, the marginal costs of preventing terrorist bomb attacks will be lower. It will be efficient to have more airports install the machines and to have extra machines at large airports to speed the screening process. Air travel will become safer because of the technological change. Similarly, if the marginal benefits of safety rise for some reason (perhaps because the president of the United States is on board), it could be efficient to take more precautions, resulting in safer air travel. Given the factors that determine the benefits and costs of safety, the result of a change in circumstances will be some determinate level of safety that generally will be associated with some risk of death or injury.

Airplanes are complex systems, and an amazing number of components can fail. Over the century or so that humans have been flying, airplane manufacturers and airlines have studied every one of the malfunctions thus far and have put into place design changes and operating procedures aimed at preventing recurring error. The efforts have paid off. Between 1950 and 2010, for example, the fatal accident rate on U.S. commercial airlines was cut by almost 97 percent.

DOES THE GOVERNMENT KNOW BEST?

Consumers have the greatest incentive to ensure that air travel is safe, and if information were free, we could assert with some confidence that the actual level of safety supplied by firms was the efficient level of safety.

Consumers would simply observe the safety offered by different airlines, the prices they charge, and then select the degrees of safety that best suited their preferences and budgets, just as with other goods. Information is not free, however. It is a **scarce good,** costly to obtain. As a result, passengers may be unaware of the safety record of various airlines or the competence of the pilots and the maintenance procedures of an airline's mechanics. Indeed, even the airlines themselves may be uncertain about the efficient level of safety, perhaps because they have no way of estimating the true threat of terrorist attacks, for example. Such possibilities have been used to argue that the federal government should mandate certain minimum levels of safety, as it does today through the operation of the Federal Aviation Administration (FAA). Let's look at this issue in some detail.

One argument in favor of government safety standards rests on the presumption that when left to their own devices, airlines would provide less safety than passengers want. This might happen, for example, if customers could not tell (at a reasonable cost) whether the equipment, training, and procedures employed by an airline are safe. If passengers cannot cheaply gauge the level of safety, they will not be willing to reward airlines for being safe or punish them for being unsafe. If safety is costly to provide and consumers are unwilling to pay for it because they cannot accurately measure it, airlines will provide too little of it. The conclusion is that government experts, such as the FAA, should set safety standards for the industry.

DO CONSUMERS KNOW BEST?

This conclusion seems plausible, but it ignores two simple points. First, how is the government to know the efficient level of safety? Even if the FAA knows the costs of all possible safety measures, it still does not have enough information to set efficient safety standards because it does not know the value that people place on safety. Without such information, the FAA has no way to assess the benefits of additional safety and hence no means of knowing whether those benefits are greater or less than the added costs.

Second, people want to reach their destinations safely. Even if they cannot observe whether an airline hires good pilots or bad pilots, they can see whether that airline's planes land safely or crash. If it is *safety* that is important to consumers—and not the obscure, costly-to-measure *reasons* for that safety—the fact that consumers cannot easily measure metal fatigue in jet engines may be totally irrelevant to the process of achieving the efficient level of safety.

Interestingly, evidence shows that consumers are indeed cognizant of the safety performance of airlines, and that they "punish" airlines that perform in an unsafe manner. Researchers have found that when an airline is at fault in a fatal plane crash, consumers appear to downgrade their safety rating of the airline (i.e., they revise upward their estimates of the likelihood of future fatal crashes). As a result, the offending airline suffers substantial adverse financial consequences over and above the costs of losing the plane and being sued on behalf of the victims. These findings suggest a striking degree of safety awareness on the part of supposedly ignorant consumers.

WHAT ABOUT TERRORISM?

Of course, this discussion leaves open the issue of how to handle safety threats posed by terrorists and other miscreants. For example, much of the information that goes into assessing terrorist threats is classified as secret, and its revelation to airlines or consumers might compromise key sources of the data. Hence, there could be an advantage to having the government try to approximate the efficient safety outcome by mandating certain screening provisions without revealing exactly why they are being chosen. Similarly, because airlines are connected in networks (so that people and baggage move from one airline to another in the course of a trip), achieving the efficient level of safety might require a common set of screening rules for all airlines. Even so, this does not inform us whether the government should impose those rules or the airlines should come to a voluntary joint agreement on them.

We began this chapter with the commonplace observation that airlines are safer than cars. Yet many people still worry for their safety every time they get on an airplane. Are they being irrational? Well, the answer, it seems, is in the eye of the beholder. Measured in fatalities per mile traveled, airplanes are about 15 times safer than cars (and 176 times safer than walking, we might add). This number masks the fact, however, that 68 percent of aircraft accidents happen on takeoff and landing, and these operations occupy only 6 percent of flight time. It is presumably this fact that quite sensibly makes people nervous whenever they find themselves approaching an airport.

DISCUSSION QUESTIONS

1. Is it possible to be too safe? Explain what you mean by "too safe."

2. Suppose it is possible to observe (or measure) four attributes of airlines: (i) the size of their planes (measured in passenger-carrying capacity), (ii) the experience levels of their pilots, (iii) the age of

their planes, and (iv) the length of the typical route they fly. Which airlines would be likely to have the fewest fatal accidents? Which would be expected to have the most?

3. Is safety likely to be a "normal" good (i.e., something people want to consume more of as they get richer)? Use your answer to this question to predict likely safety records of airlines based in North America and Europe, compared to those based in South America and Africa. Then go to www.airsafe.com to see if your prediction is confirmed or refuted by the facts.

4. Many automobile manufacturers routinely advertise the safety of their cars, yet airlines generally do not mention safety in their advertising. Can you suggest an explanation for this difference?

5. Many economists would argue that private companies are likely to be more efficient than the government at operating airlines. Yet many economists would also argue that there is a valid reason for government to regulate the safety of those same airlines. Can you explain why the government might be good at ensuring safety, even though it might not be good at operating the airlines?

6. Professional football teams sometimes charter airplanes to take them to their away games. Would you feel safer on a United Airlines plane that had been chartered by the Washington Redskins than on a regularly scheduled United Airlines flight?

CHAPTER 4

The Mystery of Wealth

Why are the citizens of some nations rich while the inhabitants of others are poor? Your initial answer might be, "because of differences in the **natural resource endowments** of the nations." It is true that ample endowments of energy, timber, and fertile land all help raise wealth. But natural resources can be only a very small part of the answer, as witnessed by many counterexamples. Switzerland and Luxembourg, for example, are nearly devoid of key natural resources, yet the real incomes of citizens of those lands are among the world's highest. Similarly, Hong Kong, which consists of a few square miles of rock and hillside, is one of the economic miracles of modern times, while in Russia, a land amply endowed with vast quantities of virtually every important resource, most people remain mired in economic misery.

A number of studies have begun to unravel the mystery of **economic growth.** Repeatedly, they have found that it is the fundamental political and legal **institutions** of society that are conducive to growth. Of these, political stability, secure private property rights, and legal systems based on the **rule of law** are among the most important. Such institutions encourage people to make long-term investments in improving land and in all forms of **physical capital** and **human capital.** These investments raise the **capital stock,** which in turn provides for more growth long into the future. Also, the cumulative effects of this growth over time eventually yield much higher standards of living.

THE IMPORTANCE OF LEGAL SYSTEMS

Consider first the contrasting effects of different legal systems on economic growth. Many legal systems around the world today are based on one of two models: the English **common law system** and the French

TABLE 4-1 Differing Legal Systems

Common Law Nations	Civil Law Nations
Australia	Brazil
Canada	Egypt
India	France
Israel	Greece
New Zealand	Italy
United Kingdom	Mexico
United States	Sweden

civil law system. Common law systems reflect a conscious decision in favor of a limited role for government and emphasize the importance of the judiciary in constraining the power of the executive and legislative branches of government. In contrast, civil law systems favor the creation of a strong centralized government in which the legislature and the executive branches have the power to grant preferential treatment to special interests. Table 4–1 shows a sampling of common law and civil law countries.

Research reveals that the security of **property rights** is much stronger in common law systems, such as observed in Britain and its former colonies, including the United States. In nations such as France and its former colonies, the civil law systems are much more likely to yield unpredictable changes in the rules of the game—the structure of **property and contract rights.** This unpredictability makes people reluctant to make long-term fixed investments, a fact that ultimately slows the economic growth of these nations and lowers the standard of living for their citizens.

The reasoning here is simple. If you know that the police will not help you protect your rights to a home or a car, you are less likely to acquire those assets. Similarly, if you cannot easily enforce business or employment contracts that you make, you are less likely to make those contracts—and hence less likely to produce as many goods or services. Also, if you cannot plan for the future because you don't know what the rules of the game will be in 10 years or perhaps even one year from now, you are less likely to make the kinds of productive long-term investments that take years to pay off. Common law systems seem to do a better job at enforcing contracts and securing property rights and so would be expected to promote economic activity now and economic growth over time.

THE ECONOMIC IMPACT OF INSTITUTIONS

Research into the economic performance of nations around the world from 1960 to the 1990s found that economic growth was one-third higher in the common law nations, with their strong property rights, than in civil law nations. Over the more than three decades covered, the standard of living—measured by real **per capita income**—increased more than 20 percent in common law nations compared to civil law nations. If such a pattern persisted over the span of a century, it would produce a staggering 80 percent real per capita income difference in favor of nations with secure property rights.

Other research has taken a much broader view, both across time and across institutions, in assessing economic growth. Institutions such as political stability, protection against violence or theft, security of contracts, and freedom from regulatory burdens all contribute to sustained economic growth. Indeed, it is key institutions such as these, rather than natural resource endowments, that explain long-term differences in economic growth and thus present-day differences in levels of real income. To illustrate the powerful effect of institutions, consider the contrast between Mexico, with per capita real income of about $15,000 today, and the United States, with per capita real income of about $50,000. Had Mexico developed with the same political and legal institutions that the United States has enjoyed, per capita income in Mexico would today be equal to that in the United States.

THE ORIGINS OF INSTITUTIONS

Given the great importance of such institutions in determining long-term growth, one might ask another important question: How have countries gotten the political and legal institutions they have today? The answer has to do with disease, of all things. An examination of more than seventy former European colonies reveals that a variety of strategies were pursued. In Australia, New Zealand, and North America, the colonists found geography and climates that were conducive to good health. Permanent settlement was attractive, so colonists created institutions to protect private property and curb the power of the state. When Europeans arrived in Africa and South America, however, they encountered tropical diseases, such as malaria and yellow fever, which produced high mortality rates. This discouraged permanent settlement and encouraged a mentality focused on extracting metals, cash crops, and other resources. As a result, there were few **incentives** to promote democratic institutions or stable long-term property rights systems.

The differing initial institutions helped shape economic growth over the years and, because of the broad persistence of those institutions, continue to shape the political and legal character and the standard of living in these nations today.

INSTITUTIONAL CHANGE TODAY

Recent events also illustrate that the effects of political and legal institutions can be drastically accelerated—in either direction. Consider China, which in 1979 began to change its institutions in two key ways. First, China began to experiment with private property rights for a few of its citizens, under narrow circumstances. Second, the Chinese government began to clear away obstacles to foreign investment, making China a more secure place for Western companies to do business. Although the institutional changes have been modest, their combined effects have been substantial. Over the years since, economic growth in China has accelerated, averaging almost 7 percent per year. If that doesn't sound like much, keep in mind that it has been enough over that period to raise real per capita income in China by a factor of 8.

For an example of the potential *destructive* impact of institutional change, we need to look no further than Zimbabwe. When that country won its independence from Britain in 1980, it was one of the most prosperous nations in Africa. Soon after taking power as Zimbabwe's first (and so far only) president, Robert Mugabe began disassembling that nation's rule of law, tearing apart the institutions that had helped it grow rich. He reduced the security of property rights in land and eventually confiscated those rights altogether. The Mugabe government has also gradually taken control of the prices of most goods and services in his nation, and has confiscated large stocks of food and much of anything of value that might be exported out of or imported into Zimbabwe. In short, anything that is produced or saved has become subject to confiscation, so the incentives to do either are—to put it mildly—reduced.

As a result, between 1980 and 1996, real per capita income in Zimbabwe fell by one-third, and since 1996, it has fallen by an additional third. Eighty percent of the workforce is unemployed, investment is nonexistent, and the annual inflation rate reached an astonishing 231 million percent. (In 2009, Zimbabwe gave up on having its own currency, and now uses American dollars and South African rand.) The fruit of decades of labor and capital investment has been destroyed because the institutions that made that progress possible have been eliminated. It is a lesson we ignore at our peril.

DISCUSSION QUESTIONS

1. Go to a source such as the CIA *World Factbook* or the World Bank and collect per capita income and population data for each of the nations listed in Table 4–1. Compare the average per capita income of the common law countries with the average per capita income of the civil law countries. Based on the discussion in the chapter, identify at least two other factors that you think are important to take into account when assessing whether the differences you observe are likely due to the systems of the countries.

2. Most international attempts to aid people living in low-income nations have come in one of two forms: (i) gifts of consumer goods (such as food) and (ii) assistance in constructing or obtaining capital goods (such as tractors, dams, or roads). Based on what you have learned in this chapter, how likely are such efforts to *permanently* raise the standard of living in such countries? Explain.

3. Both Louisiana and Quebec have systems of local law (state and provincial, respectively) that are heavily influenced by their common French heritage, which includes civil law. What do you predict is true about per capita income in Louisiana compared to the other U.S. states, and per capita income in Quebec compared to the other Canadian provinces? Is this prediction confirmed by the facts (which can be readily ascertained with a few quick Web searches)? Identify at least two other factors that you think are important to take into account when assessing whether the differences you observe are likely due to the influence of civil law institutions.

4. Consider two countries, A and B, which have identical *physical* endowments of a key natural resource. In country A, any profits made from extracting that resource are subject to confiscation by the government, while in country B, there is no such risk. How does the risk of expropriation affect the *economic* endowment of the two nations? In which nation are people richer?

5. In light of your answer to question 4, how do you explain that in some countries there is widespread political support for government policies that expropriate resources from some groups for the purpose of handing them out to other groups?

6. If the crucial factor determining a country's low standard of living is the adverse set of legal and cultural institutions it possesses, can you offer suggestions for how the other nations of the world might help in permanently raising that country's standard of living?

CHAPTER 5

Surf Gangs

What do California surfers and Maine lobstermen have in common? Hint: It's more than just salt water. In fact, both groups have devised ingenious systems to conserve natural resources. The systems not only don't require any help from the government, they actually do their work *despite* government rules that would otherwise cause those resources to be squandered.

COMMON PROPERTY

If you've ever seen a picture of the Washington Monument, you've seen an example of a **common property resource,** that is, a resource jointly owned by a group of individuals who cannot (for legal or physical reasons) divide the resource into pieces and dispose of them separately. Every owner (in this instance, every citizen of the United States) simultaneously owns the entire structure. Similarly, most highways and streets are also common property, owned by the citizens of the relevant jurisdiction, who, despite their ownership may not sell any piece of the roadway.

Common property resources do not have to be owned by a government. Indeed, many are not. For example, the members of a neighborhood swimming pool association each own common property (the swimming pool and accompanying land and buildings), but the membership in the association is limited to those people willing to pay for the right to be members, and thus is closed to those who won't pay.

ACCESS: OPEN OR CLOSED?

There is a crucial distinction between the situations just mentioned and other examples of common property resources. Both the Washington

Monument and the swimming pool association are said to be **closed access** common property. In the example of the Washington Monument, even if you are a citizen, and thus an owner, you cannot simply access the monument any time you like. Instead, you must first obtain a ticket that specifies the day and time slot when you are allowed to enter the facility. Although there is no charge for the ticket, the monument is closed to you unless you have one. Similarly, the association swimming pool has closed access: Only owners and their guests are lawfully allowed to use it. No matter how hot and humid the day, and despite the great relief you would get from a quick dip, if you are not an owner or an authorized guest, the pool is closed to you.

Now consider streets, roads, and highways. Nearly all of these (in the United States and elsewhere) are said to be **open access.** That is, day or night, anyone who wishes to is legally free to use them. You need not pay a fee to drive on the road, nor even have a ticket. This is true even if you are not an owner of the road (because, for example, you are a citizen of another nation). That is, unlike the example of closed access property, no one legally may be excluded from open access property. (Toll roads are closed access—you may not use them without paying a monetary toll. We'll note later in this chapter why some roads are operated this way.)

THE PROBLEM WITH OPEN ACCESS

The good news about open access resources is that everyone may lawfully use them at their own convenience, without directly paying for access. Not even a "free" ticket is required. But this is also the *bad* news about open access resources. Consider the example of the Washington Monument. Once it officially opened on October 9, 1888, anyone could ride the elevator or climb stairs to the top any time they wanted, during its hours of operations. Yet the monument, which was immensely popular from the outset, steadily attracted more and more visitors, and the crowds created **congestion.** Long lines formed to get inside and once there, visitors faced extended waits to use the elevator. Even though one could walk up the 897 stairs that led to the top, these were jammed with people going up and down, making the transit a slow, miserable process. The more people that packed in, the more unpleasant it became for every other visitor. Plenty of people were *visiting* the monument, but few were *enjoying* it.

This sort of congestion plagues all popular open access resources. In the case of urban highways, for example, the congestion comes in the form of huge and frequent traffic jams. These not only make drivers miserable and waste their time (and gasoline). The traffic jams also result in *less* traffic actually flowing over the highway, because people are moving so slowly. Plenty of people are *on* the road, but almost no one enjoys what they actually want—speedy travel to their intended destination.

SURF GANGS

Areas along the California coast known as "surf breaks" are locations where waves are particularly conducive to high-quality surfing. California law defines the coast as open access up to the high-tide mark. This makes surf breaks a classic open access resource, subject to congestion due to excessive entry by individuals hoping to enjoy the resource. People can (and in many places do) crowd into surf breaks in such numbers that they markedly degrade the surfing experience for everyone. In the language of economics, the heavily congested surf breaks are said to be overexploited: The total enjoyment of surfers is actually *less* than it would be if access to the breaks were restricted.

Long-time regular surfers, known as "locals" (or surf gangs), have battled back against the overcrowding at many surf breaks. They seek to limit the total number of surfers at a site and to regulate the use of waves by people who surf there. In both instances, the objective is to reduce the congestion and overexploitation of the valuable resource (high-quality waves).

Surf gangs employ two specific practices. First, they establish unwritten but unmistakable rules of etiquette for each surf break. These rules, enforced by members of the local surf gang, help establish who gets to ride which wave at a site. This reduces collisions and enhances the surfing experience. These rules are just like the rules of the road on a highway, except they are established and enforced by private individuals rather than by a government.

The second practice of the surf gangs is known as "localism." Quite simply, people who are not established surfers at a particular break are not allowed to surf in the best areas of the break. Enforcement of this practice (as well the etiquette rules) is undertaken via unpleasant verbal assaults and sometimes even physical hostility. In this way the surf breaks are converted from open access resources to closed access.

THE BENEFITS OF CLOSED ACCESS

The actions of the surf gangs create benefits and enhance **economic efficiency** in two ways. First, by limiting the number of surfers on the break and having rules of etiquette, crowding and collisions are reduced, thereby enhancing the quality of the surfing experience. Second, many locations have hidden hazards such as underwater rocks or dangerous currents, and local knowledge can reduce the harms caused by them. Understanding how to read the water at a particular location can lead to better surfing. The value of the time investment it takes to learn about such specific factors can be sharply reduced or wiped out by congestion. When excessive entry by nonlocals is prevented, local surfers are encouraged to undertake the effort to learn and master local conditions, creating knowledge that can be passed on to others. The result is greater safety and overall enjoyment of the surfing experience.

It is worth noting that surf gangs are not always successful in their efforts. When breaks are close to densely populated areas, nonlocals can simply show up in overwhelming numbers, making it impossible for the locals to prevent congestion or enforce etiquette. In these situations, overexploitation of the resource takes place, and the result is a low-quality surfing experience for all.

LOBSTER GANGS

On the opposite coast of America, lobster fishermen in Maine organize themselves into harbor (or lobster) gangs to prevent the overexploitation of the lobster fishery. Until 1997, under Maine law the lobster fishery was open access. As a practical matter, commercial fishing for lobster was open to anyone who wished to set out traps.

Many people liked the freedom offered by open access, but it led to excessive fishing, threatening the very existence of the Maine lobster. Hence, all along the Maine coast, local fishermen organized themselves into gangs, which established and enforced rules for who could fish commercially for lobster in each harbor area and how the commercial fishing could take place (such as setting permissible locations for traps). Intruders from outside a gang were initially warned with a distinctive knot tied in the line connecting the trap to the floating buoy that marked its location. If the warning failed, the line was cut (causing the loss of the $55 trap, plus line and buoy), or the trap was hauled to the surface by a gang member and permanently disabled.

Technically such actions by the gangs are in violation of Maine law. But the *effect* of the gangs has been to preserve and even enhance the population of Maine lobsters. Without the lobster gangs, indiscriminant commercial fishing by all comers under the open access regime would have decimated lobster populations.

THE GANGS AND THE MONUMENT

When the National Park Service (NPS) decided to close access to the Washington Monument by requiring tickets, it was acting completely within the law. The actions of the surf gangs and lobster gangs technically are outside the law. Nevertheless, the actions of the NPS and the gangs protected and enhanced resources, the value of which was being destroyed by the open access to them.

Under open access, a visit to the Washington Monument eventually became a tedious, often unpleasant, experience for visitors. Closed access under the ticket system has dramatically improved the quality of a visit to the monument. Moreover, because the system smoothes out the flow of visitors over the day, it actually became possible for the NPS to admit *more* total visitors to the site each year.

Under open access, even the best surf breaks yield a low-quality surfing experience, because the extreme overcrowding leads to collisions, near-misses, and long waits to get a small segment of a surfable wave. The closed access and etiquette imposed by the surf gangs have not only improved the surfing experience dramatically for local surfers. They have also improved safety, because surfers have an enhanced incentive to learn about local hazards and transmit that knowledge to their fellow surfers.

Under open access, the Maine lobster fishery was threatened with depletion, perhaps even destruction (see Chapter 25 to learn more about the global threat posed by open access to fisheries). In closing access, the harbor gangs of Maine have protected the resource by reducing fishing pressure, helping the lobster population grow to record levels.[1]

NO PAIN, NO GAIN

Of course, in each instance, there are some people who are made worse off, and thus are unhappy. People who fail to carefully plan their visits to the monument are often disappointed because they either cannot get a ticket or cannot gain entry at a time best for them. Similarly, surfers visiting breaks policed by local surf gangs find that they are relegated to the inferior portions of the break. And in Maine, outsiders may attempt to fish only at the peril of losing their fishing gear.

---

1 Since 1997, Maine has limited the number of commercial lobstermen with a license system, and also set limits on the number of traps that each person may set out. Both actions have helped close access to the fishery and thus complemented the work of the lobster gangs in protecting the population of Maine lobsters.

As a practical matter, it seems almost impossible to ensure that no one will be made worse off when an open access resource is converted to a closed access resource. Consider tolls for roads or bridges, useful in reducing vehicular congestion and increasing traffic flow. Some users are likely to have preferred slow travel and no toll to speedy travel with a toll. Some people will even choose not to pay the toll, and thus be relegated to a route that for them is inferior even to the original highly congested route. Both groups clearly lose due to the toll.

Even so, limiting access to congested or overexploited resources has been shown repeatedly to improve the well-being of the vast majority of individuals, and increase human wealth, in the broadest sense of that term. Indeed, when the open access resource in question is a natural resource (such as a fishery), limiting access is often the *only* way we can preserve the very thing that our attempts to enjoy are threatening to destroy. In a world of scarcity, this is a fact that simply cannot be avoided.

DISCUSSION QUESTIONS

1. Is access to the house or apartment in which you live open or closed? If it is currently a closed access resource, how would the house likely be treated differently if it were converted to an open access resource—one that anyone could use at any time in any way she chose? Explain.

2. Explain the sense in which your classroom is an example of a closed access resource. Explain what would happen to the quality of your education if access to the room were open—in the sense that anyone could come in during class time and, say, have a rave.

3. Referring back to the last question, raves and education are both goods. That is, people typically prefer more of each to less. Do you think it is proper that people may not hold raves in the room when your class meets? Can you suggest a general principle that could guide university administrators as to when access to your room should be closed rather than open? Would the rule you suggest make *some* people worse off? If so, who?

4. Some nominally closed resources are effectively open access. For example, to gain entry to Yellowstone National Park by automobile one must pay a fee of $25. But during the popular summer months, at this price, far more people want to drive into the park than can be readily accommodated by its roads. The result is terrible road congestion, added air pollution, and frayed tempers. In fact, the park is

then (very nearly) an open access resource, heavily visited by many but not fully appreciated by any, at least during the peak season. The National Park Service could transform Yellowstone into a closed access resource simply by raising the entry fee. Explain who would gain and who would lose by doing so. Why do you think the Park Service has thus far refused to raise the entry fee? Explain.

5. It is generally acknowledged that more people would like to attend the Super Bowl each year than in fact attend. (Presumably, many people stay away due to the high cost of the tickets, which are priced at many hundreds of dollars apiece.) Suppose a law were passed specifying that people who wished to attend need not even have a ticket, much less pay for one? How would attendance at the game change? What would determine who got into the stadium? Who would gain and who would lose due to the law?

6. Almost all privately owned resources are closed access. Many (perhaps most) government-owned or controlled resources are open access. Can you suggest any explanations for this observation? Explain.

PART TWO

Supply and Demand

Introduction

The tools of **demand** and **supply** are the most basic and useful elements in the economist's kit. Indeed, many economists would argue that the **law of demand**—the lower the price of a good, the greater the quantity of that good demanded by purchasers—is the single most powerful proposition in all of economics. Simply stated, the law of demand has the capacity, unmatched by any other proposition in economics, to explain an incredibly diverse range of human behaviors. For example, the law of demand explains why buildings are taller in downtown areas than in outlying suburbs and also why people are willing to sit in the upper deck of football stadiums even though lower-deck seats are clearly superior. The great explanatory power of the law of demand is almost matched by that of the **law of supply,** which states that the higher the price of a good, the greater will be the quantity of that good supplied by producers. The law of supply helps us understand why people receive a premium wage when they work overtime, as well as why parking places at the beach are so much more expensive during the summer months than during the winter.

SEX, BOOZE, AND DRUGS

When the laws of demand and supply are combined, they illuminate the enormous **gains from trade** that arise from voluntary exchange. In Chapter 6, we examine what happens when the government attempts to prohibit the exchanges that give rise to these gains. The consequences are often surprising, always costly, and—sadly—sometimes tragic. We find, for example, that when the federal government made alcoholic beverages illegal during the era known as Prohibition, Americans responded by switching from beer to hard liquor and by getting drunk more often when they drank. We also show that the government's ongoing efforts to prevent individuals from using drugs such as marijuana and cocaine cause the drive-by shootings that have occurred in many major cities and also encourage drug overdoses among users. Finally, we explain why laws against prostitution help foster the spread of AIDS.

All Fracked Up

Hydraulic fracturing—better known in the press as "fracking"—is revolutionizing the production of natural gas, and thus the entire energy market. According to some observers, the revolution is making us richer, cleaning the environment, and stifling climate change. Other observers are convinced that fracking will pollute the environment, hasten climate change, and ultimately make us poorer, not richer. One thing is for sure. The spread of fracking has driven down the cost of energy, and this in turn is transforming other markets. It is a classic example of **demand** and **supply** in action. It is also a story that illustrates once again that the application of just a little bit of economics will go a long way in untangling the facts.

Kidneys for Sale

Sometimes markets can create gains for humanity in the most unexpected places. One instance involves the transplantation of human organs. Many thousands of people die each year waiting in vain for the donation of a lifesaving organ. As we see in Chapter 8, one major impediment to saving their lives is the fact that although we allow voluntary organ donations at a zero price, we prohibit individuals from being paid for a human organ for transplant.

It is legal to pay the surgeons who perform the transplants, and lawful for hospitals to profit from organ transplants performed in their operating rooms. But it is against the law for you to sell a cornea, a kidney, or a lobe of your liver. It is even unlawful for your loved ones to benefit from the harvesting of any of your organs after your death. This reduces the number of human organs available for transplant and thus results in the deaths of many thousands of people. We know from the experience of other nations that paying for organs induces many more donations. Safeguards against abuse (such as involuntary "donations") are also relatively easy to implement. Moreover, paying for organs would add relatively little to the costs of the insurance programs that already pay for virtually all transplants. On balance, it thus appears that allowing payment for transplant organs would benefit the donors and, more important, save the lives of many thousands of recipients—which is surely a classic illustration of the gains from trade.

ARE WE RUNNING OUT OF WATER?

Despite abundant everyday evidence of the power of prices to stimulate production, ration consumption, and ensure the efficient allocation of scarce goods, sometimes people deny that prices can perform their wonders even for goods like water, so essential to human life. This denial appears to be based on a variety of myths that surround water—notions that the planet is somehow drying up or that water cannot (because it is essential to life) be allocated through markets or that salty ocean water cannot readily be converted into freshwater.

As we see in Chapter 9, such ideas simply can't stand up to careful scrutiny. The earth is a closed system: Water can be dirtied, cleaned up, or moved around, but when we use it, we don't destroy it. Moreover, because it *is* so precious to us, water is an *ideal* candidate for the unfettered operation of competitive markets. Any attempts to interfere with open markets for water will reduce our total wealth and will place a disproportionate share of the burden on the people who are least able to bear it—those at the bottom of the income distribution.

One important conclusion of this chapter is that the water shortages and water crises periodically afflicting various parts of the world are rarely the result of droughts. They are far more often caused by government officials who are unwilling or unable to accept the reality of the laws of demand and supply.

BANKRUPT LANDLORDS, FROM SEA TO SHINING SEA

Our final application of demand and supply analysis comes in Chapter 10. This chapter brings us back to the issue discussed in Chapters 6 and 8—the effects of government interference with free markets. Here we examine **rent controls**—legal ceilings on the rent that landlords may charge for apartments. Although the effects of rent controls are perhaps less tragic than some of the effects observed in Chapter 6 or 8, they are just as surprising and often as costly. We find, for example, that legal ceilings on rents have increased the extent of homelessness in the United States, have led to a rise in racial discrimination, and have caused the wholesale destruction of hundreds of thousands of dwelling units in our nation's major cities. We cannot escape one simple fact: Politicians may pass legislation, and bureaucrats may do their best to enforce it, but the laws of demand and supply ultimately rule the economy.

CHAPTER 6

Sex, Booze, and Drugs

Before 1914, cocaine was legal in this country. Today it is not. Alcoholic beverages are legal in the United States today. From 1920 to 1933, they were not. Prostitution is legal in Nevada today. In the other 49 states, it is not.[1] All these goods—sex, booze, and drugs—have at least one thing in common: The consumption of each brings together a willing seller with a willing buyer, creating an act of mutually beneficial exchange (at least in the opinion of the parties involved). Partly because of this property, attempts to proscribe the consumption of these goods have met with less than spectacular success and have yielded some peculiar patterns of production, distribution, and usage. Let's see why.

SUPPLY-SIDE ENFORCEMENT

When the government seeks to prevent voluntary exchange, it must generally decide whether to go after the seller or the buyer. In most cases (and certainly where sex, booze, and drugs are concerned), the government targets sellers, because this is where the authorities get the most benefit from their enforcement dollars. A cocaine dealer, even a small retail pusher, often supplies dozens or even hundreds of users each day, as did speakeasies (illegal saloons) during Prohibition; a hooker typically services three to ten "tricks" per day. By incarcerating the supplier, the police can prevent several, or even several hundred, transactions from taking place, which is usually much more cost-effective than going

---

1 These statements are not entirely correct. Even today, cocaine may be obtained legally by prescription from a physician. Prostitution in Nevada is legal only in counties that have chosen to permit it. Finally, some counties in the United States remain "dry," prohibiting the sale of beer, wine, and distilled spirits.

after the buyers one by one. It is not that the police ignore the consumers of illegal goods. Indeed, sting operations, in which the police pose as illicit sellers, often make the headlines. Nevertheless, most enforcement efforts focus on the supply side, and so shall we.

Law enforcement activities directed against the suppliers of illegal goods increase the suppliers' operating costs. The risks of fines, jail sentences, and possibly even violence become part of the costs of doing business and must be taken into account by existing and potential suppliers. Some entrepreneurs will leave the business, turning their talents to other activities. Others will resort to clandestine (and costly) means to hide their operations from the police. Still others will restrict the circle of buyers with whom they are willing to deal to minimize the chances that a customer is a cop. Across the board, the costs of operation are higher, and at any given price, less of the product will be available. There is a reduction in supply, and the result is a higher price for the good.

This increase in price is, in a sense, exactly what the enforcement officials are after, for the consumers of sex, booze, and drugs behave according to the **law of demand:** The higher the price of a good, the lower the amount consumed. So the immediate impact of the enforcement efforts against sellers is to reduce the consumption of the illegal good. There are, however, some other effects.

VIOLENCE EMERGES

First, because the good in question is illegal, people who have a **comparative advantage** in conducting illegal activities will be attracted to the business of supplying (and perhaps demanding) the good. Some may have an existing criminal record and are relatively unconcerned about adding to it. Others may have developed skills in evading detection and prosecution while engaged in other criminal activities. Some may simply look at the illegal activity as another means of thumbing their noses at society. The general point is when an activity is made illegal, people who are good at being criminals are attracted to that activity.

Illegal contracts are usually not enforceable through legal channels (even if they were, few suppliers of illegal goods would be foolish enough to complain to the police about not being paid for their products). Thus, buyers and sellers of illegal goods must frequently resort to private methods of contract enforcement, which often entails violence.[2]

---

2 Fundamentally, violence—such as involuntary incarceration—also plays a key role in the government's enforcement of legal contracts. We often do not think of it as violence, of course, because it is usually cushioned by constitutional safeguards and procedural rules.

Hence, people who are relatively good at violence are attracted to illegal activities and have greater **incentives** to employ their talents. This is one reason why the murder rate in America rose to record levels during Prohibition and then dropped sharply when liquor was again made legal. It also helps explain why the number of drug-related murders soared during the 1980s and why drive-by shootings became commonplace in many drug-infested cities. The Thompson submachine gun of the 1930s and the MAC-10 machine gun of the 1980s were just low-cost means of contract enforcement.

USAGE CHANGES

The attempts of law enforcement officials to drive sellers of illegal goods out of business have another effect. Based on recent wholesale prices, $300,000 worth of pure heroin weighs about 10 pounds, while $300,000 worth of marijuana weighs about 200 pounds. As any drug smuggler can tell you, hiding 10 pounds of contraband is a lot easier than hiding 200 pounds. Thus, to avoid detection and prosecution, suppliers of the illegal good have an incentive to deal in the more valuable versions of their product, which for drugs and booze mean the more potent versions. Bootleggers during Prohibition concentrated on hard liquor rather than on beer and wine. Even today, moonshine typically has roughly twice the alcohol content of legal hard liquor such as bourbon, scotch, or vodka. After narcotics became illegal in this country in 1914, importers switched from the milder opium to its more valuable and more potent derivative, heroin.

The move to the more potent versions of illegal commodities is enhanced by enforcement activities directed against users. Not only do users, like suppliers, find it easier (cheaper) to hide the more potent versions, but there is also a change in relative prices due to user penalties. Typically, the law has lower penalties for using an illegal substance than for distributing it. Within each category (use or sale), however, there is commonly the same penalty regardless of value per unit. For example, during Prohibition, a bottle of wine and a bottle of more expensive, more potent hard liquor were equally illegal. Today, the possession of 1 gram of 90 percent pure cocaine brings the same penalty as the possession of 1 gram of 10 percent pure cocaine. Given the physical quantities, there is a fixed cost (the legal penalty) associated with being caught, regardless of value per unit (and thus potency) of the substance. Hence, the structure of legal penalties raises the relative price of less potent versions, encouraging users to substitute more potent versions—heroin instead of opium, hashish instead of marijuana, and hard liquor instead of beer.

Penalties against users also encourage a change in the nature of usage. Before 1914, cocaine was legal in this country and was used openly as a mild stimulant, much as people today use caffeine. (Cocaine was even an ingredient in the original formulation of Coca-Cola.) This type of usage—small, regular doses over long time intervals—becomes relatively more expensive when the substance is made illegal. Extensive usage (small doses spread over time) is more likely to be detected by the authorities than intensive usage (a large dose consumed at once), simply because possession time is longer and the drug must be accessed more frequently. Thus, when a substance is made illegal, there is an incentive for consumers to switch toward more intensive usage. Rather than ingesting cocaine orally in the form of a highly diluted liquid solution, as was commonly done before 1914, people switched to snorting or injecting it. During Prohibition, people dispensed with cocktails before dinner each night; instead, on the less frequent occasions when they drank, they more often drank to get drunk. The same phenomenon is observed today. People under the age of 21 consume alcoholic beverages less frequently than people over the age of 21. But when they do drink, they are more likely to drink to get drunk. Binge drinking becomes the norm.

INFORMATION COSTS RISE

Not surprisingly, the suppliers of illegal commodities are reluctant to advertise their wares openly; the police are as capable of reading billboards and watching TV as potential customers are. Suppliers are also reluctant to establish easily recognized identities and regular places and hours of business because to do so raises the chance of being caught by the police. Information about the price and quality of products being sold goes underground, often with unfortunate effects for consumers.

With legal goods, consumers have several means of obtaining information. They can learn from friends, advertisements, and personal experience. When goods are legal, they can be trademarked for identification. The trademark cannot legally be copied and the courts protect it. Given such easily identified brands, consumers can be made aware of the quality and price of each. If their experience does not meet expectations, they can assure themselves of no further contact with the unsatisfactory product by never buying that brand again.

When a general class of products becomes illegal, there are fewer ways to obtain information. Brand names are no longer protected by law, so falsification of well-known brands ensues. When products do not meet expectations, it is more difficult (costly) for consumers to punish suppliers. Frequently, the result is degradation of and uncertainty about product quality. The consequences for consumers of the illegal goods are often unpleasant and sometimes fatal.

DANGEROUS SEX

Consider prostitution. In Nevada counties where prostitution is legal, the prostitutes are required to register with the local authorities, and they generally conduct their business in well-established bordellos. These establishments advertise openly and rely heavily on repeat business. Health officials test the prostitutes weekly for venereal disease and monthly for HIV (the virus that causes AIDS). Contrast this with other areas of the country, where prostitution is illegal. Suppliers are generally streetwalkers, because a fixed, physical location is too easy for the police to detect and raid. They change locations frequently to reduce harassment by police. Repeat business is reported to be minimal. Frequently, customers have never seen the prostitute before and never will again.

The difference in outcomes is striking. In Nevada, the spread of venereal disease by legal prostitutes is estimated to be almost nonexistent. To date, none of the registered prostitutes in Nevada has tested positive for HIV. By contrast, in some major cities outside Nevada, the incidence of venereal disease among prostitutes is estimated to be near 100 percent. In Miami, one study found that 19 percent of all incarcerated prostitutes tested positive for HIV. In Newark, New Jersey, 52 percent of the prostitutes tested were infected with the AIDS virus, and about half of the prostitutes in Washington, D.C., and New York City are also believed to be carrying the AIDS virus. Due to the lack of reliable information in markets for illegal goods, customers frequently do not know exactly what they are getting. As a result, they sometimes get more than they bargained for.

DEADLY DRUGS AND BAD BOOZE

Consider alcohol and drugs. Today, alcoholic beverages are heavily advertised to establish their brand names and are carried by reputable dealers. Customers can readily punish suppliers for any deviation from the expected potency or quality by withdrawing their business, telling their friends, or even bringing a lawsuit. Similar circumstances prevailed before 1914 in this country for the hundreds of products containing opium or cocaine.

During Prohibition, consumers of alcohol often did not know exactly what they were buying or where to find the supplier the next day if they were dissatisfied. Fly-by-night operators sometimes adulterated liquor with far more lethal methyl alcohol. In tiny concentrations, this made watered-down booze taste like it had more kick, but in only slightly higher concentrations, the methyl alcohol blinded or even killed the unsuspecting consumer. Even in "reputable" speakeasies (those likely to be in business at the same location the next day), bottles bearing the labels of high-priced foreign whiskeys were refilled repeatedly with locally (and illegally) produced rotgut until their labels wore off.

In the 1970s, more than one purchaser of what was reputed to be high-potency Panama Red or Acapulco gold marijuana ended up with low-potency pot heavily loaded with stems, seeds, and maybe even oregano. Buyers of cocaine must worry not only about how much the product has been cut along the distribution chain, but also about what has been used to cut it. In recent years, the purity of cocaine at the retail level has ranged between 10 and 95 percent; for heroin, the degree of purity has ranged from 5 to 50 percent. Cutting agents can turn out to be any of various sugars, local anesthetics, or amphetamines; on occasion, rat poison has been used.

We noted earlier that the legal penalties for the users of illegal goods encourage them to use more potent forms and to use them more intensively. These facts and the uncertain quality and potency of the illegal products yield a deadly combination. During Prohibition, the death rate from acute alcohol poisoning (due to overdose) was more than 30 times higher than today. In 1927 alone, 12,000 people died from acute alcohol poisoning, and many thousands more were blinded or killed by contaminated booze. Today, about 8,000 people per year die as a direct result of consuming either cocaine or heroin. Of that total, it is estimated, roughly 80 percent die from either an overdose caused by an unexpectedly potent product or an adverse reaction to the material used to cut the drug. Clearly, caveat emptor ("let the buyer beware") is a warning to be taken seriously if one is consuming an illegal product.

Success Is Limited

We noted at the beginning of this chapter that one of the effects of making a good illegal is to raise its price. One might well ask, "by how much?" During the early 1990s, the federal government was spending about $2 billion per year in its efforts to stop the importation of cocaine from Colombia. One study concluded that these efforts had hiked the price of cocaine by 4 percent relative to what it would have been, had the federal government done nothing to interdict cocaine imports. The study estimated that the cost of raising the price of cocaine an additional 2 percent would be $1 billion per year. More recently, Nobel Laureate Gary Becker and his colleagues have estimated that America's war on drugs costs at least $100 billion per year. And the results? The prices of heroin and cocaine are at record-low levels.

The government's efforts to halt imports of marijuana have had some success, presumably because marijuana is easier to detect than cocaine. Nevertheless, suppliers have responded by cultivating marijuana domestically instead of importing it or by bringing it in across the relatively open U.S.–Canadian border rather than from elsewhere. The net effect has been an estimated tenfold increase in potency due to the superior farming techniques available in this country and Canada, as well as the use of genetic bioengineering to improve strains.

A few years ago, most states and the federal government began restricting sales of cold medicines containing pseudoephedrine, because that ingredient was widely used for making the illegal stimulant methamphetamine in home laboratories. The restrictions succeeded in reducing home production of "meth." They also led to a huge increase in imports of a far more potent version of meth from Mexico. Overall, it is estimated that neither consumption of nor addiction to methamphetamine was reduced by the restrictions. But overdoses from the drug rose sharply because of the greater purity of the imports. Moreover, the "shake-and-bake" method of domestic production that arose after the crackdown on cold medicines had an unintended and often fatal consequence. The mixing process often goes wrong, and when it does, the ensuing explosion causes horrific and sometimes fatal burns of the head and upper torso. Many emergency rooms and hospital burn centers have been overwhelmed by these casualties.

Consider also the government's efforts to eliminate the consumption of alcohol during the 1920s and 1930s. They failed so badly that the Eighteenth Amendment, which put Prohibition in place, was the first (and so far the only) constitutional amendment ever to be repealed. As for prostitution, it is reputed to be "the oldest profession" and by all accounts continues to flourish today, even in Newark and Miami.

The government's inability to halt the consumption of sex, booze, or drugs does not mean that its efforts have failed. Indeed, the impact of these efforts is manifested in their consequences, ranging from tainted drugs and alcohol to disease-ridden prostitutes. The message instead is that when the government attempts to prevent mutually beneficial exchange, even its best efforts are unlikely to meet with spectacular success.

Discussion Questions

1. From an economic perspective, is it possible for laws restricting dangerous or destructive activity to be *too* strict? Explain. (*Hint:* Revisit Chapter 3.)

2. In recent years, more than 15 states have passed so-called medical marijuana laws. Typically, these laws permit individuals to lawfully purchase marijuana from licensed stores, provided they have letter from their doctor recommending its use. Use the reasoning in this chapter to predict how the characteristics of medical marijuana will differ from illegal marijuana. Focus specifically on price, quality, variety, and consistency (or predictability).

3. The federal government currently taxes alcohol on the basis of the 100-proof gallon. (Alcohol that is 100 proof is 50 percent pure ethyl alcohol; most hard liquor sold is 80 proof, or 40 percent ethyl alcohol, whereas wine is usually about 24 proof, and most beer is 6–10 proof.) How would alcohol consumption patterns change if the government taxed alcohol strictly on the basis of volume rather than also taking its potency into account?

4. During Prohibition, some speakeasy operators paid bribes to ensure that the police did not raid them. Would you expect the quality of the liquor served in such speakeasies to be higher or lower than in those that did not pay bribes? Would you expect to find differences (e.g., in income levels) between the customers patronizing the two types of speakeasies?

5. The markets for prostitution in Nevada and New Jersey have two important differences: (i) prostitutes in New Jersey face higher costs because of government efforts to prosecute them and (ii) customers in New Jersey face higher risks of contracting diseases from prostitutes because the illegal nature of the business makes reliable information about product quality much more costly to obtain. Given these facts, in which state would you expect the price of prostitution services to be higher? Which state would have the higher amount of services consumed (adjusted for population differences)? Explain your answer.

6. According to the Surgeon General of the United States, nicotine is the most addictive drug known to humanity, and cigarette smoking kills perhaps 300,000–400,000 people per year in the United States. Why then isn't tobacco illegal in America?

CHAPTER 7

All Fracked Up

There is an energy revolution upon us. It is neither blowing in the wind nor shining in the sky. Instead, it is a gas revolution—natural gas, that is, pouring out of the ground in unprecedented quantities. It is changing the way we power our air conditioners and heat our homes. According to some observers, the revolution is making us richer, cleaning the environment, and stifling climate change. All of this is happening because of a controversial drilling technique known as **fracking**—a technique that other observers are convinced will pollute the environment, hasten climate change, and ultimately make us poorer, not richer. Let's see what we can sort out.

FRACKING

Fracking is the informal name given to the hydraulic fracturing process in which water, sand, and small amounts of chemicals are injected deep underground to break rock apart. The process has been utilized in the oil and gas business since 1947, but its usage expanded rapidly after 1998. That is when a petroleum entrepreneur named George P. Mitchell figured out how to make fracking a commercially feasible means of extracting gas from shale rock located thousands of feet underground. The process is now widely used in Arkansas, Colorado, North Dakota, Pennsylvania, and Texas, and is spreading to other U.S. states and to other nations.

Hydraulic fracturing has become a major public issue in America and elsewhere because of its potential for "good news and bad news" on a global scale. The great promise of fracking is that it can unlock vast stores of cheap, relatively clean energy. Yet there is also a downside: the process itself is believed to cause earthquakes and has been linked to contamination of groundwater. Moreover, the natural gas produced by fracking, although clean compared to coal and oil, may not be as clean as other energy sources. So, it would seem, a classic **trade-off** exists.

First, the Good News

Between 2005 and 2010, natural gas production from fracking grew an average of 45 percent per year. Over the same period, fracked gas (more often referred to as shale gas) expanded from 4 to 24 percent of overall natural gas production in the United States, and helped natural gas grow rapidly relative to other energy sources. Not surprisingly, this **increase in supply** pushed natural gas prices down—fast and far. Natural gas costs 75 percent less than it did over the years 2003–2008. Between 2008 and 2013, the price of natural gas sank from $12 per million British thermal units (MMBtu) to about $3 per MMBtu.[1] This left the price in the United States at about one-quarter of its level in Europe and about one-eighth the amount paid in Asian markets. (The big price disparities are possible because it takes a long time to build the facilities—specialized tankers or pipelines—appropriate for transporting natural gas in large quantities.)

The sharply lower price of natural gas is changing behavior across America, as users respond in exactly the ways predicted by the **law of demand.** For example, cheap electricity from natural-gas-powered turbines is beginning to displace electricity from coal-fired plants, thereby lowering heating and cooling costs, reducing manufacturing energy costs, and cutting air pollution and carbon dioxide emissions. Natural gas is also a key ingredient for the petrochemicals industry, so the lower gas prices are bringing back to America manufacturing activities that had moved offshore. Companies have even begun to experiment with switching trucks and buses from diesel to natural gas. On all of these counts, the wealth of America is higher in every dimension, including the environmental one.

Next, the Bad News

Nothing in life is free, and fracking is no exception. One key concern about the process has been the potential for groundwater contamination. Fracking wells are drilled vertically for thousands of feet before

---

1 A British thermal unit (Btu) is the amount of energy required to heat one pound of water by one degree Fahrenheit. Thus, a million British thermal units (MMBtu) of energy would heat one million pounds of water (about 125,000 gallons) by one degree Fahrenheit.

they turn horizontally to go into the shale rock, fracture it, and retrieve the gas. Although the fracking itself occurs well away from any water sources, when the gas comes up the vertical pipe, it is possible for some of it to escape from the pipe. If the vertical well shaft passes through a surrounding aquifer from which people draw their water, the gas will contaminate the water if there is a leak.

Gas that escapes the pipe is gas that cannot be sold. Drilling companies prevent leaks by injecting cement into the well, totally encasing the pipe and sealing the gas off from any nearby aquifer (or indeed anything else). Although leaks do happen, the issue here is not fracking, *per se.* Gas can escape from virtually any gas or oil well. The key to preventing them is careful well construction. As the Environmental Defense Fund notes, "The groundwater pollution incidents . . . have all been caused by well construction problems." Overall, experts seem to agree that as long as standard drilling practices are adhered to, groundwater contamination is extremely rare.[2]

Much has been made about the potential for fracking to cause earthquakes. Indeed, it is one of many human activities known to cause temblors. As long as 90 years ago, for example, scientists realized that conventional oil and gas production can cause small quakes. More recently, it has been recognized that the production of geothermal power also induces earthquakes. Even the impoundment of large amounts of water behind a dam can put enough stress on the earth to cause earthquakes. According to the National Academy of Sciences, however, the chances are negligible that fracking would prompt an earthquake of a magnitude that would harm humans or property.

Trucks are used to haul the equipment, sand, chemicals, and even the water used in the drilling phase of the hydraulic fracturing process— trucks that are a nuisance on roads in the vicinity of the well property. The owner of the land where the drilling occurs is presumably compensated by the drilling company for this nuisance, but the neighbors generally are not. Many communities are thus enacting special truck regulations for well sites. For example, fracking trucks are often prohibited from operating at night and on the weekends, and some areas have even kept them off the roads when school buses are running.

---

2 There are photos and Internet film clips that show people igniting methane-infused tap water. Supposedly, the methane has entered the tap water from a fracking well. Naturally occurring methane in ground water supplies is fairly common in areas lying over fossil fuel reserves in places such as Pennsylvania. Indeed, setting one's water on fire has long been a party trick where the natural methane concentrations are high enough to be readily flammable. So a given example of flaming water *could* be due to a poorly constructed fracking well, but so far the chances appear to be tiny.

Such regulations are obviously imperfect, but they do seem to have calmed most objections to the truck traffic—the bulk of which lasts only a few weeks for each well. The trucks also accelerate wear and tear on local roads typically not designed for this intensity of use. Thus, local governments often insist (as part of the permitting process) that drilling companies agree to pay for upgrading or repairing the roads most affected.

WATER

There are also concerns about the amount of water used in fracking, because water is the number one ingredient in the process. A typical well requires about 4 million gallons to fracture the rocks and get the gas flowing at commercially profitable levels, after which water use halts. This sounds like a lot of water until we realize that it is less than the amount a typical golf course uses in two weeks. (We are not advocating more golf courses. We are only putting water usage in context. See Chapter 9 for more on water.)

On average, about 80 percent of the water used to create a fracking well stays underground. The rest comes back up as return flow during and immediately after the drilling process, and must be cleaned before it can be safely consumed or used in agricultural or commercial processes. Much has been made of the chemicals used in fracking, but they are typically the kinds that many people have around their homes, including those found in deodorants, glass and other cleaners, and even chewing gum and cosmetics. Thus, some of the return flow water can be cleaned in wastewater treatment facilities.

An additional complication for fracking in many areas, however, is that a variety of contaminants, including chloride and bromide salts, are brought from underground to the surface in the return flow water. Most of this contaminated wastewater is currently re-injected deep underground into separate EPA-regulated wells designated for this purpose, but a growing percentage of the contaminated water is now being recycled— cleaned with special methods and used to fracture other wells. Because the costs of such recycling have come down sharply in recent years, drillers have strong incentives to handle more of their wastewater in this way.

MORE ON THE ENVIRONMENT

Methane is regarded as a potent greenhouse gas. It is also the principal component of natural gas, and all natural gas production causes the release of some methane into the atmosphere. (This is also true of oil production, because natural gas typically provides the pressure that forces the oil to the surface.) Many critics of fracking have singled out the process as being a source of methane, but it appears that fracking releases little more methane than does conventional natural gas production. Moreover, balanced against the methane release is the fact that the natural gas produced by fracking is displacing coal as an energy source. Although coal production generates less methane than gas production, burning coal for energy generates about twice as much CO_2 per unit of energy as burning natural gas does. According to Environmental Protection Agency (EPA) estimates, replacing coal with natural gas (fracked or otherwise) likely *reduces* overall greenhouse gas emissions.

There is another key environmental issue to consider: air pollution. Coal-fired power plants are a major source of carbon monoxide, nitrogen oxides, sulfur dioxide, and particulate matter. Compared to coal, burning natural gas generates only 20 percent as much carbon monoxide and nitrogen oxides and virtually *no* sulfur dioxide or particulate matter. Fracking is displacing coal, so it is reducing air pollution.

Of course, one might argue that the relevant comparison is not natural gas versus coal, but rather gas versus wind, solar, nuclear, or hydroelectric power. The important thing to remember about these four "zero-emissions" sources of energy, however, is that each creates its own set of trade-offs. Nuclear power leaves behind spent fuel waste, which requires expensive handling to keep it from harming humans. Hydroelectric power interferes with the migration of endangered fish species, and has been used to subsidize agricultural production, which itself is a major source of water pollution due to fertilizer and pesticide runoff. Solar and wind use far more (and largely non-renewable) resources to produce energy than do natural gas, coal, nuclear, or hydro. Thus, although fracking offers clear environmental advantages over coal, trade-offs abound when it is compared to the other competing energy sources. (See Chapter 20 for more on this issue.)

Energy Independence

The fracking revolution is part of an even larger transformation of the U.S. energy industry in recent decades. Not only can natural gas be extracted from shale. So, too, can oil—and vast quantities of such shale oil are now being produced in North Dakota, Montana, and Texas. Considering all fossil fuels together—natural gas, oil, and coal—the United States now has more recoverable energy than any other nation in the world (Russia is a close 2nd). Indeed, America's reserves of fossil fuels now exceed the *combined* fossil fuel reserves of Saudi Arabia (3rd), China (4th), and Canada (6th).

All of this new energy has caused some interesting changes in trade patterns. About 20 years ago, construction began in the United States on specialized facilities designed to import natural gas from the Middle East and elsewhere. Now those same facilities are being converted to export natural gas, and more such export facilities are on the drawing boards. And it's not just natural gas. In 2011, for the first time on record, fuel, including gasoline, diesel, and jet fuel, was America's largest export commodity. Some experts are now predicting that U.S. oil production will exceed Saudi Arabia's by 2020. Although America still imports oil from the Middle East, our dependence on that region for energy has been dramatically slashed.

THE CONTRAST WITH EUROPE

Europe also sits atop shale formations that likely contain large amounts of natural gas, yet people in most countries there have turned their backs on it. France has said *"Non!"* to fracking, and, under pressure from various citizens' groups, governments in numerous other EU nations have put up substantial impediments to exploration. There are no doubt many reasons for the reluctance of Europeans to embrace fracking, but the simplest may also be among the most important: **property rights.**

In America, the rights to minerals under the surface (such as oil, gas, and gold) typically belong to whoever owns the land. The land owners can thus lease or sell these mineral rights to oil, gas, or other exploration companies. Oil and gas leases are extraordinarily lucrative for the land owners. In Europe, as elsewhere in the world, mineral rights belong not to the land owners, but to the central government. The practical implications of this difference in property rights are enormous. In America, land owners are richly rewarded for the nuisance of exploration and production on their property. In Europe, the landowners would get nothing if oil or gas were found under their lands—but would have to endure every bit as much nuisance as American landowners. It is little wonder then that people in Europe are much more likely to adopt an attitude of "Not In My Back Yard" (NIMBY) and, we should add, end up paying considerably more for their natural gas than Americans do.

THE BOTTOM LINE

The gas revolution has become a contentious public issue because, like most other things in life, it entails trade-offs. If you are the one who is subjected to a neighbor's drill site truck traffic, or your well water happens to be contaminated by an inadvertent gas leak, the trade-offs are likely to look pretty bad. For the overwhelming number of people, however, fracking seems to promise an improvement in the quality of their lives. Energy costs and air pollution are reduced, and American industry is made more competitive in world markets. So, while some people feel that the situation is "all fracked up," it seems that on balance this innovation in natural gas production will leave most of us both healthier and wealthier.

DISCUSSION QUESTIONS

1. If the property rights to food belonged not to the landowner where the food was grown, but instead belonged to the national government, how might this affect the willingness of people to let strangers grow food on their land?

2. So far, most government regulations dealing with fracking are written and enforced by state and local governments, rather than the federal government. What are the advantages and disadvantages of local and state government regulation compared to federal regulation? To what extent is the nature of the issue important to your analysis? For example, compare the issue of increased local truck traffic to the issue of increased releases of methane into the atmosphere.

3. Natural gas produced by fracking is a **substitute** for some goods, i.e., the demand for these other goods falls when the price of natural gas falls. Nevertheless, natural gas is also a **complement** for other goods—their demands rise when the price of natural gas falls. Identify at least two goods that are substitutes for natural gas and two that are complements. Considering both producers and consumers of those goods, analyze how they are either made better off or worse off as a result of the spread of fracking.

4. Pennsylvania and New York are adjacent states that both have large amounts of natural gas-rich shale underground. Coal mining has a long and important history in Pennsylvania, in contrast to New York, where there has been essentially no coal mining historically. Use economic analysis to predict how people (including politicians) in the two states have responded to the opportunities for extracting natural gas by fracking. How might attitudes toward fracking differ depending on whether the people involved lived in rural areas (where the fracking is likely to take place), or in the cities (where there will presumably be no fracking)?

5. If national governments in other nations agreed to share the profits from fracking with the landowners on whose property the drilling takes place, how might that change attitudes toward the process?

6. Russia now supplies virtually all of the natural gas used by the citizens of many European nations, and sales of natural gas and other fossil fuels account for fully 10 percent of the national income of Russia. Suppose that technological change substantially reduces the costs of shipping natural gas from the United States to Europe. Analyze the economic impacts (on Russia and on those dependent on Russian natural gas) of this technological change. Would American *consumers* of natural gas be made better off or worse off by the technological change?

CHAPTER 8

Kidneys for Sale

This year, more than 8,000 Americans will die waiting for an organ transplant. They will not die because physicians are unable to transplant organs or because their health insurance does not cover the cost of the transplant. They will die because since 1984, it has been against federal law to pay for human organs.[1] It is lawful to pay a man for his sperm, a woman for her eggs, and members of either gender for their blood. It is even lawful to donate an organ or to receive one as a gift. And it is certainly legal to pay the surgeons who perform the transplants. It is even lawful for hospitals to make a profit on organ transplants performed in their operating rooms. But it is against the law for you to sell a cornea, a kidney, or a lobe of your liver. It is even unlawful for your loved ones to be paid for any organs harvested after your death. Thus 8,000 people die every year, waiting in vain for someone to donate an organ to them.

An Overview of Organ Transplants

The transplantation of human body parts is not new. The first cornea was successfully transplanted in Austria in 1905. The first successful kidney transplant (between identical twins) was conducted in Boston in 1954. Since then, successful transplants of the pancreas, liver, heart, lung, hand, and even face have been performed. Indeed, there are now 37 different organs and types of human tissues that can be transplanted. None of this is cheap. In the United States, a kidney transplant costs about $250,000 on average, a liver transplant runs $520,000, and a heart transplant costs

---

1 This legislation was originally introduced by Rep. Al Gore (D., Tenn.), who went on to become Vice President of the United States (1993–2001).

an average of $650,000. (There are services that arrange for international transplants—performed, for example, in India or China—at prices about one-half the level available in the United States.) None of these figures include payment for the organ itself because such payments are illegal in the United States and in most other countries.

These astronomical sums are obviously out of the reach of most people. In fact, however, transplants done in the United States are generally not paid for directly by the recipients. For a person under the age of 65 with health insurance, private insurance pays for the transplant. For anyone 65 or older, the federal Medicare system pays for the transplant. For people under 65 with neither private insurance nor the wealth to pay by themselves, transplants are paid for by the Medicaid system, which is financed jointly by the federal government and the states. (Neither private insurance plans nor Medicare or Medicaid will pay for international transplants, which are generally chosen only by relatively affluent people who are unwilling to wait—or to die waiting.)

THE CASE OF KIDNEYS

Now, to begin our inquiry into the economics of organ transplants, let's consider the case of kidneys. We start here because the technical features of the transplant process have become relatively routine and because each of us is born with two kidneys but can manage quite well with only one. In fact, thanks to the technique known as dialysis, humans can actually survive for several years without functioning kidneys. In 2013, over 90,000 people were awaiting kidney transplants in the United States. In the same year, 10,000 Americans received transplants from deceased strangers. Another 6,000 received a transplant from a living donor (recall that "extra" kidney we each have), usually a close friend or relative. Tragically, more than 5,000 of the people waiting for a kidney either died or were dropped from the list because they had become too sick to qualify for a transplant. Another 3,000 died that year waiting for a liver, heart, lung, or other critical organ.

Could they be saved if it were as lawful to pay for kidneys as it is to pay for the surgeons who transplant them? Or would a market for kidneys ultimately become a black market, relying on "donated" organs removed from unwilling victims by unscrupulous brokers motivated by cash rather than kindness? This is precisely the nexus of the debate over whether we should permit people (or the relatives of just-deceased donors) to be remunerated for lifesaving organ donations.

First things first: Surely we cannot object to a market for organs because the act of donating a kidney or the lobe of a liver is potentially hazardous to the donor. After all, we currently permit people to undergo such risks under the current system with *no* monetary compensation. If it is safe enough to allow friends or family to donate without payment, why is it too risky for someone to give up a kidney or part of his or her liver in return for money?

THE CASE OF IRAN

There are, of course, many other contentious issues. To start exploring them, let's look first at a nation where it *is* legal to pay people for human organs: Iran, which just happens to have the highest living-donor rate in the world, at 23 donations per million people. Monetary compensation for organs in Iran has been lawful there since 1988, and in the ensuing decade, Iran eliminated the *entire* backlog of kidney transplant patients, something no other nation has achieved:

Under the Iranian system, a person awaiting a kidney must first seek a suitable, willing donor in his or her family. If none is forthcoming, the person must wait up to six months for a suitable deceased donor. At this point, the potential recipient can apply to the national transplant association for a kidney from a willing donor who is paid for the kidney. The donor receives from the government $1,200 plus a year of fully paid health insurance and a payment of $2,300–$4,500 from the recipient (or a charity, if the recipient is poor). Donor and recipient are also free to agree to an additional cash payment, although in most situations, the sums already mentioned are sufficient to get the job done. There are still purely altruistic donors in Iran, as well as cadaveric donations from the recently deceased. But it is the payment for organs that has permitted essentially all who seek kidney donations in Iran to get them, and the Iranian system has done so *without* leading to "back alley" donations or to people who are unable to afford a transplant because of the high cost of the organs themselves. Meanwhile, the system has saved the lives of thousands of Iranians.

THE FEAR OF INVOLUNTARY DONATIONS

Many people worry about a system of payment for human transplant because of the possibility that it would yield *involuntary* donors. That is, if there is a market for organs, some unscrupulous brokers might be tempted by profits to knock people over the head and harvest their organs for sale at the highest price. Yet it is generally agreed that the Iranian system has worked for more than 20 years without a hint of any such activities. Perhaps this should not be too surprising, given the medical techniques developed to ensure that the tissue match between organ and recipient is close enough to make transplants feasible. These and other DNA tests can now quickly ascertain with substantial certainty that "organ A" came from voluntary "donor A" rather than from involuntary "donor B."

Indeed, apart from gruesome works of fiction, most of the horror stories about the hazards of allowing markets for human organs are stories about behavior caused by the *lack* of a market for organs. In China, for example, many "transplant tourists" in the past received organs taken from the bodies of the thousands of prisoners who are executed there every year. China insisted that the prisoners' organs were used only with their "consent," a claim that many human rights groups have disputed. Of course on one point all agree: There were no payments to the prisoners or their surviving relatives. The organs were simply taken. As recently as 2012, China's Ministry of Health admitted that the practice continues, despite earlier promises to halt it.

In both the United States and Britain, there have been highly publicized cases of what amount to "body snatching"—removal of organs and other body parts from the recently deceased. Some of these cases involved body parts used in research, while other body parts were intended for sale at a profit. In each of these cases, removal was done without the prior consent of the deceased or the postmortem consent of relatives. But this amounts to theft. It is singularly horrifying, but we must remember that it is theft. Consider another form of stealing: Every year many thousands of senior citizens are defrauded of their hard-earned retirement funds by unscrupulous individuals who masquerade as "financial advisers." Should we make it illegal for anyone to pay for investment advice—or should we devote our efforts to prosecuting and incarcerating the perpetrators of such crimes?

In Pakistan and the Philippines, there were small-scale markets for transplant organs until recently, although Pakistan has now banned the trade in human organs, and transplants for non-Filipinos have been outlawed in their nation. In both countries, there were anecdotes of donors who sold kidneys for $2,000–$3,000 (about a year's worth of per capita income in either nation), but who later came to regret the transaction because of adverse long-term health effects. This would be a potential issue even with unpaid donors, and in any nation such as the United States, donors in a market for organs would surely receive at least as much medical and psychological counseling as volunteer donors receive now.

THE COSTS OF PAYING FOR ORGANS

Now, what about the added expense of allowing payments for donated organs? Would this break the budgets of Medicare or Medicaid or empty the coffers of the private insurance companies that pay for the bulk of transplants? In the case of kidneys, we have enough information from elsewhere to say the answer is probably not. In Iran, where per capita income is about $12,000 per year, payments to donors smaller than this amount have been sufficient to clear the market for kidneys. In Pakistan and the Philippines, payments equivalent to a year's worth of per capita income were enough to support a substantial transplant tourist market in both countries.

At almost $50,000 per year, average per capita income in the United States is clearly much higher than in any of these nations, suggesting that payments for kidneys would also have to be much larger to induce a substantial increase in the number of donations. Nevertheless, experts have estimated that even if the payment for a kidney were as much as $100,000, private and public insurance systems (which, as we have noted, pay for almost all of the transplants in the United States) could actually *save* money on many transplants because dialysis (at $70,000 per year) and other treatments associated with chronic kidney disease are so expensive.

It is true that allowing payments for human organs would almost surely increase the number of transplants each year—indeed, this is the very point. Payments would bring forth more organs, and this would in turn reduce deaths among people waiting for transplants. A payment system would have added costs associated with it: There would be more transplant operations (at $250,000 each for kidneys, for example, plus another, say, $100,000 for each of the organs themselves). Suppose that the payments for kidneys enabled an additional 5,000 transplants per year (assuming that the U.S. system would be as successful as the Iranian system in eliminating the excess demand for kidneys). This would yield added costs of about $1.75 billion nationwide (5,000 transplants estimated at $350,000 each).

There is a second cost: Paying for organs would cause a reduction in the number of altruistic donations. How many fewer there would be we cannot know for sure, but let us make two assumptions to be on the safe side. First, we assume that there would be *no* altruistic donations from living donors under a payment system. Second, we assume that the relatives of all deceased donors would insist on payment. Together these assumptions imply there would be an added expense of $100,000 on each of the 16,000 kidney transplants performed under the current system. The added cost here would be $1.6 billion per year, which, when added to the $1.75 billion cost of the new transplants, yields a total added annual cost of $3.35 billion for the organ payment system.

THE BENEFITS OF PAYING FOR ORGANS

In return for this sum, we would surely recoup some savings from the dialysis system, because at least 5,000 people per year would no longer be on dialysis at $70,000 per year—they would instead have a kidney to do that work for them. Moreover, the current three- to four-year delay on kidney transplants would be sharply reduced, generating additional savings. Far more important of course is that we would be saving the lives of 5,000 people every year, at a cost per life saved of but $600,000—and this number does not count any of the savings from reduced dialysis treatments.

All these calculations seem a callous way to view a human life. By the standards of medical care of today, however, allowing payments for human organs is almost surely a safe and remarkably cheap way to alleviate needless suffering and save thousands of lives every year. Once this is clear, aren't the truly callous people those who would deprive human beings of that opportunity?

DISCUSSION QUESTIONS

1. For the purposes of this question, assume that allowing payment for kidney donations would cause us to spend another $3.5 billion on kidney transplants. (This is slightly above the estimate provided in the text.) Also assume that permitting such payments saves the lives of 5,000 patients who would otherwise die waiting for a kidney? How much must we value a human life for it to make economic sense to permit payments for kidneys? How much is that number reduced if each of the 5,000 also ends up spending 18 months less on dialysis? Show all of your calculations.

2. Per capita income varies substantially across the country. If there was a free market in which payments for kidneys was permitted within the United States, would you expect there to be different prices in different parts of the country? In which areas of the countries would you expect the most organs to be offered for donation? Keeping in mind that insurance, either private or public, pays for essentially all transplants, would these same areas also be the chief "exporting" areas? Explain.

3. Why might the owners of the private insurance companies that pay for most organ transplants be in favor of a system that prohibits paying for a donated organ? Should the taxpayers of the United States, who ultimately cover the cost of Medicare and Medicaid transplants, similarly be opposed to paying for donated organs?

4. If payment for organs drives up the financial costs of transplants, is it possible that private insurance companies, and even Medicare and Medicaid, might tighten their standards for transplants so as to reduce the number of transplants each year? If they do, who would gain and who would lose compared to the current system?

5. The average waiting time on transplant lists is three to four years for kidneys (although this is expected to rise sharply, due to the rising incidence of diabetes, a major cause of kidney damage). Many of these people waiting must undergo dialysis, at a cost of $70,000 per year, paid for by private insurance, Medicare, or Medicaid. Suppose that if payment for organs were permitted, the transplant waiting time was shortened by three years, and that for the average patient, the result was 18 months less on dialysis. At what price for a kidney would a system of paying for organs be a "break-even" proposition for insurers? Show all calculations and explain your reasoning.

6. The United States currently has an "opt-in" system for organ donations from the deceased: People must explicitly choose postmortem donation ahead of time (as when they obtain their driver's licenses). Many other nations have "opt-out" systems: A desire to donate postmortem is presumed to exist unless an individual explicitly chooses ahead of time *not* to permit donation. How—if at all—would a shift to an opt-out system likely change the supply of cadaveric (postmortem) donations?

CHAPTER 9

Are We Running Out of Water?

If you believe the headlines, humans are about to die of thirst. A few samples should be enough to convince you:

"A World of Thirst" (*U.S. News & World Report*)

"Water Shortages May Lead to War" (*Financial Times*)

"Drying Up" (*The Economist*)

"Water Shortages Could Leave World in Dire Straits" (*USA Today*)

The world, it seems, is running out of water.

How can this be true? After all, about 71 percent of the earth's surface is covered with water. Lake Michigan alone contains more water than the world's population uses in two years. Even more to the point, the earth is a closed system. Using water does not destroy water. Whether we drink it, flush it, irrigate with it, or even let it evaporate, it comes back to us eventually, just as pure as the raindrops of a spring shower. In fact, every three weeks, enough rain falls to satisfy the water uses of the entire world's population for a year. So what, exactly, is the problem?

THE ULTIMATE RENEWABLE RESOURCE

Water is the ultimate renewable resource: The act of using it begins the process that returns it to us. But—and this is the crux—water is also *scarce*. That is, having the amount of clean water we want, where we want it, when we want it there is not free. We must sacrifice other resources to accomplish this. Moreover, as the level of economic activity grows, the demand for water grows, and so the costs of consuming water also grow.

In this sense, water is no different from any other **scarce good.** If we want more of it, we must sacrifice more of other things to achieve that goal. What makes water seem different is that unlike, say, broccoli, if we do entirely without it, disastrous things happen in a relatively short period of time. If water gets sufficiently scarce, people may start doing some pretty unpleasant things to each other to ensure that they, rather than their neighbors or enemies, are the ones who end up with it. Before we see if this is really something we should worry about, we had better start by learning a little more about water.

WATER, WATER EVERYWHERE

Of the enormous amount of water on the earth's surface, about 97.2 percent is ocean water, which is too saline under normal circumstances to drink or use for irrigation. Another 2.15 percent is polar ice, which is certainly not a very convenient source. Of the remaining 0.65 percent, about 0.62 percent is underground in aquifers and similar geological structures. This groundwater takes hundreds of years to recharge and so is not really a sustainable source of freshwater over the relevant time span. That leaves us with rain.

Fortunately, it rains a lot, and despite the headlines, on a *worldwide* basis, the amount of rainfall doesn't vary much from year to year. About two-thirds of the rain falls on the world's oceans, where almost no one lives. Even so, and even taking into account evaporation and the fact that much of the rain over land quickly runs off into the oceans before it can be captured, there is still a lot of usable rainfall every year. Indeed, there is enough to yield 5,700 liters per person every day—about six times as much as the average person actually consumes in all uses.

Of course, Mother Nature is not particularly evenhanded in the distribution of this usable rainfall. For example, China gets only 5 percent of it, despite having 20 percent of the world's population. Brazil, Canada, and Russia, which together have 6 percent of the world's population, receive 29 percent of the usable rainfall. Although the United States does pretty well on average, picking up 5 percent of the rain and having about 5 percent of the world's population, there are plenty of differences within our borders. Massive amounts of rain fall in southeastern Alaska and on the mountain slopes of Hawaii, while very little falls in Southern California. But the fact that people routinely choose to locate themselves in places where it does not rain highlights one of the fundamental points of this chapter: Water is an **economic good,** and the distribution and consumption of water are fundamentally economic problems, ones that can be solved in markets, just as other economic problems (such as the provision of food, shelter, and clothing) are solved in markets. To focus clearly on this point, let's examine some of the myths that have grown up around water in recent years:

Myth 1: The planet is drying up. As we have suggested earlier, there is nothing to worry about here. The cheapest (and completely sustainable) source of clean freshwater is rainfall, and roughly 113,000 cubic kilometers (3 quadrillion gallons) of the stuff falls every year on land areas around the world, year in and year out. Although small amounts of this are temporarily stored in plants and animals while they are alive, all of it eventually either recharges groundwater or evaporates, forms clouds, and precipitates—all 113,000 cubic kilometers, year after year. Sometimes, more is in Brazil and less in Sudan, and sometimes more of it inconveniently runs off in floods. Nevertheless, because the earth is a closed system, all of that water stays with us.

Myth 2: We can save water by flushing less and using less in agriculture. Remember the closed system? That applies to toilets and alfalfa, too. Flushing the toilet does not send the water to the moon. It just sends it through the sewer system to a water treatment plant and eventually into aquifers under the ground or back down on our heads in the form of raindrops. So-called low-flow toilets (and showers) have no effect on the amount of water in existence. (Because they may slightly reduce the amount of water running through water and sewer systems, they may conserve a bit on the amount of resources used in these systems. There are, however, offsets. Such devices are routinely more costly to produce than regular toilets or shower heads, and they occupy people's time—because of double flushes and longer showers. On balance, besides not "saving" water, there is thus no evidence that such devices conserve resources at all.)

Even agriculture, notorious for consuming an enormous amount of (usually subsidized) water around the world, does not destroy the stuff. Most of the water used by agriculture evaporates or runs off into rivers or soaks into underground aquifers. A small amount is temporarily stored in the crops, but this, soon enough, is consumed by animals or humans and simply returns to the same system that delivers 113,000 cubic kilometers of water onto our heads every year. There is no doubt that all of this use of water in agriculture is costly because it could be used elsewhere. Moreover, agricultural use of water is generally subsidized by taxpayers. Making farmers pay full market value for water would reduce agricultural use and raise our collective wealth by improving the allocation of resources, but it would not alter the amount of water available.

Having said this, agricultural use of water does present two important economic issues. First, as we just noted, government policies around the world routinely cause water for agriculture to be heavily subsidized. Farmers often pay as little as $10 to $–20 per acre-foot (about 325,000 gallons) for water that costs anywhere from $500 to $1,000 per acre to provide to them. Because of this huge subsidy, farmers are no doubt richer, but the losses to society are much greater, meaning that our overall wealth is lower. (For an explanation of why we get such subsidies despite this, see Chapters 23 and 27.)

Second, we not only subsidize water use for agriculture, but also routinely forbid farmers to sell or lease their water to other users, especially nonagricultural users. This is a particular problem in the relatively arid American West, where farmers effectively own most of the rights to surface and groundwater but must "use it or lose it"—if they don't put it to beneficial use on their crops, they lose their rights to it. Often this water would be much more productively "used" if it were left in the streams to help support the spawning and other essential life activities of downstream species, such as trout or salmon. Laws are slowly changing to recognize environmental uses as being "beneficial" uses, but existing restrictions on the use of water still yield lower overall wealth for us.

Myth 3: Water is different from other goods. Many people seem to think that because it is essential to life, water is somehow different from other goods—or at least that it should be treated differently in some very specific ways. Let's first get rid of the notion that water doesn't obey the laws of demand and supply. In fact, although the demand for water in some uses is relatively inelastic, usage of water in *all* uses responds as predicted by the law of demand—when the price of water goes up, people use less of it. In fact, the demand for water behaves very much like the demand for gasoline. A ten percent rise in the price of either good induces consumers to use about three to six percent less of the good in question. Thus, although the demand for water (or for gasoline) is said to be relatively **inelastic,** there is no doubt that people change their consumption patterns when price changes.

Similarly, although getting water from where it is to where people would like it to be is costly, the law of supply still holds true—when the price of water rises, suppliers of water provide more of it to consumers. Sometimes this process is as simple as diverting a stream or capturing rainfall. Sometimes it is as complicated as using reverse osmosis to convert seawater into freshwater. Nevertheless, even if the production technique is as esoteric as recycling urine into fresh, drinkable water (as is done on the international space station), the fact remains that when water becomes more valuable, people are incredibly ingenious in finding ways to make sure it is available.

Myth 4: Price controls on water protect low-income consumers. Some people claim that water should *not* be treated like other goods, specifically arguing that both the price of water received by suppliers and the price paid by consumers should be kept down by government decree. This, it is said, will protect people, especially those who are poor, from high water prices and will prevent suppliers from earning "excessive" profits. After all, some 1.1 billion people around the world currently do not have ready access to clean water, which makes an inviting target for anyone who might become a monopoly supplier to substantial numbers of these people.

It is true that governments can reduce the profits of the suppliers of water (or anything else) by limiting the prices they charge. In reality, however, this does not protect consumers, particularly not the poorest consumers. Price controls on water *reduce* the amount supplied and, especially for the poor, generally make consumers worse off. They end up with less water than if prices were allowed to reach equilibrium levels, and are forced to undergo nonprice rationing schemes (ranging from limited hours of service to getting no clean water at all). In fact, if we examine places around the world where the poor have little or no access to clean water, we find that government efforts to "protect" people from potential suppliers of water are in fact a key source of this lack of access.

In Brazil, for example, government limits on private water rates forced a major international water project company to cease operations there, reducing the supply of clean water. In India, the widespread insistence by many local governments that water be provided free of charge has effectively stalled most efforts to improve water distribution in that country. In China, government price controls have discouraged water utilities from developing new water supplies and from upgrading water distribution systems. As we see in detail in Chapter 10, government controls on prices make goods *more* scarce, not less, and it is generally the disadvantaged members of society who suffer the most as a result.

Myth 5: The ocean is too salty to drink. As a practical matter, prolonged consumption of salt water by species not specifically adapted for it is highly deleterious. But the technology for desalination of seawater is advancing rapidly, however, and the cost of desalination is falling just as rapidly—more than 95 percent over the past 20 years. In relatively arid parts of the earth (including Southern California), desalination has become price-competitive with other sources of supply, and large-scale desalination plants are in operation around the world.

The process yields highly concentrated brine as a by-product. To avoid damage to ocean species sensitive to excess salinity, this brine must be dealt with carefully (dispersed widely) when it is returned to the sea. Nevertheless, this is simply a matter of routine care. Moreover, if local conditions make wide dispersal impractical or expensive, the brine can be evaporated, and the resulting solid materials then either used or disposed of in ordinary landfills. The upshot is that with continued technological progress in desalination, water from the ocean will likely become cheaper than collecting rainfall in large portions of the world. Far from running out of water, people everywhere will then find themselves able to secure it as easily as, well, turning on the tap.

DISCUSSION QUESTIONS

1. How much water do people "need"? Is your answer the same if you have to pay their water bills?

2. Evaluate the following: "Although taxpayers foot the bill for federal water sold to farmers at subsidized prices, they also eat the crops grown with that water. Because the crops are cheaper due to the subsidized water, taxpayers get back exactly what they put in, and so there is no waste from having subsidized water for farmers." Would you give the author of this quote an A or an F in economics? Explain.

3. During the droughts that periodically plague California, farmers in that state are able to purchase subsidized water to irrigate their crops, at the same time many California homeowners have to pay large fines if they water their lawns. Can you suggest an explanation for this difference in the treatment of two different groups of citizens in the state of California?

4. If allocating water through nonprice means generally harms society, can you suggest why governments often do this?

5. Consider two otherwise identical communities; call them P and N. Suppose that in P, all homes, apartments, and businesses have meters that record the usage of water. In addition, the users of the water must pay more when they use more water. Thus, water is priced like most other goods. In community N, there are no meters and the local supplier of water charges everyone in the community a fixed amount per person, per month for their water service. Thus, using another gallon costs the user nothing additional. In which community will per capita water usage be higher? Explain, using the relevant principles of economics.

6. Referring back to the facts of the previous question: Suppose you knew that in one community water is supplied by a privately owned company, while in the other community water is supplied by the local government. In which community do you predict that water is supplied by the privately owned company? Explain.

CHAPTER 10

Bankrupt Landlords, from Sea to Shining Sea

Take a tour of Santa Monica, a beachfront enclave of Los Angeles, and you will find a city of bizarre contrasts. Pick a street at random, and you may find run-down rental units sitting in disrepair next to homes costing $800,000. Try another street, and you may see abandoned apartment buildings adjacent to luxury car dealerships and trendy shops selling high-fashion clothing to Hollywood stars. Sound strange? Not in Santa Monica—known locally as the People's Republic of Santa Monica—where stringent rent-control laws once routinely forced property owners to leave their buildings empty and decaying rather than even bothering to sell them.

Three thousand miles to the east, rent-control laws in New York City—known locally as the Big Apple—have forced landlords to abandon housing units because the laws imposed huge financial losses on owners. Largely as a result of such abandonments, the city government of New York owns thousands of derelict housing units—empty, except for rats and small-time cocaine dealers. Meanwhile, because the controls also discourage new construction, the city faces a housing gap of 200,000 rental units—apartments that could easily be filled at current controlled rental rates if the units were in habitable condition.

From coast to coast, stories like these are commonplace in the two hundred or so American cities and towns practicing some form of **rent control**—a system in which the local government tells building owners how much they can charge for rent. Time and again, the stories are the same: poorly maintained rental units, abandoned apartment buildings, tenants trapped by housing gridlock in apartments no longer suitable for them, bureaucracies bloated with rent-control enforcers, and even homeless families that can find no one who will rent to them. Time and again, the reason for the stories is the same: legal limits on the rent people may pay for a place to live.

A Brief History of Rent Controls

Our story begins in 1943, when the federal government imposed rent control as a temporary wartime measure. Although the federal program ended a few years after the war, New York City continued the controls on its own. Under New York's controls, a landlord generally could not raise rents on apartments as long as the tenants continued to renew their leases. Rent controls in Santa Monica are more recent. They were spurred by the inflation of the 1970s, which, combined with California's rapid population growth, pushed housing prices and rents to record levels. In 1979, the city of Santa Monica (where 80 percent of the residents were renters) ordered rents be rolled back to the levels of the year before and stipulated that future rents could go up by only two-thirds as much as any increase in the overall price level. In both New York and Santa Monica, the objective of rent controls has been to keep rents below the levels that would be observed in freely competitive markets. Achieving this goal required that both cities impose extensive regulations to prevent landlord and tenant from evading the controls—regulations that are costly to enforce and that distort the normal operation of the market.

It is worth noting that the rent-control systems in New York and Santa Monica are slowly yielding to decontrol. For a number of years, some apartments in New York have been subject to only "rent stabilization" regulations, which are somewhat less stringent than absolute rent controls. In addition, New York apartments renting for over $2,500 per month are deregulated when a lease ends. In Santa Monica, the state of California mandated that as of 1999, rent for newly vacant apartments could increase. Even so, in both cities, much of the rental market is dominated by rent controls. Accordingly, in this chapter we focus on the consequences of those controls.

The Adverse Effects of Rent Controls

In general, the unfettered movement of rental prices in a freely competitive housing market performs three vital functions: (1) it allocates existing scarce housing among competing claimants; (2) it promotes the efficient maintenance of existing housing and stimulates the production of new housing, where appropriate; and (3) it rations usage of housing by demanders, thereby preventing waste of scarce housing. Rent control prevents rental prices from effectively performing these functions. Let's see how.

Rent control discourages the construction of new rental units. Developers and mortgage lenders are reluctant to get involved in building new rental properties because controls artificially depress the most important long-run determinant of profitability—rents. Thus, in one recent year, 11,000 new housing units were built in Dallas, a city with a 16 percent rental vacancy rate but no rent-control statute. In that same year, only 2,000 units were built in San Francisco, a city with a 1.6 percent vacancy rate but stringent rent-control laws. In New York City, the only rental units being built are either exempt from controls or heavily subsidized by the government. Private construction of new apartments in Santa Monica also dried up under controls, even though new office space and commercial developments—both exempt from rent control—were built at a record pace.

Rent control leads to the deterioration of the existing supply of rental housing. When rental prices are held below free market levels, property owners cannot recover through higher rents, the costs of maintenance, repairs, and capital improvements. Thus, such activities are sharply curtailed. Eventually, taxes, utilities, and the expenses of the most rudimentary repairs—such as replacing broken windows—exceed the depressed rental receipts; hence, the buildings are abandoned. In New York, some owners have resorted to arson, hoping to collect the insurance on their empty rent-controlled buildings before the city claims them for back taxes. Under rent controls in Santa Monica, the city insisted that owners wishing to convert empty apartment buildings to other uses had to build new rental units to replace the units they no longer rented. At a cost of up to $50,000 per apartment, it is little wonder that few owners were willing to bear the burden, choosing instead to leave the buildings empty and graffiti-scarred.

Rent control impedes the process of rationing scarce housing. Tenants are understandably reluctant to give up controlled apartments, so one consequence of rent controls is that tenant mobility is sharply reduced. Even when a family's demand for living space changes—due, for example, to a new baby or a teenager's departure for college—there can be substantial costs in giving up a rent-controlled unit. In New York City, landlords often charge "key money" (a large up-front cash payment) before a new tenant is allowed to move in. The high cost of moving means that large families often stay in cramped quarters while small families or even single persons reside in large apartments. In New York, this phenomenon of non-mobility came to be known as *housing gridlock*. It is estimated that more than 20 percent of renters in New York City live in apartments that are bigger or smaller than they would otherwise occupy. In Santa Monica, many homeowners rented out portions of their houses in response to soaring prices in the 1970s and then found themselves trapped by their tenants, whom they could not evict even if they wanted to sell their homes and move to a retirement community.

EFFORTS TO EVADE CONTROLS

Not surprisingly, the distortions produced by rent control lead to efforts by both landlords and tenants to evade the rules. This in turn leads to the growth of cumbersome and expensive government bureaucracies whose job is to enforce the controls. In New York City, where rents can be raised when tenancy changes hands, landlords have an incentive to make life unpleasant for tenants or to evict them on the slightest pretense. The city has responded by making evictions extremely costly for landlords. Even if a tenant blatantly and repeatedly violates the terms of a lease, the tenant cannot be evicted if the violations are corrected within a "reasonable" time period. If the violations are not corrected—despite several trips to court by the owners and their attorneys—eviction requires a tedious and expensive judicial proceeding. For their part, tenants routinely try to sublet all or part of their rent-controlled apartments at prices substantially above the rent they pay the owner. Because both the city and the landlords try to prohibit subletting, the parties often end up in the city's housing courts, an entire judicial system developed chiefly to deal with disputes over rent-controlled apartments.

Strict controls on monthly rents force landlords to use other means to discriminate among prospective tenants. Simply to ensure that the rent check comes every month, many landlords rent only to well-heeled professionals. As one commentator put it, "There is no disputing that Santa Monica became younger and richer under rent control." The same pattern occurred under the rent-control laws of Berkeley, California, and Cambridge, Massachusetts.

BUREAUCRACIES FLOURISH

There is little doubt the bureaucracies that evolve to administer rent-control laws are cumbersome and expensive. Between 1988 and 1993, New York City spent $5.1 billion rehabilitating housing confiscated from private landlords. Even so, derelict buildings continued piling up at a record rate. The overflow and appeals from the city's housing courts clog the rest of New York's judicial system, impeding the prosecution of violent criminals and drug dealers. In Santa Monica, the Rent Control Board began with an annual budget of $745,000 and a staff of 20 people. By the early 1990s, the staff had tripled in size, and the budget was pushing $5 million. Who picked up the tab? The landlords did, of course, with an annual special assessment of $200 per unit levied on them. Also, even though the 1999 state-mandated changes in the law meant that apartment rents in Santa Monica can be increased when a new tenant moves in, the new rent is then controlled by the city for the duration of the tenancy. Indeed, the Rent Control Board conveniently maintains a website where one can go to learn the maximum allowable rent on any of the many thousands of rent-controlled residences in Santa Monica.

THE LOSERS FROM RENT CONTROLS

Ironically, the big losers from rent control—in addition to landlords— are often low-income individuals, especially single mothers. Indeed, many observers believe that one significant cause of homelessness in cities such as New York and Los Angeles is rent control. Poor individuals often cannot assure the discriminating landlord that their rent will be paid on time—or paid at all—each month. Because controlled rents are generally well below free market levels, there is little incentive for apartment owners to take a chance on low-income individuals as tenants. This is especially true if the prospective tenant's chief source of income is a welfare check. Indeed, a significant number of tenants appearing in New York's housing courts have been low-income mothers who, due to emergency expenses or delayed welfare checks, have missed rent payments.

Often their appeals end in evictions and residence in temporary public shelters or on the streets. Before the state-mandated easing of controls, some apartment owners in Santa Monica, who used to rent one- and two-room units to welfare recipients and other low-income individuals, simply abandoned their buildings, leaving them vacant rather than trying to collect artificially depressed rents that failed to cover operating costs. The disgusted owner of one empty and decaying 18-unit building had a friend spray-paint his feelings on the wall: "I want to tear this mess down, but Big Brother won't let me." Perhaps because the owner had escaped from a concentration camp in search of freedom in the United States, the friend added a personalized touch: a drawing of a large hammer and sickle, symbol of the former Soviet Union.

DAMAGE AROUND THE WORLD

The ravages of rent controls are not confined to the United States. In Mumbai, India, rents are still set at the levels that prevailed back in 1940. A two-bedroom apartment near the center of the city may have a controlled rent of as little as $8.50 per month. (Nearby, free market rents for an apartment of the same size can be as much as $3,000 per month.) Not surprisingly, landlords have let their rent-controlled buildings decay, and collapsing apartments have become a regular feature of life in this city of thirteen million people. Over the past decade, almost 100 people have been killed in the collapse of rent-controlled buildings. The city government estimates that a hundred or more apartment buildings are currently on the verge of collapse.

Even Communist nations are not exempt from rent controls. In a heavily publicized news conference several years ago, the foreign minister of Vietnam, Nguyen Co Thach, declared that a "romantic conception of socialism" had destroyed his country's economy after the Vietnam War. Thach stated that rent control had artificially encouraged demand and discouraged supply and that all of the housing in Hanoi had fallen into disrepair as a result. Thach concluded by noting, "The Americans couldn't destroy Hanoi, but we have destroyed our city by very low rents. We realized it was stupid and that we must change policy."

Apparently, this same thinking was what induced the state of California to compel changes in Santa Monica's rent-control ordinance. The result was an almost immediate jump in rents on newly vacant apartments, as well as a noticeable rise in the vacancy rate—exactly the results we would expect. Interestingly enough, however, prospective new tenants were less enthusiastic about the newly available apartments than many landlords had expected. The reason? Twenty years of rent controls had produced many years of reduced upkeep and hence apartments that were less than pristine. As one renter noted, "The trouble is, most of this area . . . [is] basically falling apart." Another complained, "I don't want to move into a place that's depressing, with old brown carpet that smells like chicken soup." Higher rents are changing both the ambience and the aroma of Santa Monica apartments—but only at the same rate that the market is allowed to perform its functions.

DISCUSSION QUESTIONS

1. Why do you think governments frequently attempt to control apartment rents but not house prices?

2. What determines the size of the key-money payments that landlords demand (and tenants offer) for the right to rent a controlled apartment?

3. Who, other than the owners of rental units, loses as a result of rent controls? Who gains from rent controls? What effect would the imposition of rent controls have on the market price of an existing single-family house? What effect would rent controls have on the value of vacant land?

4. Why do the owners of rental units reduce their maintenance expenditures on the units when rent controls are imposed? Does their decision have anything to do with whether they can afford those expenditures?

5. Because rent controls reduce the rental price below the market clearing price, the quantity of rental units on the market must decline. What does this imply *must* happen to the full cost of renting an apartment including "key money," harassment by the landlord, and so forth? Explain.

6. How does the percentage of voters who are renters (as opposed to owners) affect the incentives for politicians to propose rent controls? Does this incentive depend on the likelihood that renters are less likely to vote in local elections than are owners of apartments and houses? Why do you suppose renters are less likely to vote in local elections? Explain.

PART THREE

Labor Markets

Introduction

Almost everyone participates in the labor market, and most of us do so for most of our lives. In one sense, labor (or **human capital,** as it is sometimes called by economists) is no different from any other **economic good.** After all, labor is a **scarce good,** and so the basic tools used by economists can be applied to understanding the markets for it. Nevertheless, special care is sometimes required to understand what is going on in labor markets because not all aspects of these markets are what they seem to be.

(Why) Are Women Paid Less?

As you will see in Chapter 11, since the middle of the twentieth century, there has been a revolution in the labor market as women have entered in unprecedented numbers. Yet even though women now regularly work in jobs formerly closed to them, the data still suggest that they are being paid less than men. Much of this seeming discrimination in pay is attributable to the occupational choices made by women. They work in less hazardous environments and take jobs that offer greater flexibility and fewer hours of work per week. Safe, flexible employment demanding fewer hours of work per week is desirable. Once we correct for these job attributes, the real differences in pay between men and women are much smaller than they appear to be at first glance. Nevertheless, the question remains: Do women select such jobs because that is really their preferred choice, or are they forced into such work because discrimination by male business owners and managers gives women no real alternatives? This is an issue that only further study will resolve.

OVER $1 TRILLION IN COLLEGE DEBT, AND RISING

Whatever our gender, we inherit some of our human capital (such as intelligence and attractiveness) from our parents. But to acquire the rest, we must undertake **investment,** most importantly in education. Up through high school, this investment is chiefly financed from tax revenues. But once off to college, the costs are largely borne directly by students and their families. Over the past twenty years, college costs have more than *tripled*, even after taking out the effects of **inflation.**

As we see in Chapter 12, students and their families have increasingly turned to federally controlled student loans to pay the bills. Indeed, the total amount of student loan indebtedness now exceeds $1 trillion, and is rising at more than $100 billion per year. Although student loans were initially introduced to help low income families meet the high cost of college, the loan system has now become an important part of the problem. The loans are so readily available to upper income students that they have helped drive up the cost of college, and thus indirectly forced low income students *out* of the market for a college education. The high average **rate of return** to college will enable many students to repay their loans with plenty left over. Unfortunately, weaker students and those majoring in low-paying majors, or attending second-tier colleges, will find to their dismay that they would have been better off going straight from high school to the labor force.

THE EFFECTS OF THE MINIMUM WAGE

Just as the effects of college loans are not always what is claimed for them, the same is true for many government programs. We shall see this fact repeatedly in this book, including in Chapter 13, where we examine the effects of the **minimum** wage. The chief losers from the minimum wage—disadvantaged minority teenagers—are often the very people who can least afford those losses, while those who claim to support the law on altruistic grounds are in fact likely to be the biggest winners. The message of this chapter may well be this simple piece of advice: When someone claims to be doing something *for* you, it is wise to ask what that person is doing *to* you.

IMMIGRATION, SUPERSTARS, AND POVERTY

The plight of the disadvantaged is the central focus of Chapter 14. Over the past forty or fifty years, people at the bottom of the income distribution in America have experienced a rising standard of living. In more recent years, however, this rise seems to have slowed relative to the improving standard of living at the very top of the income distribution. Here we learn that several factors are likely at work, including the rising premium on education, technological changes that have helped top performers ("superstars") earn even more, and high rates of immigration that have depressed wages near the bottom of the income distribution. Sadly, it also appears that some (though not all) government programs directed at improving life for the least fortunate have had the reverse effect. Once again, we see that when it comes to important public issues, things are rarely what they appear to be.

The (Dis)incentives of High Taxes

As we see in Chapter 15, the net earnings of workers are importantly influenced by the taxes we impose on their labor income. The consequences can be large-scale and sometimes counterproductive. When we tax income more heavily, people work less. Even so, at low levels of taxes, such responses are often modest, so that a higher **tax rate** can yield more **tax revenue.** But at some point, the disincentive effects of higher taxes can so discourage suppliers of labor that revenues collected from the tax actually *fall.* When combined with the fact that the disincentive effects of taxes cause a reduction in the overall output produced in society, the result is surely a "lose–lose" outcome by any definition.

CHAPTER **11**

(Why) Are Women Paid Less?

Since the middle of the twentieth century, there has been a revolution in the job market. Women have entered the paid workforce in unprecedented numbers. In 1950, for example, only about one-third of working-age women were in the paid workforce. Today, nearly 60 percent are. Over the same period, the male **labor force participation rate** has fallen from 86 percent to 70 percent, so women now account for almost half of the paid workforce in America. There also has been an overwhelming change in the nature of paid work done by women. Fifty years ago, professional careers for women outside of nursing or teaching were unusual. Today, women comprise roughly half of the newly minted attorneys and physicians starting work each year. Over the same period, there has been a transformation of wages, too. In 1950, median earnings of women were only two-thirds those of men. Today, women earn 80 percent of what men are paid.

Reread that last sentence. On average, for every dollar a man earns, a woman gets paid 80 cents. Can this possibly be true? Consider this fact: Nearly 70 percent of employers' costs are accounted for by labor. An employer who hired only women at 80 cents on the dollar could cut labor costs by 20 percent relative to an employer who hired only men. This would yield added profits of about 14 percent of sales—which would *triple* the **profit** earned by the typical firm. If women are paid 20 percent less than men, how could any employer possibly afford to hire anyone *but* women?

IS IT DISCRIMINATION?

At this point you may be saying to yourself, "Surely, there are differences between men and women other than their sex that can help account for this 'gender gap' in earnings." You would be correct. Earnings are a reflection of experience, education, marital status, and age, for example. But even when economists control for all of these individual characteristics—using nationwide data, such as from the U.S. Census Bureau or the Bureau of Labor Statistics—unexplained differences between the pay of men and women persist. Men with the same measured individual characteristics are paid at least 10 percent more than women, and some studies find a difference twice that size.

The widespread opinion of many observers is that the unexplained gap between the pay of men and women is chiefly the result of discrimination against women. The reasoning is simple. Most business owners and senior managers are men, and given a choice between hiring a man or a woman, the "old-boy network" operates in favor of the man. According to this view, women can get the job only if they agree to accept lower wages.

Consider this fact, however: For 50 years, it has been illegal to discriminate in the workforce on the basis of race or gender. Two major federal agencies, the Equal Employment Opportunity Commission and the Office of Federal Contract Compliance, are wholly or largely devoted to ensuring that this antidiscrimination mandate is enforced. As interpreted by the courts, the law now says that if the statistical *appearance* of lower wages for women (or minorities) is present in a workplace, the employer is *presumed* guilty of discrimination and must prove otherwise. No one thinks that federal agencies do a perfect job at enforcing the law here or elsewhere, but it is hard to believe that a persistent 20 percent pay difference could escape the notice of even the most nearsighted federal bureaucrat.

A hint of what might be going on begins to emerge when economists study the payroll records of individual firms, using actual employee information that is specific and detailed regarding location of the firm, type of work, employee responsibilities, and other factors. These analyses reveal that the so-called wage gap between men and women is much smaller—typically no more than 5 percent—and often there is no gap at all. The sharp contrast between firm-level data and economy-wide data suggests that something may be at work here besides (or in addition to) outright gender discrimination.

THE IMPORTANCE OF CHILDREN

That something is actually three things. First, women's pay is extremely sensitive to whether or not they have children. In Britain, for example, where this issue has been studied intensively, the average pay earned by a woman begins to fall shortly before the birth of her first child and continues to drop until the child becomes a teenager. Although earnings begin to revive once the first child passes the age of 20 or so, they never fully recover. The earnings drop associated with motherhood is close to one-third, and only one-third of that drop is regained after the nest is empty. American data suggest that the same pattern is present on this side of the Atlantic.

The parenthood pay declines suffered by women stem from a variety of sources. Some are put on the "mommy track," with reduced responsibilities and hours of work. Others move to different employers around the time their first child is born, taking jobs that offer more flexible work schedules but offer correspondingly lower pay as well. Overall, a woman with average skills who has a child at age 24 can expect to receive nearly $1 million less compensation over her career compared to one who remains childless. It is worth emphasizing that no similar effect is observed with men. In fact, there is some evidence that men with children are actually paid *more* than men without children. These findings strongly suggest a fact that will come as no surprise to most people. Despite the widespread entry of women into the labor force, they retain the primary responsibility for child care at home, and their careers suffer as a result.

OCCUPATIONAL SELECTION

The second factor at work in explaining male–female wage differences is occupational selection. Compared to women, men tend to concentrate in paid employment that is dangerous or unpleasant. Commercial fishing, construction, law enforcement, firefighting, truck driving, and mining, to name but a few, are occupations that are much more dangerous than average and are dominated by men. As a result, men represent 92 percent of all occupational fatalities. Hazardous jobs offer what is known as a **compensating differential,** extra pay for assuming the differential risk of death or injury on the job. In equilibrium, these extra wages do no more than offset the extra hazards. So even though measured earnings *look* high relative to the educational and other requirements of the jobs, appearances are deceiving. After adjusting for risk, the value of that pay is really no greater than that for less hazardous employment—but the appearance of higher pay contributes to the measured gender gap.

HOURS OF WORK

The third key factor influencing pay is hours of work. Men are more than twice as likely as women to work in excess of 50 hours per week in paid employment. Overall, the average paid workweek for men is about 15 percent longer than it is for women. Men are also more likely than women to be in full-time, rather than part-time, paid employment, and the wage differences here can be huge. Working an average of 44 hours per week versus 34 hours per week, for example, yields more than twice the pay, regardless of gender. This substantial gender gap in hours of paid work is due in part to the "mommy track" phenomenon, but the question that remains is: Does this constitute discrimination on the part of employers, or is it the result of choices by women?

Although we cannot answer that question definitively, there is reason to believe that some differences in occupational choice (and thus in pay) are due to discrimination. For example, the highest-paying blue-collar jobs are typically union jobs, and industrial and crafts unions have had a long history of opposition to women as members. Or consider medicine. Women are becoming much more numerous in specialties such as dermatology and radiology, where schedules tend to be more flexible, hours of work can be limited, and part-time practice is feasible. But many physicians would argue that the noticeable underrepresentation of women in the high-paying surgical specialties is partly the result of discrimination against women, rather than reflecting the occupational choices preferred by women. If this argument is correct, then even if women in a given specialty are paid the same as men in that specialty, the exclusion of women from high-paying slots will lower their average wages and make them worse off.

The extent of gender discrimination in the workplace is unlikely to be definitively settled anytime soon. Measured earnings differences, even those that account for experience, education, and other factors, clearly overstate the true pay gap between equally qualified men and women. Just as surely, however, given the heavier parenting demands typically made on women, even when they receive equal pay, it is not for equal work.

Discussion Questions

1. Suppose an employer offers a base wage of $20 per hour for the first 40 hours of work each week and overtime pay of $30 per hour for any hours beyond 40 per week; the employer allows workers to choose their own hours of work. Suppose employee A chooses to work 36 hours per week and employee B chooses to work 42 hours per week. Compute the average weekly earnings for employees A and B and the "earnings gap" (in percentage terms) between them. In your view, does this observed earnings gap constitute discrimination? Justify your conclusion.

2. A recent British study found that married men earned more than unmarried men, but only if their wives did *not* have full-time paid employment. Suggest an explanation for this finding. (*Hint:* In which case is a man more likely to share in the household responsibilities, including child care?)

3. Women who own their own businesses earn net profits that are only half as large as the net profits earned by men who own their own businesses. First, consider why women would be willing to accept lower profits. Could this reflect poorer options for women as employees? Alternatively, could it reflect other attributes of self-employment that women might find more advantageous than men do? Then think about why women earn lower profits. Is this evidence of discrimination? If so, by whom? If not, what else might account for the lower profits?

4. Why do you think we have laws that prohibit discrimination in pay based on gender or race but permit employers to discriminate in pay based on education or experience?

5. Suppose you own a company. If you hire ten men, each of them at $70,000 per year, your firm will be able to sell $1,000,000 in output this year, and you will be able to earn $50,000 in profits, an amount that is normal for a firm of your size in your industry. (Your firm's other costs, such as for rent and advertising, will be $250,000 this year.) Now assume that you could hire ten women for $56,000 each, instead of hiring the men. What would your total profits be if you hired the women and they were just as productive as the more expensive men? Show all calculations.

6. Refer back to the last question. Based on the discussion in the chapter, what would you want to know about these women to satisfy yourself that they will be at least as productive as the men? List the key factors and explain briefly.

CHAPTER 12

Over $1 Trillion in College Debt, and Rising

In any given year, new student debt increases by well over $100 billion. The amount of student debt outstanding now exceeds all car loans. It even exceeds all outstanding credit card balances. Indeed, the total of all student loans outstanding now exceeds the amount by which the federal government adds to its debt each year. In light of this massive, mounting debt load, it is perhaps not surprising, then, that newspaper and other media outlets are starting to label the situation as a student loan debt "education bubble."

Bubbles Usually Burst

When the word "bubble" is used to describe any financial situation, the implication is that at some point it will burst. When real estate prices rose dramatically in the first part of this century, a real estate bubble was declared. Indeed, it did burst over the period 2006–2009—the housing market collapsed. If the student loan build-up means that there will be a collapse, that is, loan recipients will just refuse to pay, the implications are serious. Why? Because for the most part, student loans are offered or controlled by the federal government. Any collapse in that loan market would mean that all taxpayers would be "on the hook." Given the amount of red ink that continues to flow on the federal government's books, the last thing cash-strapped taxpayers can afford is yet more government spending, this time to bail out students.

Actually, it is hard to imagine that the buildup in student loan debt can simply crash. For example, even individuals who believe that they have truly "crushing" student-loan repayment obligations can only rarely have them forgiven through **bankruptcy** proceedings. Moreover, the federal government is stringent in collecting on student-loan debt. For example, the federal government can and does withhold money from the rapidly growing number of **Social Security** recipients who are behind on their federal student loans. Now, you must be wondering to yourself, aren't Social Security payments only for older people? Yes, that is generally correct. But many of those older people contracted for student-loan debt to defray education costs for their children or other dependents. As you read this, several hundred thousand retirees' Social Security checks are being reduced to help cover interest and principle payments that are overdue.

Given that more than 20 percent of student loans are in default, the federal government is increasingly utilizing all sorts of modern debt-collection tools. For example, the U.S. Department of Education can do the following to collect on your student debt:

- Keep your tax refund, if you have one.
- Garnish your paycheck without obtaining a court judgment.
- Withhold money from any federal disability payments you are receiving.
- In some states, ensure that any professional licenses you have are revoked.
- Bring a lawsuit against you and if it wins, collect judgment from your bank accounts or place a **lien** on any **real property** you have.

Rising College Debt Among Upper-Income Families

According to the latest studies, the slow-moving economy and rising college costs have caused upper–middle-income families to take on more student-loan debt than other groups. These are families in the 80th to 95th percentiles of all households nationwide—people who may not be wealthy, but do have substantial incomes. Before the economic recession hit really hard, less than 20 percent of these households had college debt outstanding. Today, that number is closer to 26 percent. These relatively well-off families now owe on average about $35,000 in college loans, up one-third since 2007. Overall, there are more than three million households that owe at least $50,000 in student loans.

The reality is that five out of six college students today opt for some form of college loans. When those who receive student loans find that they cannot manage their monthly payments, they will often be allowed to put them off, even for years. But that means the amount owed rises in the meantime as the **deferred interest** is added to the total bill. Eventually, the burden can be truly daunting.

The Rising Real Cost of a College Degree

The authors of this book remember when college tuition was measured in the thousands, rather than in the tens of thousands of dollars per year. Of course, as we all know, during modern times, there has been **inflation**—an increase in the average level of all prices. So to get a good handle on what has really happened to the cost of a college degree, we have to adjust for inflation, yielding what economists call the **real,** or **inflation-adjusted, cost.**

Well, the results are quite shocking—the rate of increase in the real cost of college has been even greater than the rate of increase in real health-care costs. Indeed, over the last 30 years, the price of a college degree after correcting for inflation has more than *tripled.* And over the last 10 years, the inflation-corrected cost of a college degree has actually accelerated its rapid ascent.

So, why has a college degree become so expensive?

Student Loans Are Part of the Problem

According to Dr. Richard Vedder, Director of the Center for College Affordability and Productivity, rising student loans are part of the problem rather than the solution to dealing with increasing higher education costs. It is a simple matter of demand and supply.

The expansion of student loans encourages colleges to engage in an academic "arms race." The growing availability of college loans has made it easier for students to finance their education, and thus increased the demand for a college education. Just as happens anytime the demand for a commodity increases, the price has risen. Indeed, while student loan programs have been sold as a means of benefiting students, many of those benefits have been captured by colleges and universities as they raise their tuition and fees.

But matters are even worse for lower-income students. Initially, the federal loan and grant programs put into effect in the early 1970s had the stated goal of increasing the proportion of college degrees awarded to students who came from lower-income families. But Dr. Vedder's examination of the data reveals that just the *opposite* has occurred. The proportion of recent graduates coming from the bottom 25 percent of the income distribution is lower today in the 2010s than it was in 1970s. Indeed, Vedder argues that to redress this imbalance, the federal government should simply eliminate loan eligibility for all students from highly affluent families.

The Economic Value of a College Degree

Those who claim that the education loan bubble is about to burst are really saying that "it's not worth it," where "it" means borrowing and spending big bucks to obtain a college degree. The data tell us otherwise. The **earnings premium** for a college degree relative to a high school degree almost doubled in the last three decades. In addition, the **unemployment rate** for college graduates is only about half of what it is for high school graduates.

For most young people, the decision to go to college is the single largest investment decision that they will make. Does this big investment pay off? For most people, the answer is, yes. Even though college graduates start their careers several years later than do high school graduates, their higher annual earnings more than make up the difference—much more. After correcting (or adjusting) for the time value of income (called the **discount rate**), the average college graduate will earn $1.2 million in earnings (net of tuition costs) compared to only $780,000 for the high school graduate. According to Professors Christopher Avery and Sarah Turner:

> "Expected lifetime earnings associated with a college degree have increased markedly over time. As the investment value of a college degree rises, it is natural to think of individuals increasing their willingness to borrow to achieve these higher returns."

Even so, as we shall see, whether college is a good investment for *you* depends on several key factors beyond simple averages.

What's Your Major?

Students commonly ask each other the question, "What's your major?" As it turns out, the answer to that question helps to predict whether borrowing for (or even getting) a college education is worth it. Just because the average college graduate makes a relatively high **rate of return** for investing in a college degree does not mean that *every* graduate does. It depends heavily on your major. A few years ago, the *New York Times* ran a story about a 26-year-old graduate from New York University with almost $100,000 in outstanding student loans. She had obtained an interdisciplinary degree in religious and women's studies. She was earning $22 an hour working as a photographer's helper. Obviously, given the high cost of living in the New York area, she was not going to easily pay off her student loans.

This woman's story is not unique. In general, the expected lifetime earnings of those who major in the humanities is quite a bit less than those who major in information sciences, business, engineering, and math. Of course, this means two things if you plan on a humanities major. First, college is less likely to be a good financial investment. Second, any loans you obtain will be that much tougher to pay.

BUT THERE'S MORE

It's not just your major that is important in assessing the investment potential of your degree. Where you receive your degree also matters. Expenditures for an education at average or below average private universities or for-profit institutions have a much lower payoff than if you attend a highly respected public university or a top-level private school. That is, if you go to a second- or third-tier school, especially if it is out-of-state or private, you are unlikely to see the wage premiums enjoyed by people at top schools. And if you borrowed the money to finance that lower-tier education, you will likely have to sacrifice plenty in other areas of your life to make those loan payments.

Then there is the matter of just who you are. Intelligence and work ethic are simply not distributed equally among all people. Therefore, the rate of return to higher education varies widely, even for the same major at the same institution. It is important that students ask themselves: Is college a good investment for *me*? Because if the answer is "no," you may want to think twice before signing on the dotted line for that student loan.

COLLEGE IS FUN

Even though the inflation-adjusted cost of college has tripled in recent decades, this definitely does not mean the quality of the education received has risen at the same rate. In fact, as colleges and universities have competed more intensely for students, many of whom have access to federally subsidized loans, the **amenities** offered by colleges have skyrocketed. The typical college campus today looks much different from the campus of 30 or 40 years ago. Dorms are much more luxurious, the food served on campus is higher quality, and the student center offers a variety of leisure activities unheard of before. And, of course, the sports facilities are almost always first rate.

Thus, if you are thinking of borrowing tens of thousands of dollars to go to college, you may want to understand that not all of what you are spending constitutes an **investment.** A significant part of the price of college goes to covering a more luxurious day-to-day student living environment away from home. When you **consume** by going to a movie, you typically do not believe that there is any financial pay-off to doing so, above the immediate pleasure you receive. Why should it be any different when you lounge around a spacious new student activity center with the latest in flat screen TVs, video games, and the like? So, if you've borrowed the money for all that fun, don't complain to us when the bills come due.

DISCUSSION QUESTIONS

1. Discuss how much of your college experience is consumption and how much is investment. Briefly explain your rationale for why some of your own consumption spending is consumption rather than investment.

2. If you were not going to college, would you still have to eat and have a place to live? How many people not in college do you think borrow to pay for meals and their apartment rent? Why do college students routinely borrow funds to pay their room and board?

3. What is the proper way to calculate whether borrowing an extra $10,000 per year to go to a "good" college or university is worth the additional debt?

4. Some people believe it is not fair that those who major in the humanities almost always have an expected lifetime earnings that is much less than those who major in information sciences and computers. What do you think? More importantly, what do you think the consequences would be if the government prohibited employers from paying humanities majors less than they pay other majors?

5. Is there any way for government to prevent colleges and universities from spending so much on improvements in dorms, student restaurants, and student activity centers?

6. Even as college graduates job prospects faltered over the period from 2007 through 2013, more students went to college and more of them borrowed to do so. How can you explain this?

CHAPTER 13

The Effects of the Minimum Wage

Ask workers if they would like a raise, and the answer will likely be a resounding yes. But ask them if they would like to be fired or have their hours of work reduced, and they would probably tell you no. The effects of the minimum wage are centered on exactly these points.

Proponents of the **minimum wage**—the lowest hourly wage firms may legally pay their workers—argue that low-income workers are underpaid and therefore unable to support themselves or their families. The minimum wage, they say, raises earnings at the bottom of the wage distribution, with little disruption to workers or businesses. Opponents claim that most low-wage workers are low-skilled youths without families to support. The minimum wage, they say, merely enriches a few teenagers at the far greater expense of many others, who can't get jobs. Most important, opponents argue, many individuals at the bottom of the economic ladder lack the skills needed for employers to hire them at the federal minimum. Willing to work but unable to find jobs, these people never learn the basic job skills needed to move up the economic ladder to higher-paying jobs. The issues are clear—but what are the facts?

BACKGROUND

The federal minimum wage was instituted in 1938 as a provision of the Fair Labor Standards Act. It was originally set at 25 cents per hour, about 40 percent of the average manufacturing wage at the time. Over the next forty years, the legal minimum was raised periodically, roughly in accord with the movement of market wages throughout the economy. Typically, its level has averaged between 40 and 50 percent of average manufacturing wages. In response to the high inflation of the late 1970s, the minimum wage was hiked seven times between 1974 and 1981, reaching $3.35 per hour—about 42 percent of manufacturing wages. President Ronald Reagan vowed to keep a lid on the minimum wage, and by the time he left office, the minimum's unchanged level left it at 31 percent of average wages. Legislation passed in 1989 raised the minimum to $3.80 in 1990 and $4.25 in 1991. Five years later, Congress raised it in two steps to $5.15 per hour. Over the period 2007–2009, the minimum was hiked in three steps to its current level of $7.25 per hour.

About 1.7 million workers earn the minimum wage. Another 2.2 million are paid even less because the law doesn't cover them. Supporters of the minimum wage claim that it prevents exploitation of employees and helps people earn enough to support their families and themselves. Even so, at $7.25 per hour, a full-time worker earns only about two-thirds of what the government considers enough to keep a family of four out of poverty. In fact, to get a family of four with one wage earner up to the poverty line, the minimum wage would have to be above $11.00 per hour.

Yet opponents of the minimum wage argue that such calculations are irrelevant. For example, 98 percent of married people earn *above* the minimum wage, and single people paid the minimum earn enough to put them 30 percent above the poverty cutoff. Overall, about one-quarter of minimum wage workers are teenagers, most of whom have no financial obligations, except perhaps clothing and automobile-related expenditures. Thus, opponents argue that the minimum wage chiefly benefits upper middle class teens who are least in need of assistance at the same time that it costs the jobs of thousands of disadvantaged minority youths.

RECENT EVIDENCE

The debate over the minimum wage intensified a few years ago when research suggested that a change in the New Jersey minimum wage had no adverse short-run impact on employment. Further research by other scholars focusing on Canada reveals more clearly what actually happens when the minimum wage is hiked. In Canada, there are important differences in minimum wages both over time and across different provinces. These differences enabled researchers to distinguish between the short- and long-run effects of changes in minimum wages. The short-run effects are indeed negligible, as implied by the New Jersey study. But the Canadian research shows that in the long run, the adverse effects of a higher minimum wage are quite substantial. In the short run, it is true that firms do not cut their workforce by much in response to a higher minimum. But over time, the higher costs due to a higher minimum wage force smaller firms out of business, and it is here that the drop in employment shows up clearly.

The Canadian results are consistent with the overwhelming bulk of the U.S. evidence on this issue, which points to a negative impact of the minimum wage on employment. After all, the number of workers demanded, like the quantity demanded for all goods, responds to price: The higher the price, the lower the number desired. There remains, however, debate over how many jobs are lost due to the minimum wage. For example, when the minimum wage was raised from $3.35 to $4.25, credible estimates of the number of potential job loss ranged to 400,000.

When the minimum was hiked to $5.15, researchers suggested that at least 200,000 jobs were at stake. More recently, economists have estimated that the latest increase in the federal minimum wage to $7.25 from $6.55 caused 300,000 people to lose their jobs. With a workforce of over 155 million persons, numbers like these may not sound very large. But most of the people who don't have jobs as a result of the minimum wage are teenagers. They comprise less than 5 percent of the workforce but bear almost all the burden of foregone employment alternatives.

The Big Losers

Significantly, the youths most likely to lose work due to the minimum wage are disadvantaged teenagers, chiefly minorities. On average, these teens enter the workforce with the fewest job skills and the greatest need for on-the-job training. Until and unless these disadvantaged teenagers can acquire these skills, they are the most likely to be unemployed as a result of the minimum wage—and thus least likely to have the opportunity to move up the economic ladder. With a teen unemployment rate triple the overall rate and unemployment among black youngsters close to 40 percent, critics argue that the minimum wage is a major impediment to long-term labor market success for minority youth.

Indeed, the minimum wage has an aspect that its supporters are not inclined to discuss: It can make employers more likely to discriminate on the basis of gender or race. When wages are set by market forces, employers who would discriminate face a reduced, and thus more expensive, pool of workers. But when the government mandates an above-market wage, the result is a surplus of low-skilled workers. It thus becomes easier and cheaper to discriminate. As former U.S. Treasury secretary Lawrence Summers noted, the minimum wage "removes the economic penalty to the employer. He can choose the one who's white with blond hair."

Critics of the minimum wage also note that it makes firms less willing to train workers lacking basic skills. Instead, companies may choose to hire only experienced workers whose abilities justify the higher wage.

Firms are also likely to become less generous with fringe benefits in an effort to hold down labor costs. The prospect of more discrimination, less job training for low-skilled workers, and fewer fringe benefits for entry-level workers leaves many observers uncomfortable. As the economist Jacob Mincer noted, the minimum wage means "a loss of opportunity" for the hard-core unemployed.

Living Wages?

Despite these adverse effects of the minimum wage, many state and local governments believe that people with jobs should be paid a wage on which they can "afford to live." In fact, some states and localities mandate that minimum wages (sometimes called "living wages") be even higher, at levels above $10 an hour in Santa Fe, New Mexico, and San Francisco, California (amounts that are adjusted up in both cities to reflect inflation each year). Somtimes, as in Baltimore, Maryland, the local minimum wage applies only to workers at firms that do business with the relevant government entity. But in the case of the Santa Fe and San Francisco minimum wages, as well as all state-determined minimum wages, the law applies to all but a few firms that are exempt due to their very small size or their industry (such as agriculture).

When politicians decide to raise the minimum wage, it is only after heated battles often lasting months. Given the stakes involved—an improved standard of living for some and a loss of job opportunities for others—it is not surprising that discussions of the minimum wage soon turn to controversy. As one former high-level U.S. Department of Labor official said, "When it comes to the minimum wage, there are no easy positions to take. Either you are in favor of more jobs, less discrimination, and more on-the-job training, or you support better wages for workers. Whatever stance you choose, you are bound to get clobbered by the opposition." When Congress and the president face this issue, one or both usually feel the same way.

Discussion Questions

1. Are teenagers better off when a higher minimum wage enables some to earn higher wages but causes others to lose their jobs?

2. Are there methods other than a higher minimum wage that could raise the incomes of low-wage workers without reducing employment among minority youngsters?

3. Why do you think organized labor groups, such as unions, are supporters of a higher minimum wage, even though all their members earn much more than the minimum wage?

4. Is it possible that a higher minimum wage could ever *increase* employment?

5. Even without a minimum wage, the unemployment rate would almost surely be higher among teenagers than among adults. Suggest at least two reasons why this is so.

6. Why is it teenagers (rather than members of any other age group) who are most likely to lose their jobs (or get turned down for employment) when the minimum wage is raised?

CHAPTER **14**

Immigration, Superstars, and Poverty

In 1960, the poorest 20 percent of households in the United States received a bit over 4 percent of total income. Today, after nearly five decades of government efforts to relieve poverty, the bottom 20 percent receive a bit less than 4 percent of total income. About forty million Americans lived in poverty in 1960. About forty million U.S. citizens *still* live in poverty, despite the expenditure of hundreds of billions of dollars in aid for the poor. In the richest country in the world, poverty seems remarkably resilient.

START WITH THE FACTS

If we are to understand why, we must begin by getting the facts straight. First, even though the absolute number of Americans living in poverty has not diminished over the past five decades, population growth has brought a sizable reduction in the *proportion* of impoverished Americans. As conventionally measured, more than 22 percent of Americans lived in poverty in 1960. Today, as we emerge from one of the worse recessions in our history, about 14 percent of the population is below the poverty line.

Second, traditional methods of measuring poverty may be misleading because they focus solely on the *cash income* of individuals. In effect, government statisticians compute a "minimum adequate budget" for families of various sizes—the "poverty line"—and then determine how many people have a cash income below this line. Yet major components of the federal government's antipoverty efforts come in the form of **in-kind transfers** (transfers of goods and services rather than cash) such as Medicare, Medicaid, subsidized housing, food stamps, and school lunches. When the dollar value of these in-kind transfers is included in measures of *total* income, the standard of living of persons at lower income levels has improved substantially over the years.

There is disagreement over how much of these in-kind transfers should be included in measures of the total income of recipients.[1] Nevertheless, most observers agree that these transfers, plus the **Earned Income Tax Credit** (which gives special tax rebates to low-income individuals), are major sources of income for people at the bottom of the income distribution. Adjusting for these transfers and taxes, it seems likely that over the past fifty years, the proportion of Americans living below the poverty line has been cut roughly in half. Just as important, the standard of living for the poorest 20 percent of the population has more than doubled since 1960. In short, the number of poor individuals in this country has declined significantly, and those who remain poor are generally much better off than the poor of fifty years ago.

INCOME MOBILITY

Whatever measure of income we use, it is crucial to remember that most Americans exhibit a great deal of **income mobility**—they have a tendency to move around in the income distribution over time. The most important source of income mobility is the "life-cycle" pattern of earnings: New entrants to the workforce tend to have lower incomes at first, but most workers enjoy rising incomes as they gain experience on the job. Typically, annual earnings reach a maximum at about age fifty-five. Because peak earnings occur well beyond the **median age** of the population (now about thirty-seven), a "snapshot" of the current distribution of earnings will find most individuals on the way up toward a higher position in the income distribution. People who have low earnings now are likely, on average, to have higher earnings in the future.

Lady Luck is another major source of income mobility. At any point in time, the income of high-income people is likely to be abnormally high (relative to what they can expect on average) due to recent good luck— they may have just won the lottery or received a long-awaited bonus. Conversely, the income of people who currently have low incomes is

---

1 There are two reasons for this disagreement. First, a given dollar amount of in-kind transfers is generally less valuable than the same dollar amount of cash income, because cash offers the recipient a greater amount of choice in his or her consumption pattern. Second, medical care is an important in-kind transfer to the poor. Inclusion of all Medicaid expenditures for the poor would imply that the sicker the poor got, the richer they would be. Presumably, a correct measure of the income added by Medicaid would include only those medical expenses that the poor would have to incur if they were *not* poor and thus had to pay for the medical care (or medical insurance) out of their own pockets.

likely to be abnormally low due to recent bad luck, for example, because they are laid up after an automobile accident or have become temporarily unemployed. Over time, the effects of Lady Luck tend to average out across the population. Accordingly, people with high incomes today will tend to have lower incomes in the future, while people with low incomes today will tend to have higher future incomes. This means that many people living below the poverty line are there temporarily rather than permanently.

The effects of the forces that produce income mobility are strikingly revealed in studies examining the incomes of individuals over time. During the 1970s and 1980s, for example, among the people who were in the top 20 percent (quintile) of income earners at the beginning of the decade, less than half were in the top quintile by the end of the decade. Similarly, among the people who were in the bottom quintile at the beginning of the decade, almost half had moved out of that bracket by the end of the decade. Although income mobility has diminished somewhat over the past 40 years, it remains robust. From 1996 to 2005 (the decade most recently studied), more than half of the people who were in the bottom 20 percent income bracket in 1996 had moved out of that bracket by 2005.

INCOMES AT THE TOP

Nevertheless, there are several forces that have either increased income inequality in the United States or given the appearance of such an increase, so it is best to be clear on the nature of these. Consider first that a rising proportion of the population is *far* above the poverty line. In 1969, for example, about 4 percent of all people in America had earnings six times greater than the poverty level. Today, about 6 percent of Americans have earnings that high (above $150,000 for a family of four). Much of this jump in incomes at the top of the income distribution has come at the very top. Thirty years ago, for example, people in the top 10 percent of earners in America pulled in about 31 percent of total income; today they garner 37 percent. Most of this jump is in even more rarified company. The top 1 percent of earners used to account for 9 percent of total income; today they take in 17 percent of income. Thus, although inflation-adjusted incomes are rising across the board, they appear to be rising the fastest at the very top. This pattern, which first became apparent during the 1990s, is one that economists are seeking to explain. Much work remains to be done, but a few answers are emerging.

First, some key demographic changes are occurring. America is aging, and an older population tends to have more income inequality than a young population, because older people have had more time to experience rising or falling fortunes. Americans are also getting better educated, and this tends to increase income inequality. People with little education have incomes that tend to cluster together, while the incomes of well-educated people spread out: Some choose to convert their human capital into much higher incomes, while others convert it into added leisure time. Taken together, these two demographic changes (aging and education) can account for more than 75 percent of the *appearance* of greater income inequality.

Second, a substantial part of the rapid income growth at the top has really been a matter of accounting fiction, rather than reality. Until the late 1980s, there were substantial tax advantages for the very wealthy to have a large portion of their incomes counted as corporate rather than personal income. In effect, a big chunk of income for the wealthy used to be hidden, not from the tax authorities, but from the policymakers who worry about the distribution of income. Subsequent changes in the tax laws have since encouraged people to report this income as personal rather than corporate income. Their incomes haven't really changed; it just looks to policymakers like they have.

Nevertheless, it is clear that there are more people in the rarified upper reaches of the income distribution, in part due to the so-called superstar effect. Technological changes have vastly expanded the size of the market that top performers can serve. Because of cell phones, video-conferencing, and e-mail, for example, top business managers can effectively direct far larger enterprises than used to be the case. Sports and entertainment stars can now use cable and satellite TV and the Internet to reach audiences of tens (or hundreds) of millions, far more than the tens of thousands who can attend a live performance. These additional customers are each willing to pay for these services, so the incomes of those at the very top have multiplied correspondingly.

Incomes at the Bottom

So much for incomes at the top. What about those at the bottom? Well, between 1990 and 2005, there was a huge influx of immigrants to the United States. New immigrants typically earn far less than long-term residents. When large numbers of them are added to the mix of people whose incomes are being measured, *average* income can fall, even when the incomes of all individuals are rising. Thus, immigration created downward pressure on *measured* incomes at the bottom of the distribution. But new immigrants during the 1990s and early 2000s also added to competitive pressures in labor markets for less-skilled individuals. On balance, it appears that immigration probably lowered the wages of high school dropouts in America by some 4–8 percent. Although this seems small, remember that it is occurring among people whose incomes are already low.

Recent developments suggest that immigrants' impact on income distribution may be changing. First, the recession of 2007–2009 induced many recent low-income immigrants to return to their homelands. Second, the composition of new immigrants to America is changing. Since 2008, there has been an upsurge in arrivals from Asia, including China, India, and Korea. The higher educational and income levels of these new immigrants has shifted the competitive pressures from the bottom of the income distribution to the middle and upper reaches.

Oddly enough, public policy has taken its toll on the incomes of people at the bottom. The war on drugs, for example, has saddled literally millions of individuals with criminal records, and the impact has been disproportionately greatest on African Americans, whose incomes were lower to begin with. For example, since 1990, more than two million African American males have served time in jail on serious (felony) drug charges. Once they return to the workforce, they find that their felony records exclude them from most jobs—and not just jobs in the middle or at the top. Often convicted felons cannot find positions that pay more than $8 per hour. The result is that the incomes of such individuals are sharply diminished, which means more poverty.

The expansion of Social Security Disability Insurance (SSDI) has also likely contributed to income stagnation at the bottom. Originally established in 1956 as a program to help individuals under age sixty-five who are truly disabled, SSDI has become the federal government's fastest-growing transfer program. It now accounts for about $130 billion in federal spending per year. It allows even those who are not truly disabled to receive payments from the government when they do not work. Since 1990, the number of people receiving disability payments from the Social Security Administration has tripled to almost nine million. This is not surprising when you consider that the real value of the monthly benefits a person can collect has gone up more than 60 percent in the last thirty-five years, and eligibility requirements have been eased. The federal government spends more on disability payments than it does on food stamps or unemployment benefits.

What does this mean? Simply that people who might have worked through chronic pain and temporary injuries—particularly those without extensive training and education—now choose to receive a government disability benefit instead. The average Social Security disability payment is nearly $1,200 per month, tax-free. For many at the lower echelon of the job ladder, $1,200 per month seems pretty good. For the truly disabled, SSDI and related federal disability programs have definitely made life better. But experts believe that many disability recipients are now being drawn out of higher-paying jobs by the tax-free status of disability pay, combined with the fact that it enables them to spend more time with family and friends. This development also means that measures of income inequality have risen: Even though disability recipients are clearly better off as a result of the program, their incomes as measured by government statisticians are markedly lower.

A NOTE OF OPTIMISM

There is one definite bright spot on the poverty policy front: the "welfare reform" program undertaken in 1996. Previously, low-income families had been eligible to receive—for an unlimited duration—federal payments called Aid to Families with Dependent Children. The program was converted in 1996 to Temporary Assistance to Needy Families. Limits were placed on the length of time individuals could receive payments, and all recipients were given additional **incentives** and assistance to enhance their job skills and enter or reenter the labor force. The full impact of this policy change is still being studied, but it now appears that it has modestly raised incomes among individuals at the bottom of the income distribution.

Although the resilience of poverty in America is discouraging to the poor and to analysts who study their plight, it is useful to consider these issues in an international context. In other industrialized nations, such as Japan and most countries in Europe, people at the bottom of the income distribution sometimes (but not always) fare better than the poor in America. Although the poor typically receive a somewhat larger *share* of national income than in America, the national income in which they are sharing is lower. Thus, compared to America, the poorest 10 percent of the population has a higher average income in Japan and Germany but a lower average income in the United Kingdom and Italy.

In developing nations—which is to say, for the vast majority of people around the world—poverty has a completely different meaning than it does in America. In Africa and much of Asia, for example, it is commonplace for people at the bottom of the income distribution to be living on the equivalent of $400 per *year* or less—in contrast to the $10,000–$15,000 per year they would earn in America. As we noted in Chapter 4, this staggering difference in living standards is due to the vast differences in legal and economic **institutions** that are observed around the world. In America, as in many other industrialized nations, these institutions both give people the incentives to put their talents to work and protect them from having their assets confiscated by the government. Thus, the best antipoverty program anyone has ever seen is the creation of an institutional environment in which human beings are able to make maximum use of the talents with which they are endowed.

Discussion Questions

1. Why do most modern societies try to reduce poverty? Why don't they do so by simply passing a law requiring everybody to have the same income?

2. How do the "rules of the game" help determine who will be poor and who will not? (*Hint:* How did the Civil Rights Act of 1964, which forbade discrimination on the basis of race, likely affect the incomes of African Americans compared to the incomes of white Americans?) Explain your answer.

3. Which of the following possible in-kind transfers do you think raises the true income of recipients the most: free golf lessons, free transportation on public buses, or free food? Why?

4. Consider three alternative ways of helping poor people get better housing: government-subsidized housing costing $6,000 per year, a housing **voucher** worth $6,000 per year toward rent on an apartment or a house, or $6,000 per year in cash. Which would you prefer if you were poor? On what grounds might you make your decision?

5. Why don't official counts of who is below the poverty include in people's incomes the value of the in-kind transfers they receive?

6. The current poverty line for a family of four is about $23,000. If we lowered that threshold to, say, $15,000, what would happen to the number of poor people in the United States? Does that mean that we are better (or worse) off? Explain.

CHAPTER 15

The (Dis)incentives of Higher Taxes

Politicians always seem to be looking for additional ways to raise tax revenues. Most often, politicians talk (and even act) as if their taxing decisions have no effect on the quantity supplied or the quantity demanded of whatever good or service they wish to tax. Indeed, there is a saying among economists that politicians believe all demand curves and supply curves are **perfectly inelastic.** In such a world, higher taxes would have no effect on either quantity demanded or quantity supplied. What a wonderful world that would be—for politicians.

The Luxury Tax

In the real world, however, changes in taxes cause changes in **relative prices,** and individuals in their roles as consumers, savers, investors, and workers react to these relative price changes. Consider a truly telling example: the luxury tax enacted by Congress in 1991. Members of Congress were looking for additional revenues to reduce the federal budget deficit. What better way to raise these hoped-for revenues than with new taxes on the purchases of high-priced luxury items, such as big boats, expensive cars, furs, planes, and jewelry. After all, rich people don't really care how much they pay, right? So Congress passed a 10 percent luxury surcharge tax on boats priced over $100,000, cars over $30,000, aircraft over $250,000, and furs and jewelry over $10,000.

The federal government estimated that it would rake in $9 billion in extra revenues over the following five-year period. Yet just a few years later, the luxury tax was quietly eliminated. Why? Because the actual take for the federal government was almost *nothing.*

Rich people, strange as it may seem, react to relative price changes, too. For high-priced new boats, for example, they had alternatives. Some bought used luxury boats instead of new ones. Others decided not to trade in their older luxury boats for new ones. Still others bought their new boats in other countries and never brought them back to the United States to be taxed. The moral of the story for politicians is that the laws of supply and demand apply to everyone, rich and poor, young and old, whatever their description might be.

Static versus Dynamic Analysis

The discrepancy between the fantasyland of politics and the reality of human behavior can be traced in part to the fact that politicians routinely engage in **static analysis.** They assume that people's behavior is static (unchanging), no matter how the constraints they face—such as taxes—might change. If the politicians who had pushed for the luxury tax had used **dynamic analysis,** they would have correctly anticipated that consumers (even rich ones) were going to change their buying decisions when faced with the new taxes.

Dynamic analysis takes into account that the impact of the tax *rate* on tax *revenue* actually collected depends crucially on the **elasticity** of the relevant demand or supply curves. That is, even a high *rate* (measured in tax per item, or as a percentage of the value of the item) can yield relatively little *revenue* (total dollars collected) if consumers are highly responsive to the tax-inclusive price of the good. For example, in the case of the luxury tax, the **elasticity of demand** for new, high-end boats was relatively high: When the tax per boat went up, the quantity demanded fell so far that tax collections were negligible.

Income Taxes and Labor Supply

Now let's shift from the demand side of this taxing issue to the supply side. Does quantity supplied react to changing relative prices? Yes, but you might not know it from listening to politicians. The first modern federal personal income tax was imposed in 1916. The highest rate was 15 percent. Eventually, the top federal personal marginal income tax rate reached an astounding 91 percent, during the years 1951–1964. This marginal tax rate was cut to 70 percent in 1965. In 1980, it was lowered to 50 percent. For much of the 1980s and since, the highest federal marginal income tax rate has ranged from 31 percent to about 40 percent.

Often politicians (and even some members of the general public) believe that the income tax rates paid by America's richest individuals do not matter to them because they are so rich that even after paying taxes, they are still very rich. The underlying "theory" behind such a belief is that the supply of labor is completely unresponsive to the after-tax price received by the providers of labor. Stated another way, if you were to draw the **supply curve** of labor, it would be a nearly vertical line for each individual at some fixed number of work hours per year. Supposedly, then, the **elasticity of supply** of labor is low.

To be sure, you might know somebody who loves work so much that she or he will work with the same intensity and for the same number of hours per year no matter what the income tax rate is. But changes occur at the margin in economics (meaning in the real world). If there are *some* individuals who respond to higher federal marginal tax rates by working less, then the overall supply curve of labor is going to be upward-sloping even for the ultrarich—just like all other supply curves for goods and services.

The Evidence Is Clear

The data seem to confirm our economic predictions. In 1980, the top marginal income tax rate was 70 percent. The highest 1 percent of income-earning Americans paid 17 percent of all federal personal income taxes in that year. In 2009, when the top tax rate was 35 percent, the richest 1 percent paid more than double that share. How can this be explained? The answer is relatively straightforward: Lower marginal income tax rates create an incentive for people to work more and harder because the rewards of doing so are greater. Also, in their role as risk-taking entrepreneurs, individuals are almost always going to be willing to take bigger risks if they know that success will yield greater after-tax increases in their incomes.

Data from Europe suggest that exactly the same incentives are at work across a broad spectrum of income earners. Researchers have found that a tax increase of just over 12 percentage points induces the average adult in Europe to reduce work effort by over 120 hours per year—the equivalent of almost four weeks' work. Such a tax change also causes a sharp reduction in the number of people who work at all and causes many others to join the underground economy. Overall, then, higher tax rates cause lower output and higher unemployment and also induce marked increases in efforts devoted to tax evasion.

Incentives Apply to Everyone

It is also true that what we have been talking about applies even among people who are at the very bottom of the income distribution. In many countries today, and in many circumstances in the United States, poorer individuals receive benefits from the government. These benefits can be in the form of food stamps, subsidized housing, subsidized health care or health insurance, and direct cash payments (often referred to as "welfare"). Those who receive such government benefits typically pay no income taxes on these benefits. In the United States, they may even receive an **Earned Income Tax Credit,** which is a type of **negative tax** or **tax credit.**

If such individuals were to accept a job (or a higher-paying job, if they are already employed), two things will normally occur. First, they will lose some or all of their government benefits. Second, they may have to start paying federal (and perhaps state) personal income taxes. They understand that the loss of a benefit is the equivalent of being taxed more. And when they also have to pay explicit taxes, they know that the result is effectively double taxation.

A Lesson from Ireland

Just as at the top end of the income ladder, the quantity of labor supplied by people at the lower end is affected by changes in the marginal income tax rates they face. If taking a good job and getting off the welfare rolls means losing benefits plus paying income taxes, the person on welfare has less incentive to accept a job. A good case in point is Ireland, which for most of the past 25 years was the fastest-growing economy in Europe. In the late 1980s, its economy was a disaster, one of the poorest among European countries. One of the problems was that individuals on welfare faced an effective (implicit) marginal income tax rate of about 120 percent if they got off the dole and went back to work. Obviously, they weren't directly taxed at 120 percent, but with the actual income tax that did apply, combined with the loss in welfare benefits, the *implicit* marginal tax rate was indeed 120 percent. Stated differently, their available spendable income would drop by about 20 percent if they went back to work! Needless to say, large numbers of poorer Irish stayed on the welfare roles until the program was completely overhauled.

Interestingly enough, this overhaul of the incentives facing low-income individuals was accompanied by an overhaul of the tax rates (and thus incentives) facing high-income corporations, with much the same results. In the 1990s, the Irish slashed the corporate profits tax to 12.5 percent, the lowest in Europe and only about one-third as high as the U.S. rate of 35 percent. Beginning in 2004, the Irish government also began offering a 20 percent tax credit for company spending on research and development, offering high-tech firms an opportunity to cut their taxes by starting up and expanding operations in Ireland. Almost immediately, Ireland became a magnet for new investment and for successful companies that didn't want to hand over one-third or more of their profits to the tax collector.

The combination of lower corporate tax rates and tax breaks on research and development induced hundreds of multinational corporations to begin operations in Ireland. They brought with them hundreds of thousands of new jobs (and this to a nation of only four million residents), and Ireland quickly became number one among the European Union's fifteen original members in being home to companies that conduct research and development. And tax revenues of the Irish government? Well, despite the drastic cut in tax rates, tax revenues actually soared to levels never seen before. Indeed, measured as a share of gross domestic product, Ireland soon collected 50 percent more tax revenues out of corporate profits than America did, despite Ireland's lower tax rate.

The lesson of our story is simple. It is true that "nothing in life is certain but death and taxes." But it is equally true that higher tax rates don't always mean higher tax revenues. This is a lesson that politicians can ignore only at their own peril.

DISCUSSION QUESTIONS

1. Suppose the government spends more this year than it collects in taxes, borrowing the difference. Assuming that the government will repay its debts, what does this imply about what must happen to taxes in the *future*? How might people adjust their behavior to account for this predicted change in taxes?

2. Consider three scenarios. In each, your neighbor offers to pay $500 if you will clear brush out of his backyard this week.

   Scenario 1: If you decline the offer, you can collect $200 in unemployment benefits this week. If you accept the offer, you get to keep the entire $500, without having to pay taxes on it.

   Scenario 2: If you decline the offer, you can collect $100 in unemployment benefits this week. If you accept the offer, you must pay $100 in income taxes out of your earnings from work.

   Scenario 3: If you decline the offer, you collect no unemployment benefits. If you accept the offer, you must pay $200 in income taxes out of your earnings from work.

   What is the net monetary gain from working in each of these three scenarios? How, if at all, do your incentives change between scenarios? Explain briefly.

3. If you found yourself in the 91 percent federal personal income tax bracket in 1951, how great would have been your incentive to find legal loopholes to reduce your federal tax liabilities? If you found yourself in the lowest federal personal income tax bracket of, say, 15 percent, would your incentive to find loopholes to reduce your tax bill be the same? Explain.

4. Explain how the incentive effects of each of the following hypothetical taxes would cause people to change their behavior. Be sure to explain what people are likely to do *less* of and what they are likely to do *more* of in response to each tax:

   (a) A $1,000,000-per-story tax on all office buildings more than two stories tall

   (b) A $2,000-per-car tax on all red (and only red) cars

   (c) A $100-per-book tax on all *new* college textbooks

5. Suppose that federal marginal personal income tax rates will rise significantly over the next 10 years. Explain the ways in which individuals at all levels of income can react over time, not just immediately after taxes are raised. How will the size of the response differ, say, a year after the rise in tax rates compared to a week after the increase? Is it possible that some people will actually change their behavior *before* the higher tax rates go into effect? Explain.

6. How does a country's tax structure affect who decides to immigrate into the nation or emigrate out of the nation? Contrast, for example, nations A and B. Assume that nation A applies a 20 percent tax on every dollar of income earned by an individual. Nation B applies a 10 percent tax on the first $40,000 per year of income and a 40 percent tax on all income above $40,000 per year earned by an individual. Start by computing the tax bill in each country that must be paid by a person earning $40,000 per year and the tax bill that must be paid by a person earning $100,000 per year. Then consider the more general issue: If the language, culture, and climate of the two nations are similar, and if a person can choose to live on one side or the other of a river separating the two nations, who is more likely to choose to live in A and who is more likely to choose to live in B? To what extent does your reasoning apply if an ocean, rather than a river, separates the two countries? Does it apply if the language, culture, or climate in the two nations differs? Explain.

PART FOUR

Market Structures

Introduction

The competitive model employed in our discussion of **demand** and **supply** assumes that firms on both sides of the market satisfy the conditions of **pure competition.** For the seller of a good, this means the **demand curve** it faces is **perfectly elastic:** Suppliers must take the market price as given because any attempt by them to raise their price above the market price will result in the loss of *all* of their sales. Similarly, each purchaser in the competitive model faces a **supply curve** that is also perfectly elastic. The market price is given, and any attempt by buyers to purchase at less than that price will be unsuccessful—no one will sell to them.

The conditions of pure competition imply that buyers and sellers have no effect individually on market prices. Even a casual glance at the world suggests that the conditions of pure competition are not always met. Sometimes, as is the case for major corporations, the firms are large enough relative to the market that significant changes in their purchase or sale decisions will have an effect on prices. In other situations, buyers or sellers are "unique," in that no other buyer or seller offers exactly what they do. (Classic examples include the superstars of sports and entertainment, who will sell less of their services if they raise their prices but will still sell some.) Sometimes firms that would otherwise be pure competitors join to form a **cartel,** acting as a single decision-making unit whose collective output decisions affect the market price.

When a seller's decisions affect the price of a good, economists usually call the firm a **monopoly.** Literally, this means "single seller," but what is actually meant is that the firm faces a downward-sloping demand curve for its output, so that its decisions affect the price at which its output is sold. When a buyer's decisions affect the market price, we term the firm a **monopsony,** or "single buyer." This means that the firm

107

faces a positively sloped supply curve, so that its purchasing decisions affect the price at which it buys goods. (Some economists use the term **price searcher** to mean any firm, buyer or seller, whose decisions affect market prices and who must therefore search for—or decide on—the price that maximizes the firm's profits. Following this terminology, a pure competitor would be called a **price taker,** for such a firm takes the market price as given.)

PATENT TROLLS AND SEED MONOPOLIES

The starting point for our examination of market structures is Chapter 16. One lawful source of monopoly in the United States is a patent. This is a set of exclusive rights granted by the federal government to an inventor for a limited period in return for public disclosure of the invention. Patents ensure inventors that they can lawfully protect, and thus profit from, the commercial value of their ideas. And because the inventor must reveal the details of the invention to the public, other people have the opportunity to be inspired by it and perhaps create useful products. But because the patent owner has a monopoly on the invention, the owner can charge a monopoly price for the product, which may be well above the price of the item if it were supplied by many competing firms. This fact creates the trade-off of patents, and thus the policy tension regarding them. People especially worry about monopoly pricing with patents when several, or several hundred, of them are combined in the hands of a patent aggregator (or "patent troll" as they are sometimes called).

The common view is that patent trolls just collect money for doing nothing but being monopolists. In fact, however, by bringing many patents together under the same roof, they may be able to vastly increase the productivity of the patents compared to the situation in which ownership of the patents is widespread. Besides, the monopoly pricing potential of a patent arises only to the extent to which it markedly outperforms competing ideas. If workers, ranging from fruit pickers to baseball stars, are paid for the value of what they produce, why shouldn't inventors be paid in accord with the value of what *they* produce?

CONTRACTS, COMBINATIONS, AND CONSPIRACIES

As you will see in Chapter 17, the rigors (and low profits) of competition are such that firms often try to devise ways to avoid competing. One of the most popular is the cartel, which is simply a collective agreement by many or all firms in an industry to reduce total output so that the price of the product—and thus the profits of the cartel's members—can be increased.

Cartels are generally illegal in the United States, but the National Collegiate Athletic Association (NCAA) is a cartel that is both legal and flourishing. Cartels are more commonly observed in international markets. Here we examine three international cartels, in the markets for oil, diamonds, and caviar. Each time, we find that although the **incentives** to form cartels are great, even greater are the incentives to cheat on the cartels almost as soon as they are formed. The overriding message of this chapter is that despite their enormous profit potential, competitive pressures make cartels inherently unstable and thus generally short-lived.

COFFEE, TEA, OR TUITION-FREE?

Whatever the degree of competition, firms are always seeking ways to raise profits. Often this means developing new products and striving to offer superior service. But sometimes, as you will see in Chapter 18, it simply means adjusting prices on existing products. The practice of charging prices that differ among customers in ways not due to differences in the marginal costs of supplying them is called **price discrimination.** Although technically illegal in the United States, it is routinely observed in markets ranging from airline travel to college financial aid. In the case of air travel, you are almost certainly the beneficiary of price discrimination, paying a lower price than you would if price discrimination were completely eliminated. But don't feel too smug: By the time you start traveling for business rather than for pleasure, you are likely to be on the wrong end of the price discrimination, paying plenty so that the college kid in the seat next to you can enjoy spring break in a sunny clime.

KEEPING THE COMPETITION OUT

As Chapter 19 demonstrates, enlisting the government to hamstring or exclude competitors is probably the most reliable means of ensuring that you are protected from the rigors of competition. Perhaps for this reason, the array of markets in which the government stifles competition is nothing short of remarkable. Here we examine just a handful, ranging from taxicabs to hair braiding, but the list could have gone on and on. In each instance, the method is the same: Usually under the guise of "consumer protection," the government prevents entry by some firms into a market, thereby reducing supply in that market. The effect is much the same as that produced by a fully enforced cartel. Firms thus protected by the government enjoy both a higher price for their product and a larger **market share.** The consumers, supposedly "protected" by their government, are usually the big losers due to higher product prices and reduced selection among suppliers.

CHAPTER 16

Patent Trolls and Seed Monopolies

Nathan Myhrvold is a patent troll. Monsanto Corporation is a seed monopoly. Or so their critics claim. Myhrvold, formerly the chief technical officer at Microsoft, founded Intellectual Ventures, which creates and invests in inventions. Monsanto, which got its start by creating the artificial sweetener saccharin, is now the world's leader in creating genetically modified (GM) seeds for agriculture. Whatever their history, however, both Myhrvold's company and Monsanto regularly make headlines because of the many patents they each own.

The Nature of Patents

A **patent** is a set of exclusive rights granted by a national government to an inventor for a limited period in return for a public disclosure of the invention.[1] The notion of a patent dates back at least 2,500 years to the Greek city of Sybaris. Patents have been a part of U.S. history since our nation's inception. Article 1, section 8, clause 8 of the U.S. Constitution specifically authorizes Congress to issue exclusive rights to new ideas, and the Patent Act of 1790 laid out the first rules for doing so in this country. (Thomas Jefferson, in his role as Secretary of State from 1790 to 1793, was our first Patent Commissioner.) Originally, patents in the United States were issued for 14 years. In the nineteenth century, this was raised to 17 years, and in 1994 to 20 years. During the period of the patent, the inventor has exclusive rights to the commercial use of the

---

1 **Copyrights and trademarks** are similar to patents. The former grant exclusive rights to authors or creators of books (such as this one), songs, or other original works. The latter protect distinctive signs or indicators used by businesses to identify their products or services to consumers. (A famous example is McDonald's "Golden Arches.")

patented item, but the inventor must publicly disclose all of the details of the patented item.

Devising new ideas is an uncertain, costly business. For people to undertake this risky investment, they must have some reasonable expectation of a reward if they are successful. A patent increases the chance of reward by granting the inventor a **monopoly** on the use of his or her new idea. For the duration of the patent, its owner has the exclusive rights to the patented process, design, or good. Anyone else who wants to use the design or process or manufacture the product must compensate the patent's owner.

The Costs and Benefits of Patents

The advantages of patents are twofold. First, they ensure inventors (such as the famous Thomas Edison) that they can lawfully protect, and thus profit from, the commercial value of their ideas. Second, because the inventor is required to publicly reveal all elements of his or her idea, other people have the opportunity to be inspired by it and perhaps create other useful products. On both counts, patents tend to foster invention (the creation of new ideas) and innovation (the successful commercial application of new ideas).

But patents may come at a cost. Because the patent owner has a monopoly on the patented item, the owner can charge a monopoly price for the item, which may be well above the price that would be observed if the product were supplied by many competing firms. Hence, the output of the patented item is less than if it were supplied competitively. This in turn implies that the total **gains from trade** associated with the product are lower than they would be if anyone were free to sell it.

This, then, is the **trade-off** of having patents. We get more inventions because the profits are higher for inventors. But we enjoy smaller gains from trade on each individual invention because of the monopoly pricing of them. As a matter of logic, it seems possible that offering patent protection might either raise or lower the total gains from trade arising from inventions.

Patents as Property Rights

There is another way to think of patents, however. Imagine you own a piece of land that is hilly and covered with scrub trees, weeds, and rocks. In its current condition, it is useful for almost nothing. Now imagine that you clear the weeds, trees, and rocks from the site, and rent a bulldozer to level out the worst of the hilly areas, so that now the property is something on which a residence or business might easily be constructed. Given that you own the land, you can sell or lease it for "whatever the market will bear." You would likely be surprised if anyone objected to your "monopoly" over this piece of land—and quite upset if someone argued that you should not be allowed to profit from all of your hard work on the property.

Well, a patent can be viewed as nothing more than a **property right** that entitles the inventor to profit from the hard work and expense that he or she puts into creating the invention. It is true that you (the hypothetical landowner) and the inventor each have a "monopoly" over the item you own. But neither of you will be able to charge a price much above the competitive level unless the item in question is appreciably different from or superior to other items in the market. Even in this situation, nothing prevents other people from continuing to do what they were doing before the land was cleared or the invention was created. Hence, it is difficult to see what damage to society can come from granting patent rights.

In contrast, as we saw in Chapter 4, it is easy to understand the damage that is done when property rights (such as patents) are either nonexistent or are costly to enforce or transfer. In particular, economic growth is diminished, and in the long run we are poorer as a result. In the absence of patent protection, the damage arises because there is less investment in the creation of new ideas.

ALTERNATIVES TO PATENTS

Patents have not always existed, and they do not exist in all nations today. Yet in their absence, there is still innovation. How does this occur? There are two important ways that inventors can profit from their ideas, even without patent protection.

The first method is simply by getting a product to the market first. Even if competitors are free to copy a product, it will still take them time to do. Until they do so, the inventor will have a monopoly on the item, and hence be able to charge a monopoly price and thereby profit. This method is an important source of profits for fashion designers, whose new creations each year are quickly copied by imitators—but often not before the designers have profited handsomely by being the first to market.

A second and more long-lived way to profit in the absence of a patent is by keeping the essence of an invention secret. **Trade secrets** have long been an important means of protecting **intellectual property.** A famous example of this is the formula for Coca-Cola. When he first concocted the beverage back in 1886, John Pemberton did not seek to patent it and, as far as anyone knows, the formula may not even be something that *could* be patented. But Pemberton and all successive owners of the formula have managed to keep it secret, and thus despite the lack of patent protection the profits have kept rolling in.

Of course, both of these alternatives to patents have significant drawbacks. Being first to market often yields significant profits for a short period of time, perhaps only weeks or months. Long-term profitability in such a setting requires that the innovator keep coming up with one new—and profitable—idea after another, time after time. Few people are able to maintain such a pace of creative endeavor over long periods. As the Coca-Cola example suggests, it is sometimes possible for trade secrets to help avoid this problem, but they present their own problem. If the formula for Coca-Cola is ever revealed, there is nothing to prevent another company from imitating the original, grabbing business by cutting prices, and eliminating Coca-Cola's profits.

Patent Trolls

Let's now return to the cast of characters that started our story. As the term "patent troll" is commonly used, it is taken to mean an individual or firm that enforces its patents in a manner that is seen as unduly aggressive or opportunistic. Often the trolls don't actually manufacture anything. They just hold portfolios of patents and collect payments from firms that want to use them—or that simply don't want to be sued by the troll for supposed patent infringement.

But it is difficult to see the difference between a patent troll and, say, computer giants HP and Apple. Both of these companies earn hundreds of millions of dollars from their patents every year, and both of them aggressively enforce their patents. Moreover, in today's world of sophisticated computer and communication systems, it is hard to imagine a setting in which companies didn't cooperate one way or another in their use of patents. Modern electronic devices typically rely on dozens of patented ideas that may have been created by just as many inventors. Each of the patents individually might be almost worthless, yet when combined in a single product may yield something of great value.

Bringing together the owners of many different patents and getting them to agree to act in a common purpose can be a costly, sensitive business. Whether or not they manufacture anything, there is thus a potentially important economic role for companies such as Nathan Myhrvold's firm. Such "patent aggregators" (as they are also known) bring together portfolios of patents and negotiate agreements between patent holders, whose inventions are worth far more when combined with other patents than when separate.

SEED MONOPOLIES

What then of our seed monopoly? Monsanto, which for many years focused its business on industrial chemicals, now directs much of its attention to creating genetically modified (GM) seeds. The company's original interest in this line of work came about because of a potent weed killer called Roundup, which the company began selling in 1976. Because Roundup can also kill the plants it is designed to protect, farmers were limited in when and how they could use the herbicide. Monsanto thus began developing and patenting GM seeds for crops, such as soy beans, which would be resistant to the Roundup. This strategy succeeded so well that sales of "Roundup Ready" seeds now account for 40 percent of the company's revenues.

Just as importantly, the company learned a great deal about the process of genetic modification, and began looking for other ways to apply it. One result was patented GM corn resistant to most of the insects that normally attack it. The superiority of Monsanto's genetic innovations is such that Monsanto's patented genes are now being inserted into roughly 95 percent of all soybeans and 80 percent of all corn sold in the United States.

With market share numbers like these, it is no surprise that Monsanto has been pricing its seeds accordingly. Indeed, over the past decade, the company has raised the average price of its seeds by about 80 percent in inflation-adjusted terms. Some farmers have said they wished Monsanto charged less for their seeds. No surprise there. But the biggest complainers about Monsanto, it turns out, are Monsanto's *competitors*, who argue that the company is engaged in "unfair competition."

Let's consider the implications of such competitor complaints. If Monsanto seeds were, say, 50 percent superior to those of other firms and it raised its prices by 80 percent, then farmers would indeed be harmed by Monsanto's patent monopoly. But competitors would benefit because Monsanto would effectively be pricing itself out of the market. Now imagine that Monsanto seeds are, say, 100 percent better than those of competitors and it chooses to raise its prices by "only" 80 percent. In this case, competitors will indeed be harmed (Monsanto is outcompeting them on quality-adjusted price), but only because Monsanto is *benefiting* the farmers who buy its seed. Our inference from this is that the loud complaints from Monsanto's competitors are the surest sign yet that Monsanto's seed monopoly is actually making farmers better off, not worse off.

Look Out for Mother Nature

In an ironic twist, Monsanto's Roundup Ready crops are so successful that they have become the dominant variety for many crops. This has helped Monsanto's Roundup remain the most heavily used herbicide in the United States. But the heavy use of Roundup has provoked natural selection in favor of weeds relatively resistant to the herbicide. In the long run, this resistance may destroy the value of Monsanto's monopoly of both Roundup and Roundup Ready seeds. While there is no evidence yet that insects are adapting to Monsanto's insect-repelling corn, don't count Mother Nature out here just yet, either.

Discussion Questions

1. Suppose property rights to new buildings were limited to 20 years. How would this affect the incentive to invest in new buildings?

2. What is it about innovations that make them more likely to be subject to monopoly pricing than are, say, new buildings?

3. It is possible to produce GM "terminator seeds" that yield healthy crops that are sterile. The crops are perfectly suitable for consumption, but farmers cannot use the seeds from the crops to grow another generation of crops. What is the potential advantage to Monsanto in using "terminator seeds"?

4. Referring back to question 3, what is the potential *disadvantage* to Monsanto from using terminator seeds?

5. If patents are best thought of as strengthening property rights, what are the other legal and institutional characteristics you would expect to see in nations with strong patent laws? (*Hint:* Refer back to Chapter 4.)

6. New pharmaceutical drugs are protected by patents. When the patents expire, other firms are free to produce chemically identical versions of the brand name, formerly patented drug. These are referred to as "generic" versions of the drug. What do you predict will be the price of these generic drugs, compared to the price of the branded drug while it was on patent? What do you predict will happen to the price of the branded drug when its patent ends and the production of generic drugs begins? Explain.

CHAPTER 17

Contracts, Combinations, and Conspiracies

The Sherman Act of 1890 outlaws any "contract, combination, . . . or conspiracy, in restraint of trade or commerce" in the United States. Translated from the legalese, this means that firms in America cannot lawfully join with competitors to form a **cartel** to raise prices above the competitive level.[1] Because successful cartels have the potential for great **profits,** there are strong **incentives** to form them. Usually, however, if the government discourages them, or even if it does not actively encourage them, cartels are difficult to keep together. This is because a cartel must meet four requirements for success:

1. *Share.* It must control a large share of actual and potential output, so that other producers of the good it sells will not be able to depress prices by expanding output significantly.

2. *Substitutes.* Consumers must regard alternatives to the cartel's product as relatively poor substitutes, and these substitutes must be few in number and relatively inelastic in supply. Such factors reduce the **elasticity of demand** facing the cartel, helping it raise prices.

3. *Stability.* There must be few outside factors disturbing **cost** or **demand** conditions in the industry, so that the cartel does not continually have to make new price and output decisions in response to changing conditions.

4. *Solidarity.* It must be relatively easy for the cartel to maintain solidarity by identifying and punishing members who cheat on the cartel agreement with price cuts.

---

1 Despite this, many American agricultural producers are legally permitted to collectively agree to raise their prices on products ranging from almonds to oranges. They do so under the umbrella of "marketing orders," which are effectively cartels approved and enforced by the U.S. Department of Agriculture.

All successful cartels have been able to meet these requirements to some extent. Conversely, a breakdown in one or more of these factors has been the downfall of each one that has failed. Most successful cartels are international. They are either effectively beyond (or exempt from) national laws forbidding them, or encouraged by or made up of governments themselves.

THE OIL CARTEL

One of the most famous and most successful cartels has been the Organization of Petroleum Exporting Countries (OPEC). Formed in 1960, its members have included many major oil-producing countries, such as Algeria, Indonesia, Iran, Iraq, Kuwait, Libya, Nigeria, Saudi Arabia, and Venezuela. OPEC had little impact on the price of oil until the outbreak of the Middle East war in 1973 provided the impetus for cohesive action. Saudi Arabia, Kuwait, and several other Arab nations sharply reduced their production of oil. Because the **demand curve** for oil is downward-sloping, this reduction in supply pushed oil prices—and thus the profits of OPEC members—up sharply. On January 1, 1973, one could buy Saudi Arabian crude oil for about $10 per barrel (in 2013 dollars). Within one year, the price of crude had risen to $33 per barrel. By the next year the price was $43, and by the end of the decade it was $83 per barrel, with no end in sight.

Several forces combined to send oil prices in the opposite direction by the mid-1980s. At least partly in response to the high prices charged by OPEC, worldwide output of oil from other sources began to grow, led by rising production on Alaska's North Slope and by aggressive marketing of the oil flowing out of the Norwegian and British fields located in the North Sea. Eventually, this additional production significantly reduced the **market share** controlled by OPEC members and thus helped reduce their stranglehold on price.

The most important problem for OPEC, however, as for so many cartels, has been cheating on the cartel agreement by its members. Whenever there are numerous members of a cartel, there will always be some who are unhappy with the situation, perhaps because they think they are not getting enough of the profits. They cheat by charging a slightly lower price than the one stipulated by the cartel, a move that will result in a very large increase in the cheater's revenues (and thus profits). The potential for cheating is a constant threat to a cartel's existence, and when enough of a cartel's members try to cheat, the cartel breaks up.

In the case of OPEC, war between the member nations of Iran and Iraq during the 1980s precipitated a major outbreak of cheating as those two nations expanded production beyond their **quotas,** using the extra sales to finance large military expenditures. Expressed in 2013 dollars, the price of crude oil plunged to less than $20 per barrel in 1986, when cheating on output quotas spread throughout the cartel. Saudi Arabia, the world's largest producer of crude, finally restored order when it threatened to double its output if other OPEC members did not adhere to their quotas. Crude oil prices hovered around $25–30 per barrel from then until early 2004, when they started a sharp climb due to rising world demand. After peaking at over $140 per barrel in 2008, prices subsequently dropped back below $100 in response to worldwide recession.

The Diamond Cartel

The difficulties faced by cartels are also illustrated in the diamond market. DeBeers, the famous diamond company, once controlled as much as 80 percent of the world diamond supply, but now can claim only a 40 percent share. DeBeers itself produces about 25 percent of the world's diamond output and controls the marketing of another 15 percent through a cartel called the Diamond Trading Company (DTC). Under the direction of DeBeers, the DTC has long restricted the sale of rough-cut diamonds to keep their prices at levels that maximize the profits of its members. After many years of profitable success, however, the diamond cartel hit rough times in the 1980s and 1990s. Cartel profits spurred searches for new sources of supply, and major discoveries were made in Australia and Canada. Moreover, Russia, which accounts for about one-fourth of world output, defected from the DTC cartel to market its diamonds through the Lev Leviev Group, the top DTC competitor. The combined effect of increased supplies and cartel defections pushed the inflation-adjusted price of top-quality diamonds down by 50 percent. Since 2000, the rapid growth of demand in China has helped drive prices back up to record levels.

The Caviar Cartel

The Russians have had troubles with their own historically successful cartel, the one that controls—or controlled—the supply of fine caviar. The principal source of some of the world's best caviar is the Volga River delta, where Kazakhstan and Russia (both former members of the Soviet Union) share a border at the northern end of the Caspian Sea. Both the temperature and the salinity of the water in the delta make it the ideal spawning ground for sturgeon, the long-nosed prehistoric fish whose eggs have for centuries been prized as the world's finest caviar. Originally, the Russian royal families ran the show, eating what they wanted of the harvest and then controlling the remaining supplies to their advantage.

When the Russian Revolution disposed of the Romanov dynasty in 1917, the new Communist regime quickly saw the potential profits achievable from cornering the market on caviar. Hence, for the next seventy-five years or so, a Soviet state–dominated cartel controlled the nation's caviar business from top to bottom. Although the Soviet sturgeon were considerate enough to produce an annual catch of some 2,000 tons of caviar, the Communist cartel allowed only 150 tons out of the country. As a result, a state-supplied kilogram (2.2 pounds) of top-grade black caviar costing $5 or less on the Moscow black market commanded $1,000 or more in New York.

The demise of the Soviet Union spawned trouble, however, for **competition** reared its ugly head. As it turns out, the largest sturgeon fisheries fell under the jurisdictions of two different autonomous republics—Russia and Kazakhstan—each of which wanted to own and operate its own lucrative caviar business. Moreover, a variety of individuals, including enterprising Caspian Sea fishermen from these republics, staked private claims and in some instances set up their own **export** channels (behavior officially termed "black market piracy"). The effect of this capitalist behavior was a 20 percent drop in the official caviar export price during the first year of autonomy, plus an escalation of competition since then.

Caviar consumers were pleased at this turn of events, but old-line suppliers were not so happy. "We don't need this kind of competition," complained one. "All of these small rivals mean that prices will fall and the market will be ripped apart. This is a delicacy—we need to keep it elite." Recent years have seen a sharp upswing in world caviar prices, although not because Russia and Kazakhstan have managed to get competition under control. Instead, it turns out that pollution from leftover Soviet industry in the area has sharply reduced the region's sturgeon population. The resulting decline in the amount of harvestable caviar drove costs and prices up and profits even lower. Adding insult to injury, American firms have entered the caviar market in response to the higher prices, intensifying the price–cost squeeze that the former Soviet republics are suffering. So, just as Soviet citizens found that communism wasn't all that it was cracked up to be, it appears some of them are now learning that capitalism may be more than they bargained for—but perhaps no less than Karl Marx warned them about.

THE COLLEGE SPORTS CARTEL

Oddly enough, despite the Sherman Act and other tough antitrust laws, one of the longest-running cartels can be found right here in the United States. The National Collegiate Athletic Association (NCAA), which operates under a special exemption from the antitrust laws, sets the rules not only for how intercollegiate sports competition takes place but also for how athletes are recruited and paid. And under NCAA rules, college athletes are not paid much. Indeed, as a practical matter, compensation for collegiate athletes is limited to the cost of room, board, books, and tuition at their university or college, an amount that typically ranges from $30,000 to $60,000 per year. This might sound like pretty good pay to you, and indeed, for a field hockey player or college wrestler, it probably is. But for the so-called revenue sports of college athletics, most notably football and basketball, such sums amount to a pittance compared to what these athletes would bring on the open market. (This, of course, is exactly the point: Universities are joined together in the NCAA in part simply to keep down the costs of college athletics.)

In the case of football, this issue has been studied quite intensively, so we actually have a good idea of what top college players are worth. A player who ends up getting drafted by a professional team is underpaid by $2 million over the course of his college career. And while lesser players are underpaid by lesser amounts, numbers like these make it clear that despite encouraging open competition on college playing fields, when it comes to competition in the marketplace, the NCAA is guilty of unsportsmanlike conduct.

DISCUSSION QUESTIONS

1. Why are all cartels inherently unstable?

2. Would it be easier to form a cartel in a market with many producers or one with few producers?

3. What happens to the producers of caviar made from other types of fish eggs (such as salmon, whitefish, and trout) when the price of the finest sturgeon caviar changes? Would these firms ever have an incentive to help the governments of Russia and Kazakhstan reestablish the caviar cartel?

4. If the members of your class were to attempt to form a study-reduction cartel in which everyone agreed to study less, which individuals would have the most to gain from the cartel? Which ones would have the greatest incentive to cheat on the cartel?

5. The economy of India (with a population of one billion) has begun to industrialize, and per capita income there is rising. What impact will this growth have on the demand for oil and diamonds—and thus on their prices? Explain.

6. Suppose there is a decline in marginal costs for one member of a cartel. What impact will this have on the incentive of that firm to cheat on the cartel agreement? Explain.

CHAPTER 18

Coffee, Tea, or Tuition-Free?

A few years ago, the Internet retailing giant Amazon.com received some unwanted publicity when it was revealed that the company was charging different prices for movies sold to different customers. Amazon insisted that the price differences were random and amounted to an effort to simply test the market. But some customers complained that Amazon was using the practice to tailor prices to customer characteristics, charging more to people who were likely to be willing to pay more. The flap over Amazon's "market test" soon died out. But as time passes, Internet firms and other companies are finding it almost impossible to resist regularly charging different prices to different customers, on everything from consumer electronics to razor blades. The reason is simple: By tracking people's buying habits, firms can get a pretty good idea of how to engage in **price discrimination** among their customers and thus increase their **profits.**

Shouldn't price discrimination be illegal? Actually, it *is* illegal, at least under some circumstances. Nevertheless, it is routinely practiced by businesses of all descriptions—and perhaps even by the college you attend. Interestingly, although price discrimination definitely benefits the firms (or colleges) that engage in it, you may benefit, too. Let's see how.

THE BASICS OF PRICE DISCRIMINATION

First things first: Price discrimination is defined as the existence of price differences across customers for the same good that are not due to differences in the **marginal costs** of supplying the customers. Price discrimination can occur when marginal costs are the same across customers but prices are different or when prices are the same despite differences in marginal costs. An example of the former occurs when pharmacies or movie theaters charge lower prices to "senior citizens" than to other customers. An example of the latter can be found at "all-you-can-eat" buffets, where the price is the same for all diners, even though some eat much more food than others.

Three conditions must exist for a firm to engage in price discrimination. First, the firm must be, at least to some extent, a **price searcher**—it must be able to raise price above marginal cost without losing all of its sales to rivals. Second, there must be identifiable differences across customers in their willingness (or ability) to pay different prices for the same good. Third, the firm must be able to prevent customers who pay lower prices from reselling the good to customers who otherwise would be charged higher prices—or else customers eligible for the lowest price will buy on behalf of all customers.

The objective of price discrimination is, of course, higher profits for the firm that engages in it. To see how this might work, consider a firm selling to two identifiable groups of customers, say, retirees and working people. Also suppose that the retirees have lower income and so perhaps have a higher **price elasticity of demand** for the good—that is, they tend to be more sensitive to changes in price. In this situation, it may be possible for the firm to reallocate sales among customer groups, lowering prices slightly to retirees and raising them somewhat more to working people, thereby getting more revenue at the same costs, and so earning higher profits. Of course, to accomplish this, the firm must be able to distinguish between the two groups. (This ability is often approximated by offering the lower prices only to persons who can prove they are older and thus more likely to be retired.) The firm also must be able to prevent resale from low-price buyers to other customers. When pricing prescription medicines, pharmacies are aided by federal and state laws that forbid such resale. Movie theaters prevent resale by requiring that to get a lower price one must attend the movie personally. (This helps explain why movie rental companies such as Netflix are less likely than movie theaters to offer senior citizen discounts: It would be too easy for seniors to rent movies on behalf of younger people who wish to avoid the higher prices applicable to them.)

PRICE DISCRIMINATION BY AIRLINES

If you have ever traveled on an airplane, you are likely to have been a beneficiary of price discrimination (although your parents—or their employers—may have been victims of such discrimination if they fly on short-notice business trips). Before 1978, the fares charged by airlines in the United States were regulated by the federal government, so all airlines offered the same government-approved fares; discounts were rare beyond late-night ("red-eye") or weekend flights.[1] Once deregulation occurred, airlines quickly discovered that there were large differences in the price elasticity of demand across customers. Business travelers typically had a lower price elasticity of demand and hence were willing to pay higher fares than leisure travelers. Fares charged to business travelers are now higher than they used to be, even though leisure fares are significantly lower than they were in the days of government regulation.

The precision and effectiveness with which the airlines engage in price discrimination have been rising steadily over time, thanks to a process known as "yield management." Combining sophisticated statistical techniques and massive historical databases, together with computerized up-to-the-minute bookings, the airlines can predict with almost pinpoint accuracy how many business customers will want seats on a given flight and how much they'll be willing to pay. As a result, says one industry insider, "high fares get higher and low fares get lower."

YIELD MANAGEMENT IN ACTION

The process begins months before a flight ever departs, as the airline divides the seats on a plane into as many as seven or more different fare classes, or categories. Initial fares on a flight are established for each of the categories, and the yield management computers begin the process of monitoring the reservations, comparing them to historical patterns. If advance bookings are slow, the airline will move seats to low-fare categories. But if business travelers buy higher-priced, unrestricted tickets sooner than expected, the yield management computer removes seats from discount categories and holds them for last-minute business passengers who are predicted to show up.

A host of techniques are used to optimize the blend between filling the seats on a plane and getting the highest fare for each seat. In the weeks leading up to a flight, the level of fares assigned to each category may be adjusted up or down based on the latest moves by competitors, and as the flight date approaches, lower-priced categories are likely to be closed out altogether. Moreover, some people seeking reservations may be told a given flight is "sold out" even though passengers using that flight as a connector to another of the airline's routes may find ample seating—for a price, of course. The result of all this fine-tuning is that

---

1 Adjusted for inflation, average fares were also considerably higher than they are today, because the federal government agency responsible for regulating the airlines prevented them from competing on the basis of price.

passengers on the same flight from, say, Chicago to Phoenix may pay round-trip fares that vary by a factor of 5—ranging, say, from $280 for the lowest-priced seats to $1,400 for the top fares.

You might think that all of these pricing tactics generated big profits—but you'd be wrong. Competition among airlines is so fierce that the profit on a 100-passenger flight amounts to the price of a single ticket. Is it any wonder, then, that the companies are trying to get as much as they can for it?

PRICE DISCRIMINATION BY COLLEGES

Interestingly, the same yield management techniques refined by the airlines are now being used by universities when they decide on financial aid packages offered to students. After all, given the nominal tuition at a university, a more generous financial aid offer can be thought of as a lower price, and students, like everyone else, behave according to the **law of demand.** Universities have found, for example, that they can offer less generous aid packages to students who apply for early admission because such students are more eager to attend. As one financial aid consultant notes, "Those who have the most interest in the school are going to be less price sensitive." In a similar vein, some colleges have found that people who come for campus interviews are more interested in attending. The response has been to offer slightly less generous aid packages to such students, even though the colleges routinely recommend that students come for interviews.

In addition to these regular features of price discrimination in financial aid offers, universities also monitor their enrollment figures each year, just as the airlines watch bookings by fare category. If a school is getting, say, too many premed students and not enough in the humanities, financial aid offers will be adjusted accordingly, with bigger than usual aid offers being made to the students the school is trying to attract. Schools that are noted for excellence in one area but are trying to maintain a balanced mix of majors have become particularly adept at the financial aid game. As the enrollment vice president for Carnegie Mellon University notes, without sophisticated adjustments to the blend of aid packages offered, "I'd have an institution full of engineers and computer scientists and I wouldn't have anybody in arts and design." Carnegie Mellon also recognizes the importance of competition in determining the prices it charges. After admitted students are notified of their aid offers in the spring, they are invited to fax the school any better offers they receive from other colleges. The university generally meets competing offers received by desirable students.

PRICE DISCRIMINATION BY DRUG COMPANIES

Price discrimination can even be practiced on a worldwide scale. Most major pharmaceutical companies price discriminate based on the nationality of the people buying their drugs. Partly because incomes in other nations are lower than in the United States, people in other nations have higher elasticities of demand than American citizens. Consequently, pharmaceutical companies sell prescription drugs elsewhere at lower prices than they do in the United States. But one of these other nations is Canada, and American senior citizens have found that by getting on a bus (or even just visiting the Web site of a Canadian pharmacy), they can save a bundle on their prescriptions.[2] Although this practice is technically illegal, neither the United States nor Canada has stopped it. In fact, by the time you read this, Congress may have legalized the importation of prescription drugs from other nations.

Price discrimination certainly profits the firms that practice it, but there is an entirely different question—one that cannot be answered by economics—as to whether it is fair. Most student travelers who can stay over a Saturday night or make reservations a month in advance probably don't mind the lower fares made possible by price discrimination. But business travelers are far from pleased with the high fares they must pay to get where they want, when they want, usually on short notice. "They've got you, and they know it," says one executive. The flip side, of course, is that without the extra revenue generated by price discrimination, some companies or colleges would be hard-pressed to survive. Indeed, when asked about the equity of fine-tuning aid packages to willingness to attend rather than ability to pay, one financial aid official noted he had little choice in the matter: "I could make it very fair—and be out of business."

DISCUSSION QUESTIONS

1. First-class passengers generally pay higher fares than coach passengers, even when they take advantage of advance-purchase discounts. Is this price discrimination? (*Hint:* Seats in first class are generally leather rather than fabric and are about 50 percent wider than coach seats. Also, there are more flight attendants per passenger in the first-class section.)

---

2 Another reason for lower prices in Canada is that it has a nationalized health-care system, meaning that the government buys drugs on behalf of all Canadians. This practice makes the Canadian government a **monopsonist** (literally, "single buyer"), with the power to force drug prices below what they otherwise would be.

2. Is it price discrimination when a professional football team charges, say, $150 per ticket for 50-yard-line tickets in the lower deck and $50 per ticket for upper-deck tickets overlooking the end zone?

3. What factors other than income are likely to affect willingness to pay? How will differences in these factors among its customers affect the likelihood that a firm will engage in price discrimination?

4. Consider the following data from three different firms (1, 2, and 3) each selling to two different customers (A and B). Shown are the price (P) per unit charged each customer and the marginal cost (MC) of producing each unit for the customer. (Thus, for example, Firm 1 has different marginal costs between customers and charges different prices.)

	Customer A	Customer B
Firm 1		
Price ($)	100	150
Marginal cost ($)	100	150
Firm 2		
Price ($)	200	200
Marginal cost ($)	100	150
Firm 3		
Price ($)	150	200
Marginal cost ($)	100	100

Which firms are engaged in price discrimination? Explain. Extra credit: For each firm, rank-order the elasticity of demand of the two customers.

5. Suppose a firm starts off with selling a uniform product to two different customers at the same price per unit for each. Now it decides to engage in price discrimination by raising the price to one customer and lowering the price to the other customer. Why doesn't the profit lost due to lowering the price for one customer eliminate all of the higher profits achieved by raising the price to the other customer?

6. Suppose a local beverage shop charges $6 for a six-pack of your favorite beverage, and charges $15 for a case (containing four six-packs) of that same beverage? Is this price discrimination?

CHAPTER 19

Keeping the Competition Out

Most competitors hate **competition.** And who can blame them? After all, if a firm can keep the competition out, **profits** are sure to rise. How high they will rise obviously varies by industry, but the lowly taxicab market gives some indication of what is at stake.

TAXICAB MEDALLIONS

In New York City, the number of taxicabs is limited by law—limited, in fact, to one cab for every six hundred people, in a town where many people don't own cars. To legally operate a taxi in New York, one must own a taxi medallion, a city-issued metal shield affixed to the cab's hood. Although the number of taxi medallions in New York is fixed by law, you are free to buy one from a current owner, assuming that you can come up with the prevailing market price, about $700,000. This price, we should note, does not include the taxi itself, although it does entitle you to the right to work long hours, subject to robbery, rude customers, and the erratic driving habits of other cabbies.

Lest you think New York taxi drivers are crazy to pay such sums, keep this in mind: Because the city keeps the competition out, the taxi business is so lucrative that the medallions can be used as collateral to borrow at favorable interest rates, and any cabbie who wants to leave the business can immediately find a buyer for his or her medallion, usually at a price that will bring even more profit. In fact, the long-run **rate of return** on New York taxi medallions compares favorably with the long-run rate of return on stocks listed on the New York Stock Exchange.

Keeping the competition out works quite simply. Reducing the number of firms in an industry decreases the **supply** of the good, thus driving up its price. Firms that remain thus enjoy both a higher price for their product and a larger **market share.** Consumers lose, however, suffering from higher prices and fewer alternative sources of supply from which to choose. The firms that are excluded also lose. Their owners are forced to go into lower-paying pursuits for which they are not as well suited. The higher profits enjoyed by the firms protected from competition thus come at the expense of consumers and excluded competitors. The net result is also an overall loss to society as a whole because the limit on competition reduces the total extent of mutually beneficial exchange.

Note that we said that the number of taxi medallions in New York is limited by the government. This is typical. Even though many government agencies (for example, the Federal Trade Commission and the Department of Justice at the federal level) are supposed to promote competition, getting the government involved is usually the most effective way to *stifle* competition. Consider telephones. It used to be that both long-distance and local telephone markets were regulated by the federal government. In 1984, the long-distance market was deregulated, and AT&T had to begin competing with MCI and Sprint for customers. The result was a 40 percent drop in inflation-adjusted long-distance rates. Local telephone service continued to be regulated by the Federal Communications Commission (FCC), however, and over the same period of time, local phone rates *rose* 40 percent in real terms—chiefly because the FCC kept competition out of the local phone service market.

OCCUPATIONAL LICENSING

Keeping the competition out seems to be growing in popularity across America. As the economy has moved from manufacturing to services, the number of people working in licensed professions has risen sharply. Thirty years ago, there were about 80 occupations for which one or more state governments required a license. Today, there are roughly 1,100 occupations that require a license in at least one state, ranging from secretaries in Georgia to wallpaper hangers in California. Roughly 30 percent of the U.S. labor force, about forty-five million individuals, now belongs to a licensed profession. Officially, of course, this is all done to protect the consumer from unscrupulous or incompetent practitioners. In fact, such licensing requirements serve chiefly—if not solely—to keep the competition out and raise the earnings of those who manage to get licensed.

Many of the decision makers who work for the government agencies that limit competition are lawyers, so it is not surprising that competition among lawyers is limited. For example, in every state but one (California), the number of law schools is capped by state law, thereby restricting entry into the profession and driving up earnings. Real estate agents are also well represented among the members of state legislatures, and so it may come as no surprise that they, too, have been successful in keeping the competition out. In addition to having to pass examinations to be licensed, real estate agents are prohibited—at their own request—from engaging in all sorts of competitive behavior. In a dozen states, agents are prohibited from discounting their prices even if they perform less than the usual amount of services for their customers. In eight states, real estate agents are not permitted to perform fewer services than the local realty association specifies, even if the customer does not want those services. These crimps on competition make life both comfortable and profitable for real estate agents, but it's not such a good deal for home buyers and sellers. In the United States, the average real estate agent's commission is 5.1 percent of the sale price of the home; the average commission in other countries is 3.6 percent. Thus, by restricting competition, real estate agents in America are able to charge over one-third more for their services.

SOME HAIRY COMPETITION

Sometimes the government gets involved in some unlikely markets in its efforts to prevent the ravages of competition from taking their toll. Consider hair braiding. Some African Americans like to have their hair straightened in beauty shops, a procedure that requires a touch-up every four weeks, for an average monthly cost (excluding cutting and styling) of about $100. An alternative is to get one's hair braided at a braiding salon. There are now about ten thousand of these salons across the country. Braids need maintenance only once every ten weeks, cutting the cost to $50 per month.

The same low cost and convenience that make braiding salons attractive to consumers also make them threatening to the conventional beauty shops that straighten hair, especially in fashion-conscious California. Claiming that they are seeking to protect consumers, agents of the California Barbering and Cosmetology Board regularly raid the salons of unlicensed hair braiders. Not surprisingly, the hair braiders think the state is actually trying to protect state-licensed cosmetologists at beauty shops, who must spend $6,000 for sixteen hundred hours of training to get their licenses. Indeed, one of the braiders, Ali Rasheed, argues that the marketplace is better than state licensing boards at protecting consumers. "It's simple," he says. "If I mess up your hair, you don't come back. You spread the word. And very quickly I'd be out of business." Perhaps so, but it looks like the state of California doesn't want to give consumers that option.

Licensing is even tougher for would-be braiders in Utah. There, the "Barber, Cosmetology/Barber, Esthetics, Electrology and Nail Technology Licensing Board" requires them to undergo 2,000 hours of training in cosmetology—even though none of the certified schools in Utah actually teach hair braiding. It sounds like the barbers and cosmetologists in Utah are as serious about their profession as those in Michigan, where the director of one barber school noted that "I'm not saying we are as important as doctors, but we are the closest you can get."

GOVERNMENTS DON'T LIKE COMPETITION EITHER

Back in New York, there is an example of the fact that the government likes to protect itself from competition, too. New York City is well known for its massive public transit system, comprising both subways and bus lines. What is not so well known is that mass transit in New York City started off as private enterprise. The first horsecars and elevated trains in the city were developed by private companies. Moreover, even though New York's first subway was partly financed by a loan from the city, it was otherwise a private operation, operated profitably at a fare of a nickel (the equivalent of less than a dollar today).

New York's politicians refused to allow fares to rise during the inflation of World War I, yielding financial losses for the private transit companies. Promising to show the private sector how to run a transit system efficiently while simultaneously offering to protect the public from the "dictatorship" of the transit firms, the city took over the subway, merged it with the bus line, and promptly started raising fares. Despite fare increases double the inflation rate, however, costs have risen even faster, so that today, even though the basic single fare is $2.50, the city *loses* about as much on each passenger because fares don't cover costs.

Enter the jitneys, privately owned vans that operate along regular routes, like buses, but charge as little as $1 a passenger and make detours for pickups and drop-offs on request. Actually, we should have said "attempted entry" by the jitneys because the New York City Council—at the insistence of the public transit system—has denied operating permits to almost all jitney operators who have applied. The council says it is only seeking to prevent the vans from causing accidents and traffic problems, but even fully insured drivers who have met federal requirements for operating interstate van services are routinely denied permits. Thus, most of the hundreds of jitneys operating in New York City are doing so illegally. Even the few jitneys that have managed to get licensed are forbidden from operating along public bus routes—in the name of public safety, of course.

Transportation economists such as Daniel Klein have argued that public transit systems could once more be profitable—instead of losing an average of 50 cents on the dollar—if the jitneys were given a chance. "Government has demonstrated that it has no more business producing transit than producing cornflakes. It should concentrate instead on establishing new rules to foster competition," says Klein. Unfortunately for the jitneys and their customers, however, that competition would come at the expense of New York's public transit system. Thus, for the foreseeable future, it seems the jitneys will have to compete only by breaking the laws because, like most competitors, the New York City mass transit system just hates competition.

Discussion Questions

1. Consider two different ways of beating your competition. One way is to offer your customers lower prices and better service. The other is to get a law passed that raises your competitors' costs—for example, by imposing special operating requirements on them. Can you see any difference between these two methods, assuming that both succeed in keeping your competition out?

2. Although governments at all levels sometimes act to prevent some individuals from competing with others, the federal government is probably the most active in this role, state governments are less active, and local governments are the least active. Can you explain this pattern?

3. Is there any difference between prohibiting entry by a group of firms and levying a special tax on those firms?

4. Manicurists and pedicurists are required to be licensed in both California and Florida. In California, people practicing these occupations must take 600 hours of classroom training; in Florida, they must take only 240 hours of classroom training. *Ceteris paribus* (that is, holding other factors constant), in which state would you expect pedicures and manicures to be more expensive? Explain. How could you use per capita consumption of pedicures and manicures in the two states to help you decide whether the classroom training requirement was chiefly designed to improve the quality of pedicures and manicures or to keep the competition out?

5. Although New York City's mass transit system is the largest in the country, it is not the only one that is heavily subsidized by taxpayers—in fact, as far as we know, *all* mass transit systems are heavily

subsidized by taxpayers. Suggest at least one economic and one political reason why these systems are heavily subsidized.

6. Labor unions are a device for limiting competition, in this instance competition among workers. The union bargains on behalf of all members, presumably resulting in a higher wage for workers and higher costs for employers. Use this fact, combined with the fact that international trade has played an increasing role in the American economy over the last fifty years, to explain the observation that union membership has declined as a share of private sector employment over this period in the United States. Your explanation should be consistent with the fact that union membership has *not* declined as a share of *public* sector employment over this period.

PART FIVE

Political Economy

Introduction

The chief focus of economics has always been on explaining the behavior of the private sector. Yet dating back at least to the publication of Adam Smith's *Wealth of Nations* in 1776, economists have never missed an opportunity to apply their theories to additional realms of behavior. For the past fifty years or so, much of this effort has been devoted to developing theories that explain the actions of governments, as well as the consequences of those actions. This undertaking is often referred to as the study of **political economy,** for it often involves a mixture of politics and economics. As the selections in Part Five hint, economists do not yet have a unified theory of government. Nevertheless, they are making progress and are sometimes able to offer surprising insights.

THE DECEPTION OF GREEN ENERGY

The essence of good politics lies in making costs and benefits appear to be whatever it takes to accomplish one's objectives. But the essence of good economic policy lies in making accurate evaluations of costs and benefits. Sometimes good politics and good policy coincide. More often than not they don't, however, and **green energy** is one of those instances.

Politicians decided ahead of time that "doing something" about the environment was good politics. Given this objective, all that was left was to sell electric cars and wind and solar electricity generation as policies that had high environmental benefits and low resource costs. Sadly, green energy seems to offer neither of these promises. Someday this conclusion may change, but in the meantime we need to remind ourselves that this is one of those examples of the simple adage that good politics is not always good policy.

Save a Turtle, Kill a Person

Flimsy, disposable grocery bags are cheap, convenient, and seemingly ubiquitous. But they litter our streets, trees, and yards, and when the bags reach the sea they can threaten the well-being of the wildlife that encounter them. In an effort to reduce litter and protect sea life, some nations around the world and localities across America have begun banning them and taxing other disposable shopping bags. Hence, many people are tuning to reusable cloth bags.

Sadly, it turns out that bans or taxes on disposable bags waste natural resources, and add to air and water pollution. More disturbingly, the reusable cloth grocery bags replacing the disposable bags are an ideal breeding ground for the *Salmonella*, *E. coli*, and other deadly microbes that sometimes contaminate fresh meats, fruits, and vegetables. Thus, the "bag bans" indirectly threaten the health and lives of human beings. To choose between seals and sea turtles on the one hand and human beings on the other hand is not an easy choice to face. But it is one we make every time we answer the question "cloth or plastic?"

Raising Less Corn and More Hell

Shifting our attention to rural America, it is fair to say that farmers have exploited the nuances of political economy as well as anyone in this nation, a point we elaborate on in Chapter 22. More than seventy years ago, American farmers convinced the federal government to guarantee that farmers receive prices for their crops well above the **equilibrium prices** and that taxpayers and consumers of food should bear the costs of making these high prices stick. Ever since, consumers have faced higher prices for many crops because of various **target prices** and **price-support programs,** and taxpayers have faced higher tax bills as well. Indeed, the average American household pays about $500 per year in higher food prices and higher taxes due to federal programs benefiting "farmers"—even though most of this money actually ends up in the pockets of shareholders in giant agribusiness corporations. Moreover, as the experience of New Zealand reveals, government farm programs are *not* necessary to protect the vitality or **productivity** of the farm sector.

Thirty years ago, New Zealand brought a halt to all of its efforts to protect farmers from **competition.** The result was innovation, cost cutting, and aggressive international marketing by New Zealand farmers, who are now stronger and more productive than ever before.

The Pension Crisis

Promises are easy to make and difficult to fulfill. Nowhere is this old saying truer than in politics. And when the promises offer benefits now and don't entail most of the costs until later, we have the recipe for a policy disaster. As we see in Chapter 23, this is exactly what is brewing in state and local governments all over America. These governments have made promises of generous pensions to government employees and, for decades, have been racking up financial obligations implied by these promises. Well, now that the baby boomer generation is starting to retire, the promises are coming home to roost. The result is a series of financial crises spreading across cities, counties, and states all over America. No one yet knows how the crises will be resolved, but of one fact we can be sure: The resolution will be painful for everyone involved.

The Graying of America

For thirty years, the nation struggled with the baby boom generation as it graduated from bassinets to BMWs. For the next thirty years, we will have to grapple with the problems that arise as the boomers progress from corporate boardrooms to nursing homes. As we note in Chapter 24, the United States is aging at the fastest rate in its history. As the nation ages, two major problems in political economy are emerging. First, there is the matter of paying the Social Security and Medicare bills of the rapidly growing elderly portion of the population. Second, as increasing numbers of people retire, there will be fewer workers capable of bearing the growing tax burden. America must learn new ways of harnessing the productive capabilities of the elderly and accept that as much as we may wish otherwise, the elderly may largely have to fend for themselves.

CHAPTER **20**

The Deception of Green Energy

If good intentions were all that were necessary to create "green" power, we would have so much of it today that we would not need to use coal, oil, natural gas, or nuclear power. Of course, it is also true that if wishes were horses, beggars would ride.

In the last decade or so, the federal government has poured tens of billions of dollars into "green" energy projects. The results have neither noticeably reduced our dependence on foreign oil, nor cleaned our air and water of pollutants. They have not even made a dent in the atmospheric buildup of greenhouse gases. What we *have* accomplished by using up all of these scarce resources on solar, wind, and battery power is a convincing demonstration that while green energy may make for great politics, it also makes for lousy environmental and economic policy.

GREAT GOALS, BUT NOT MUCH SCIENCE OR ECONOMICS

Anyone who is worried about the environment—meaning each of us— is concerned about potential global warming as well as pollution that occurs with many sources of energy. Environmental quality is a valuable resource and it is important that both environmental and economic policy treat it as such.

Enter the era of **green energy,** which refers to processes that can be harnessed to meet our energy needs with little pollution. Most observers would include in green energy, at a minimum, wind power, solar power, tidal and wave power, and geothermal power. Others might add hydroelectric and nuclear power to this list, although plenty of people would exclude these two on the grounds that (i) hydropower

138

threatens the long-term survival of some fish species and (ii) nuclear power yields hazardous spent-fuel waste. More generally, green power is said to be a type of sustainable (or renewable) energy—although only rarely do people define what they mean by either "sustainable" or "renewable."[1]

A Problem with the Concept of *Needs*

Notice in the above definition of sustainable energy the use of the word *needs*. One of the first concepts that anyone studying economics learns is that there is no useful definition of the term *need*. Even when we talk about the basics, such as food, water, and oxygen, it is possible to survive without them for roughly 40 days, 8 days, or 8 minutes, respectively. And human tolerance for doing without clothing or shelter is, in many latitudes and seasons, remarkably high. It is thus much more useful to think in terms of the notion of **want,** and people's **willingness to pay** for goods. Thus, we assert, no one *needs* to set a thermostat at 70 degrees during a hot summer day, even though one might greatly enjoy the resulting cool air. Moreover, even if you might think you need such a cool environment, we are confident that if the price of achieving this outcome suddenly became $100 an hour, you would quickly agree that your needs were not what you thought they were.

The point is that the amount of energy we want to consume changes remarkably depending on the price of energy we face. In countries where the price of electricity is many times what it is in the United States, per person electricity needs are miraculously less than in the United States. In the United States itself, as the price of natural gas falls, as it has over the last several years, we are finding more uses for natural gas. Trucks and busses are being converted to run on natural gas rather than gasoline, and those who heat with natural gas have discovered that it is okay to enjoy their home at 72 degrees Fahrenheit in the winter, instead of, say, 68 degrees. With lower natural gas prices, propulsion with natural gas and a more comfortable thermostat setting in the winter both cost quite a bit less than they did ten years ago. (You learned about why the price of natural gas has gone down in Chapter 7 on fracking.)

---

1 For example, it is commonplace to say that wind power is renewable but fossil fuel power is not, because the time it takes for natural processes to renew the fossil fuel is far beyond the human time horizon, whereas the wind renews itself as soon as we use it. But this argument ignores the fact that most of the resources used to manufacture and maintain the equipment used to produce "renewable" power are not themselves renewable.

Indeed, without even considering sustainable or green energy issues, we know one thing for certain. If the energy used in factories, transportation, and heating and cooling leads to undesirable environmental results, we can reduce energy consumption and thus the magnitude of the environmental damage. How? We just make sure that the prices of conventional energy sources are higher than they are today. A large tax on energy will lead to a lower **quantity demanded** and consumed. This conclusion follows immediately from the **law of demand.**

GREEN ENERGY DECEPTION #1—WIND POWER

The wind is free, right? Perhaps when you think of a windy day, that's what you imagine. But wind power is definitely not free if we are generating "green" energy from large windmill turbines. In the first place, windmills require significant amounts of steel, fiberglass, and cement. So their creation is not free. Wind turbines also require the construction of new pylons for the transmission of the turbine-created electricity. Additionally, a widespread version of the wind turbine (called direct-drive) requires the use of neodymium—eight tons of the stuff in a typical wind farm. This rare earth is produced only in Inner Mongolia. To refine it, one must boil ore in a special acid. This production process leaves behind lakes of lethal radioactive debris.

There is also a problem of the visual pollution that comes with wind farms. Wind turbines must be put where there is lots of wind, often on the tops of hills, where they may be visible for up to 40 miles. The ocean is another good place for wind farms, but because they must be close to the shore to make power transmission feasible, they again become a visual blight. (This was a key item in the controversial fight over a 24-square-mile wind farm proposed for the middle of Nantucket Sound, off Martha's Vineyard.)

There is yet another problem. The wind does not blow all the time, so city electric grids attached to wind farms require backup power stations. This backup power must start and stop—which generates much more pollution than if these power stations ran continuously. Hence, wind power is not a complete replacement for traditional energy sources, and is more polluting than you might think. How then can a nation such as Denmark rely on wind power for 20 percent of the electricity it produces? Because it sits between (and relies upon) the hydropower stations of Norway and Sweden to the north, and the coal-powered generating stations in Germany to the south.

Here is the big catch for wind power (and every other "green" source of energy): Wind power uses up to three times as many resources as natural gas turbines, and offshore wind farms use at least six times more resources than gas turbines. The enormous amount of resources gobbled up in the production of wind power means only one thing and you probably have guessed what it is by now. Government has to subsidize wind power to get anyone to build wind farms. Such **subsidization**—taxpayer dollars—has created inefficiency in the use of our scarce resources. The bottom line is that the resources that go into generating wind power vastly exceed the value of the energy they produce. This simple fact means that wind power is in fact *not* sustainable, because it leaves us with fewer resources available for the future.

Green Energy Deception #2—Solar Power

Until the world exists no longer, the sun will shine on us. Doesn't that mean we should take advantage of nature's gift? Sure—as long as it is worth it. If we can harness the sun's power in a way that creates benefits that at least equal the cost of doing so, then that is what we should be doing. The costs of solar facilities are not trivial, though. Their manufacture and installation use large amounts of energy and other resources—far more than would be required for the implementation of conventional sources, such as natural gas turbines. They must be used where there is lots of sun, and because the solar panels take up so much land area (a minimum of twenty square feet per household—plus backup conventional power), one has to cover a *lot* of desert to generate solar power in commercial quantities.

Consider one solar project built by NRG Energy halfway between Los Angeles and San Francisco. This company has installed a million solar panels, designed to produce electricity for about 100,000 homes. The cost of the project is $1.6 billion. But NRG Energy is not bearing this cost. Instead, the entire tab is being picked up by taxpayers and by electricity consumers in northern California (even those who are not consumers of NRG), who are getting a 50 percent surcharge added to their bills. Overall, taxpayers are forking over about $1.1 billion, while the electricity surcharge will extract almost $500 million from ratepayers—whether they get their electrons from NRG or not.

That it took $1.6 billion in subsidies to get this project off the ground is a clear signal that the project is unlikely to achieve its advertised objectives. We must remember that **wealth** (as that term is used by economists) simply means the sum total of productive capacity. The fact that the project must be subsidized to even exist implies that its costs exceed the benefits it yields. Hence this project destroys wealth, and is thus unsustainable.

WHAT ABOUT THE ENVIRONMENT?

Now, one might think that solar energy's great advantage is that it is "renewable." Indeed, the sun's rays will be there tomorrow for us, even if we use them for electricity generation today. But this ignores the fact that almost *none* of the non-human resources (such as silicon, aluminum, steel, concrete, and copper) going into constructing and maintaining the solar grid are renewable. And because it takes roughly *three times* as much of these other resources to generate electricity with solar power as it does with, say, natural gas, the claim that solar is more "renewable" than natural gas seems pretty unlikely.

But there is still the matter of air pollution and of carbon dioxide (which plays a role in determining the earth's temperature). Here, at first blush, solar seems to have the big edge over even clean-burning natural gas. After all, burning natural gas to make electricity does produce carbon dioxide (about half as much as coal), and other air pollutants. With solar, we are not burning anything . . . until we remember all of those extra resources that go into turning the sun's rays into a usable form. All of the steel and aluminum and glass and other components have to be produced, and all of that production generates pollution and carbon dioxide. Again, taking this additional manufacturing into account, it seems (at best) highly implausible that solar is cleaner than natural gas or even contributes less to global warming.

But, you might say, improvements in solar panels may lead to lower costs per panel and more output per panel, and thus lower resource usage down the road. That is indeed what a cutting-edge solar technology firm called Solyndra told the government when it received a $528 million federal loan guarantee. Solyndra went bankrupt trying to prove this point, as have hundreds of other solar firms around the world. Make no mistake: The resource usage involved with solar power is coming down and there is little doubt that solar will *eventually* be both economically and environmentally preferable in many applications. That time has not come and—significantly—there is *no* evidence that the pace of innovation in solar power has been accelerated in any way by expensive government (i.e., taxpayer) subsidies.

INDUSTRIAL POLICY BY ANY OTHER NAME

When the government, any government, decides to subsidize, guarantee loans, or institute new regulations to support the growth of an industry, we call it **industrial policy.** Industrial policy means (an attempt at) picking winners, presumably because the private sector won't. History has shown, though, that industrial policy generally fails. As former Obama advisor economist Larry Summers said when he argued against federal loan guarantees to Solyndra, "the government is a crappy venture capitalist." In other words, governments in general don't make good bets on commercial ventures. Otherwise stated, trendy politically directed investments rarely lead to the efficient use of resources.

This conclusion is hardly surprising. We actually design government institutions to *insulate* government decision makers from considerations of commercial feasibility, and the demands of making a profit from what they do. Who, after all, wants the budget of the local police force to be dependent on its speeding ticket revenue? So here we have the basic flaw in every industrial policy: By design, governments, bureaucrats, and even elected officials have no "skin in the game," compared to a private entrepreneur or investor. Hence, the bureaucrats and politicians are far more likely to make an error when trying to pick winners in the marketplace.

GREEN ENERGY DECEPTION #3—ELECTRIC CARS

As part of the most recent push for technologies that are supposed to be pollution-free, the electric car has become the poster child. General Motors' Volt was heralded as a way to save that company from decline, and as a way to save the environment. This and other electric cars (such as the Nissan Leaf) are considered a centerpiece of the green energy revolution because, it is said, they conserve resources and cause less pollution.

But the cars have not lived up to expectations. Consider the Volt, which has a sticker price in the $40,000 to $45,000 range, depending on options. In the hopes of getting people to buy an otherwise ordinary Chevrolet priced like a Lexus, the federal government offers a $7500 tax credit to buyers (paid for by you, the taxpayer). Even with the boost from this tax credit, sales were so slow that GM and its dealers had to offer discounts of up to 25 percent off the car's list price. Even this was not enough: During 2012 alone, GM had to shut down the Volt production line three times because of the car's lagging sales. The sad part of all this, according to the Congressional Budget Office, is that the Volt "will result in little or no reduction in the total gasoline use and greenhouse gas emissions of the nation's vehicle fleet."

Indeed, when one takes the broad view, electric cars are not really "green." Considering the full cycle of their production, including their large, expensive batteries, they create just as much carbon as do standard cars with internal-combustion engines for at least the first 80,000 miles of operation. Even this calculation ignores what electric car advocates hate to talk about. Fifty percent of the electricity used to charge the cars when they are plugged in is generated by coal-fired power plants—and coal generates far more carbon emissions and pollutants than does gasoline.

POLICY AND POLITICS

The essence of good politics lies in making costs and benefits appear to be whatever it takes to accomplish one's objectives. But the essence of good policy lies in making accurate evaluations of costs and benefits. Sometimes good politics and good policy coincide. But often they don't, and the case of green energy is one of those cases.

Politicians decided ahead of time that "doing something" about the environment was good politics. Given this objective, all that was left was to sell electric cars and wind and solar electricity generation as policies that had high environmental benefits and low resource costs. Green energy seems to offer neither of these promises. Someday this conclusion may change, but in the meantime we need to remind ourselves that this is one of those examples of the simple adage that good politics is not always good policy.

DISCUSSION QUESTIONS

1. Can you think of any situations in which the use of taxpayer dollars to subsidize industrial production of one type or another might benefit the nation in the long run?

2. What do we mean when we say that industrial policy leads to inefficient use of resources?

3. Why does the federal government have to provide subsidies to entice private companies to build and maintain wind farms?

4. What are some of the arguments that you could use to justify the expansion of wind power and solar power?

5. What are the benefits to consumers who purchase electric cars?

6. Why don't drivers of conventional cars with internal-combustion engines care about whatever pollution they generate?

CHAPTER 21

Save a Turtle, Kill a Person

Flimsy plastic bags are the packaging of choice at grocery stores, pharmacies, and many other retailers. The bags are commonplace because they are cheap to manufacture and convenient to use. But they also show up in roadside litter, and some animals, including marine mammals and endangered sea turtles, ingest pieces of the bags, with potentially lethal consequences. Both to reduce litter and to "Save the Sea Turtle," some cities and even nations have banned or sharply restricted the use of lightweight (disposable) plastic bags. These "bag bans" typically also require shops to charge a nickel or a dime for each paper bag or heavyweight plastic bag they hand out, so customers instead often choose to shop with reusable (e.g., cloth) grocery bags.

Plastic bags are made from petroleum, so the bag bans sound like a winner all around: Litter is reduced, turtles and other animals are protected, and we use less non-renewable oil. But there is a dark side to this story: Not only do reusable bags actually use *more* resources than the plastic bags they replace, they have the capacity to kill—not turtles, but humans.

A Brief History of the Plastic Bag

The word plastic was first used in 1909, but it was not until after World War I that products made from plastic appeared in any numbers. The first commercial plastic bag—a sandwich bag—appeared in 1959, followed in 1969 by the plastic produce bag. The now-commonplace plastic grocery bag came into existence in 1977. Whatever their weight or intended use, all plastic bags are composed of polyethylene, made from either oil or natural gas.

Disposable plastic bags became a staple of daily life for many reasons. They are so cheap to make that retailers willingly hand them out, even double-bagging upon request, at no charge to the consumer. The bags can be loaded quickly at the check stand, which keeps customers moving smoothly and saves on labor costs. And they are strong, durable, and versatile. After coming home from the grocery store, shoppers can deploy them as trash bags in the car or house—or even use them to safely haul dirty diapers or scoop poop while walking the dog. All in all, the bags are a veritable wonder product.

Not long after plastic bags became widely used, however, they began to show up in roadside litter. This was particularly true for the lightest weight bags, which can fly off an improperly secured truckload of trash or out a car window. There was also a growing belief that the fossil–fuel-based plastic bags created an added environmental burden above that of recyclable paper bags. Even more ominously, reports surfaced suggesting that marine animals, particularly sea turtles, were ingesting pieces of bags that had made their way to the ocean. In small doses, the plastic simply passes through the digestive track, but some instances were recorded in which large-scale ingestion appeared to have contributed to the deaths of the marine animals. All of these factors contributed to an emerging sense that disposable plastic bags might not be quite as beneficial as once thought.

BAN THE BAG

Ireland was the first nation to enact legislation intended to reduce use of plastic bags. In 2002, it imposed a tax of 15 euro cents (about 20 U.S. cents) on lightweight grocery bags. Other countries, including China, Italy, South Africa, Spain, and Wales, have since enacted a variety of taxes, restrictions, and even prohibitions on the use of lightweight plastic bags. In Wales, the tax applies to all "single use" bags, whether they are plastic or starch-based compostables. In Italy, shops have been prohibited from handing out polyethylene bags. In China, prior to the 2008 Olympics, plastic bags less than a minimum thickness were banned outright, while retailers were required to charge a government-mandated minimum price for any heavier plastic bags distributed to consumers.

The first action by a large American city came in San Francisco. In 2007, that city adopted the Plastic Bag Reduction Ordinance (PBRO), which prohibited the distribution of non-compostable plastic bags by larger supermarkets and pharmacies. The ordinance has since been expanded to all retail and food establishments within the city, and now requires establishments to charge at least 10 cents for *any* bag that they distribute. Similar laws have since been enacted by several other American cities, including Malibu, Palo Alto, and Seattle. The chief justification given for these laws has been to reduce litter and to protect marine sea life, especially turtles.

There seems little doubt that the prohibitions, restrictions, and taxes aimed at disposable plastic bags have reduced their use in the affected locales. Ireland, for example, estimated that the bag tax initially cut disposable plastic bag use by more than 90 percent, and the nation recently hiked the bag tax to 22 euro cents to discourage use even further. But the drop in flimsy bag use has also been met by a rise in the use of heavier plastic bags and paper bags, which weigh from four to ten times as much as the bags they replace. The heavier bags consume much more energy to produce, generate more solid waste, produce more atmospheric emissions, and cause the creation of far more waterborne wastes.

Thus, even though fewer *bags* are used, the overall adverse environmental impact of bags likely *rises* due to the bag bans. Moreover, while there is a consensus that the ordinances sharply cut disposable plastic bag litter, there is an accompanying rise in durable plastic and paper bag litter. Indeed, a trash audit by the City of San Francisco in 2008 found that bags comprised a *higher* proportion of its trash after enactment of the PBRO compared to before.

The Spread of the Reusable Grocery Bag

Perhaps the most visible response to the taxes and restrictions on disposable plastic bags has been the emergence of the reusable bag, most commonly made of cotton or polyester cloth. In Ireland, for example, few grocery shoppers use anything but reusable bags, and this behavior is spreading steadily in San Francisco, Seattle, and other locales that have more recently acted against disposable plastic bags.

Despite the widespread opinion that bag bans have reduced litter, the United Kingdom Department of Environment has also noted a disturbing feature of reusable bags. The Department found that, to offset the higher initial resource and environmental costs of reusable bags, they would each have to be used 131 times. Yet the same study found that in fact shoppers used them only 52 times on average before discarding them. Moreover, if the reusable bags were washed between uses, the resulting water pollution and energy used added to the environmental damage done by the bags. Fortunately for the environment, almost no one washes their reusable grocery bags. But this same behavior has some quite *unfortunate* consequences for the users of those bags: human beings.

Cloth Kills

Reusable cloth bags are often used to bring food items home from grocery stores. Perishable foodstuffs that go in the bags are sometimes contaminated with infectious microorganisms that can have serious adverse health effects. *Escherichia coli* can be found in beef, while fresh chicken frequently harbors *Salmonella*. Both organisms are also found on a variety of fruits and vegetables, as are a host of other infectious pathogens, including *Listeria*, *Shigella*, and *Cyclospora*. Significantly, these organisms are commonly transferred to the inside of bags that are used to transport them, and they not only survive, but thrive between washings. Indeed, a minor contamination brought home on one trip to the store can turn into a major one, especially if contaminated bags are stored in an automobile trunk until the next shopping trip. The consequences for the bags' users can range from diarrhea and vomiting, to hospitalization or even death.

One early study of this problem found that a reusable grocery bag was the point source for a norovirus outbreak among members of an Oregon soccer team participating in a tournament in Washington State. A contaminated cloth grocery bag was used to store food items later consumed by the team members, seven of whom contracted the pathogen. A much larger study of the issue randomly sampled reusable grocery bags from consumers in grocery stores in California and Arizona. *Coliform* bacteria were found in 51 percent of the bags, with the particularly dangerous *E. coli* version present in 8 percent of the bags. Moreover, if the bags were stored in automobile trunks—a fairly common practice—the bacteria grew at a faster rate, and thus presented greater hazards. While careful washing of the bags between uses can significantly reduce risks, 97 percent of the individuals indicated that they *never* washed their reusable grocery bags.

Subsequently, a detailed analysis of the adverse health consequences of the San Francisco PBRO has revealed that the hazards of reusable grocery bags are neither isolated nor hypothetical. For example, after controlling for other factors that might be responsible, researchers found that the PBRO appears to be responsible for a 6 percent increase in emergency room (ER) visits due to *Salmonella*, and a 24 percent increase in ER visits for *Campylobacter* infections. For the particularly lethal *E. coli* bacterium, the bag ban has led to a 27 percent rise in ER admissions. Tragically, not everyone goes home from the emergency room. The researchers found that San Francisco's PBRO has led to a 40 percent increase in deaths due to intestinal diseases in the city.

WHAT ABOUT THE TURTLES?

While it is true that bag bans have led to the use of more resources, likely caused more air and water pollution, and been responsible for sickening and even killing people, they are not without benefit. Locales implementing these laws generally report reduced plastic bag litter, and it is widely believed that the laws also protect marine mammals and sea turtles. In fact, the evidence on behalf of this particular belief is much weaker than one might suppose. For example, it is widely claimed that 100,000 marine mammals and large numbers of sea turtles are killed every year by plastic debris in the world's oceans.

There are two problems with this claim. First, there have been *no* large-scale systematic studies to document it. The claim is instead based on anecdotal episodes that, at best, have been simply extrapolated to invent a "worldwide" number. Do not misunderstand: There are numerous, well-documented case studies in which marine mammals, birds, and sea turtles have died due to the ingestion of plastics, and some of these cases involve the ingestion of disposable plastic grocery bags. The point, rather, is that there is no systematic scientific basis for any estimate of the worldwide hazards of plastics for marine mammals, bird, or sea turtles. In fact the so-called estimate of 100,000 marine mammal fatalities first appears not in a scientific journal, but in a December 1984 article in *The New York Times*, and has simply been parroted ever since.

The second problem with claims regarding the threats posed by disposable grocery bags is that most of the documented harmful episodes have nothing to do with disposable plastic bags. It is instead entanglement in plastic fishing nets and nylon or plastic fishing lines that poses the greatest threat to marine mammals and sea turtles. It is true that sea turtles routinely ingest plastic debris at sea (along with almost every other imaginable type of floating debris). It is also true that there are documented instances in which both juvenile and adult marine mammals and sea turtles have died as a result of such ingestion. But the overwhelming majority of documented deaths, disfigurements, and strandings attributable to "plastic" are due to fishing nets and lines, and *not* to plastic bags of any description.

The position in which we find ourselves is that when we use disposable grocery bags, they end up littering our streets, trees, and yards. And when the bags reach the sea, they can threaten the well-being of the wildlife that encounter them. But bans or taxes on such bags waste natural resources, add to air and water pollution, and indirectly threaten the health and lives of human beings. To choose between seals and sea turtles on the one hand and human beings on the other hand is not an easy choice to face. But it is one we make every time we answer the question "cloth or plastic?"

DISCUSSION QUESTIONS

1. How do you suppose that a number reported in a *New York Times* article has come to be accepted as a supposedly well-established scientific fact?

2. Do you think politicians were aware of the threats posed by reusable grocery bags when they chose to tax, restrict, or prohibit them? If not, try to formulate an estimate of the number of people who will have to die or be hospitalized in a given jurisdiction to lead to repeal of such an ordinance. Explain your methods.

3. Referring back to the previous question, do you think this number is smaller or larger than the number it would take to *prevent* the initial passage of such an ordinance? Explain.

4. Economists use a concept called the "value of a statistical life" (VSL) to establish a dollar figure for the valuation that individuals seem to place on their own lives, based on those individuals' personal choices about the risks of death they are willing to face. The U.S. Environmental Protection Agency, for example, currently uses $8.4 million as the value of a statistical life when assessing policies. Considering strictly the dollars and cents involved, if a bag ban that led to the death of one human being also saved the lives of, say, 100 sea turtles, how much would a turtle have to be worth to make the benefits of that policy greater than the costs? Show your calculations. Are there other factors that you think should be taken into account when deciding on such a ban? Explain.

5. A number of non-profit environmental organizations use the 100,000-marine-mammals-saved figure in campaigns for new bag bans and in their solicitations for donations. Yet no such organizations of which we are aware also mention the *costs* (monetary and otherwise) of bag bans. Drug companies are required by law to prominently list the adverse effects of their products when they market them. Are there good economic or other reasons why we might (or might not) want non-profit organizations or politicians to reveal the adverse (as well as the beneficial) effects of their proposed policies?

6. Instead of taxing or banning disposable bags, what would be the advantages and disadvantages of an ordinance simply requiring that prominent warnings be printed on the bags, noting the hazards they pose for birds, marine mammals, and sea turtles? Explain.

CHAPTER **22**

Raising Less Corn and More Hell

When politician Mary Lease stumped the Kansas countryside in 1890, she urged the farmers to raise "less corn and more hell," and that is just what they have been doing ever since.

A Brief History of American Farming

The two decades before World War I witnessed unparalleled agricultural prosperity in the United States. This "golden age of American farming" continued through the war as food prices soared. The end of the war, combined with a sharp recession in 1920, brought the golden age to a painful halt. Even the long economic recovery from 1921 to 1929—the Roaring Twenties—did little to help American farmers. European countries were redirecting their resources into agricultural production, and new American **tariffs** on foreign goods severely disrupted international trade. Because food **exports** had been an important source of farmers' incomes, the decline in world trade reduced the **demand** for American agricultural products and cut deeply into food prices and farm income.

The sharply falling food prices of the 1920s led farmers to view their problem as one of overproduction. Numerous cooperative efforts were thus made to restrict production, but virtually all of these efforts failed. Most crops were produced under highly competitive conditions, with large numbers of buyers and sellers dealing in products that were largely undifferentiated. One farmer's corn, for example, was the same as any other farmer's corn. Thus, producers were unable to enforce collective output restrictions and price hikes on a voluntary basis. But what farmers failed to do by voluntary means in the 1920s, they accomplished via government directives in the 1930s. An effective farm **price-support**

program was instituted in 1933, marking the beginning of a policy of farm **subsidies** in the United States that continues today.

THE MARKET FOR AGRICULTURAL COMMODITIES

We can understand the results of price supports and other government farm programs by first examining the market for agricultural commodities in the absence of government intervention. In that competitive market, a large number of farmers supply any given commodity, such as corn. The sum of the quantities that individual farmers supply at various prices generates the **market supply** of a commodity. Each farmer supplies only a small part of the market total. No single farmer, therefore, can influence the price of the product. If one farmer were to raise the price, buyers could easily purchase from someone else at the **market-clearing, or equilibrium, price.** And no farmers would sell below the market-clearing price.

Thus, every unit of output sold by farmers has the same price. The price received for the last (*marginal*) unit sold is exactly the same as that received for all the rest. The farmer will produce corn up to the point that if one more unit were produced, its production cost would be greater than the price received. Notice that at higher prices, farmers can incur higher costs for additional units produced and still make a **profit.** Because all farmers face the same basic production decision, all farmers together will produce more at higher prices. Indeed, no farmer will stop producing until he or she stops making a profit on additional units. That is, each farmer will end up selling corn at the market-clearing price, which will equal the costs of production plus a normal profit.[1]

PRICE SUPPORTS

Now, how has the price-support program worked? Under such a program, the government has to decide what constitutes a "fair price." Initially, this decision was linked to the prices farmers received during "good" years—such as during agriculture's golden age. Eventually, the government-established price was determined through intense negotiations between members of Congress from farm states and those from nonfarm states. The key point here is that except for the years of World War II, the "fair" price decreed by the government generally has been well above the equilibrium price that would have prevailed in the

---

1 For society as a whole, normal profit is actually a **cost** of production because it is required to keep the farmer growing corn instead of changing to an alternative occupation.

absence of price supports. This has encouraged farmers to produce more, which ordinarily would simply push prices back down.

How has the government made its price "stick"? There have been two methods. For the first several decades of farm programs, it agreed to buy the crops, such as corn, at a price, called the **support price,** which was high enough to keep farmers happy but not so high as to enrage too many taxpayers. As a practical matter, these purchases have been disguised as "loans" from a government agency—loans that never need to be repaid. The government then stored the crops it purchased, sold them on the world market (as opposed to the domestic market) at prices well below the U.S. support price, or simply gave them away to foreign nations under the Food for Peace program. In each instance, the result was substantial costs for taxpayers and substantial gains for farmers. Under the price-support system, the American taxpayers routinely spent more than $10 billion *each year* for the benefit of corn farmers alone. Smaller but still substantial subsidies were garnered by the producers of wheat, peanuts, soybeans, sorghum, rice, and cotton, to name but a few.

RESPONSES TO PRICE SUPPORTS

In an effort to keep the size of the **surpluses** down, the government has often restricted the number of acres that farmers may cultivate. Under these various **acreage-restriction programs,** farmers wishing to participate in certain government subsidy programs have been required to keep a certain amount of land out of production. About eighty million acres, an area the size of New Mexico, have at one time or another been covered by the agreements. Enticed by high support prices, farmers have found ingenious ways to evade acreage restrictions.

For example, soybeans and sorghum are both excellent substitutes for corn as a source of livestock feed. So farmers agreed to cut their corn acreage and then planted soybeans or sorghum on the same land. This action forced the government to extend acreage restrictions and price supports to soybeans and sorghum. Similarly, faced with limitations on the amount of land they could cultivate, farmers responded by cultivating the smaller remaining parcels of land far more intensively. They used more fertilizers and pesticides, introduced more sophisticated methods of planting and irrigation, and applied technological advances in farm machinery at every opportunity. As a result, agricultural output per man-hour is now *twelve times* what it was sixty years ago.

There were a couple of problems with the original price-support system. First, because it kept crop prices high, it kept consumers' food bills high as well. People were spending an extra $10 billion or more on food each year. Another problem with the price-support system was that the surplus crops were piled up year after year in government warehouses. Not only was storing the surpluses expensive, but it also eventually became politically embarrassing. For example, at one point, the federal government had enough wheat in its storage bins to make seven loaves of bread for every man, woman, and child *in the world.*

TARGET PRICES

In the early 1980s, the federal government switched to a second system, in which it set a **target price** that was guaranteed to farmers but let the price paid by consumers adjust to whatever lower level it took to get consumers to buy all of the crops. Then the government simply sent a check to farmers for the difference between the target price and the **market price.** This brought consumers' food bills down, and eliminated government storage of surplus crops, but it also meant that the cost to taxpayers—up to $25 billion per year—was painfully clear in the huge checks being written to farmers.

The original price-support program hid its subsidies by making it appear as though the crop surpluses were the result of American farmers' simply being "too productive" for their own good. With the direct payments made under the target-price system, however, it became apparent that the government was taking cash out of taxpayers' pockets with one hand and giving it to farmers with the other. Moreover, the target-price system, like our other agricultural programs, geared the size of the subsidies to the amount of output produced by the recipients. Thus, small farmers received trivial amounts, while giant farms—agribusinesses—collected enormous subsidies. The owners of many huge cotton farms and rice farms, for example, received payments totaling more than $1 million apiece.

This fact illustrates who actually benefits from federal farm programs. Although these programs have traditionally been promoted as a way to guarantee decent earnings for low-income farmers, most of the benefits have in fact gone to the owners of very large farms, and the larger the farm, the bigger the benefit. In addition, *all* of the benefits from price supports ultimately accrue to *landowners* on whose land price-supported crops are grown.

MORE POLICY TINKERING

In 1996, Congress made what turned out to be a futile attempt to reduce agricultural subsidies, enacting the seven-year Freedom to Farm Act. The reforms were supposed to increase farmer flexibility and remove market distortions by moving away from price-support payments for wheat, corn, and cotton. In their place, farmers would receive "transition payments." The taxpayer was supposed to save billions of dollars.

It was not to be. Beginning in 1998, Congress passed large farm "supplemental bills" every year, each costing billions of dollars per year that go directly from your paycheck to the bank accounts of the largest agribusiness corporations in America. Then, in 2002, Congress passed what was then the most expensive farm bill in the history of the United States, with an advertised price tag of over $191 billion for a ten-year period. President Bush said, when he signed the bill, "This nation has got to eat." He further said, "Our farmers and ranchers are the most efficient producers in the world. . . . We are really good at it."

Congress got even better at subsidizing farmers in 2008 when, despite a veto by President Bush, it passed the Food, Security, and Bio-energy Act—with an advertised ten-year cost of more than $300 billion. The new legislation gave the growers of many crops a choice of federal subsidy programs. Depending on the crop, they can select a mix of what amount to target-price or support-price programs, or they can choose a program offering guaranteed revenues. If crop prices are high, farmers get to sell at those prices, but if prices are low, they get a check that increases their earnings to the guaranteed level.

THE REALITY OF FARM SUBSIDIES

One of the claims often used to promote farm subsidies is that farming earns its practitioners relatively low incomes. In fact, farmers' household incomes have been averaging 20 percent *above* household incomes of nonfarm families over the past decade, and given the size of the subsidies, it is not hard to see why. In one recent year, when farm profits were $72 billion, the federal government handed out $25 billion in subsidies to farmers, almost 50 percent more than it spent on welfare payments for poor families. Millionaires such as Ted Turner and David Rockefeller receive hundreds of thousands of dollars per year in taxpayer-financed agricultural subsidies. When we add the billions in direct subsidies to the billions in higher food prices that result from the farm program, we find that the average American household will pay more than $5,000 in higher food prices and taxes under the latest farm bill. At the same time, two-thirds of all farm subsidies will go to the top 10 percent of farms, most of which earn over $250,000 annually. Thus, large agribusinesses continue to be the chief beneficiaries of our generous agricultural policy.

Farmers can now receive payments for *not* growing crops they used to grow. In fact, if they sell their land to someone else, the right to receive these payments goes with the land. So in many cases, even if the land is subsequently carved up into lots on which people build homes, the happy homeowners are eligible for these "direct payments," made because years ago the land was used to grow, say, rice. The price tag in one recent year: $1.3 billion. Farmers also receive payments to compensate them for losses they don't actually incur. To see how this works, let's suppose the government's target price for corn is $4.00 per bushel, and that a farmer manages to sell his crop for $5.00 per bushel during a period of the year when prices were a bit higher than usual. If at any time during the year, the price per bushel fell below $4.00, say, to $3.40, the farmer can claim a "deficiency payment" from the government. In this case, the farmer would be eligible for 60 cents per bushel ($4.00 – $3.40) for every bushel produced, even though the corn actually sold for $5.00.

Farm Policy in Other Nations

Perhaps we should not complain too much about farm programs in the United States, for at least we don't have Japanese farm programs. In Japan, a combination of subsidies for domestic farmers and tariffs on imported food has pushed farm incomes to a level roughly *double* the average income in the country as a whole. The subsidies and tariffs also have driven up the price of an ordinary melon to $100 (yes, one hundred dollars). Even the Europeans seem to find lavishing largesse on farmers irresistible. In recent years, Americans have been shelling out about $40 billion per year for farm subsidies. The European Union (EU) has been spending more than $130 billion per year on farm subsidies. To be sure, the EU is about 50 percent more populous than the United States, but even adjusting for this, the huge spending there means that the average EU citizen is spending twice as much subsidizing farmers as we spend here.

Politicians from the farming states argue that we cannot abandon our farmers because the United States would end up with too many bankrupt farms and not enough food. But there is evidence from at least one country that such a scenario is simply not correct. In 1984, New Zealand's government ended all farm subsidies of every kind, going completely "cold turkey" without any sort of transition to the new era of free markets for food. Agricultural subsidies in New Zealand had accounted for more than 30 percent of the value of agricultural production, even higher than what has been observed in the United States. The elimination of subsidies in New Zealand occurred rapidly, and there were no extended phaseouts for any crops. Despite this, there was no outbreak of farm bankruptcies. Indeed, only 1 percent of farms have gone out of business in New Zealand since 1984. Instead, the farmers responded by improving their techniques, cutting costs, and aggressively marketing their products in export markets.

The results have been dramatic. The value of farm output in New Zealand has increased by more than 40 percent (in constant-dollar terms) since the subsidy phaseout. The share of New Zealand's total annual output attributed to farming has increased from 14 percent to 17 percent. Land **productivity** has increased at about 6 percent per year. Indeed, according to the Federated Farmers of New Zealand, the country's experience thoroughly debunked the myth that the farming sector cannot prosper without government subsidies.

Are any members of the U.S. Congress listening?

DISCUSSION QUESTIONS

1. American corn farmers receive billions of dollars in taxpayer subsidies each year. These subsidies allow them to sell their grain at prices below what it costs to produce it, particularly for export markets. How do U.S. corn subsidies hurt Mexican farmers?

2. If it is so obvious that farm subsidies hurt consumers, why do such subsidies continue to be voted in by Congress? (*Hint:* See the discussion of **rational ignorance** in Chapter 27.)

3. What groups would be the major beneficiaries if farm subsidies in the United States were eliminated?

4. Why do you suppose that farmers, rather than economists, receive subsidies from the federal government? (*Hint:* If you are tempted to answer that there are more farmers than economists, ask yourself, what would happen to the number of self-proclaimed economists if the federal government started offering subsidies to economists?)

5. What are the likely environmental impacts of our farm programs? Explain.

6. Under the federal Duck Stamp program, waterfowl hunters pay a fee to the federal government each year, the proceeds from which are used to purchase land for waterfowl habitat. Do you think farmers support or oppose the Duck Stamp program? Explain.

CHAPTER 23

The Pension Crisis

It is never too early to think of your future. We refer not to your future classes or what you will do when you graduate. Nor do we speak of your future family, should you choose to have one. And not your self-imposed plan to stay healthy in the future. Rather, you might want to start thinking about how big your pension will be when you retire. That may seem a long way off, but for some—those who go to work for some cities and for some states—your pension might start in just twenty years.

CALIFORNIA ISN'T CALLED THE "GOLDEN" STATE FOR NOTHING

Today, as it struggles to recover from one of its most serious fiscal crises ever, California taxpayers are footing the bill for former police officers, firefighters, and prison guards who can retire at age fifty with a pension that equals 90 percent of their final year's salary. There are more than 15,000 government retirees in California who receive pensions that exceed $100,000 per year (and this does not count payments from federal taxpayers through the Social Security system).

Consider the odd case of Gary Clift. He spent 26 years in the California Department of Corrections & Rehabilitation. Then he retired. He now collects 78 percent of the $112,000 salary he earned in his last year of work. He also gets full health care coverage for life, which adds a tidy sum to his retirement package. Ironically, Clift spent his last two years at work analyzing legislation that would raise the state's expenditures on retirement benefits. He got nowhere when he raised a red flag about increasing pension costs. As he said, "It's just taxpayers' money, so nobody cares."

Before we go any further with the relationship between government pension payments and California's fiscal problems, let's first look at the concept of retirement and pensions.

To Retire, Normally You Have to Save

If we look back in time far enough, the concept of retirement did not exist. Individuals worked until they were physically unable to continue, and died soon thereafter. That was back when just about everyone in the world was poor. Those who could not work were often cared for by family members in large households. Not surprisingly, in very poor countries today, having lots of kids continues to be a form of retirement security—in fact, they may be the only thing standing between a retiree and starvation.

Through **economic growth,** individuals in many nations have been able to **save** to create **wealth** that can be used later on. If you do not **consume** everything that you earn, you can put aside funds to purchase houses and to make investments. Hence, when you choose to give up gainful employment, you have a stock of wealth that you can draw down during your remaining years.

If you work for a large company or a government, your retirement benefits will likely come from a pension plan run by your employer. Hopefully (for you), your employer will put aside funds in investments that will yield enough income to provide you with your promised pension. If the actual **rates of return** on these investments turn out to be as predicted by the pension plan, then there will be enough funding for all employees who retire to receive their promised pensions. If this condition is satisfied, we say that the employer (company or government) has a **fully funded pension liability.** Whenever employers do not set aside enough funds to cover future pensions, we say that they have **unfunded liabilities.** Now let's go back to the state of California to see how it has become the king of unfunded liabilities.

The Golden State Turns Red

The term "red ink" usually refers to losses being suffered by a private company or to current year **budget deficits** incurred by a government entity. In recent years, California's red ink of this variety has been in the neighborhood of $10–$20 billion per year. But current California budget deficits are peanuts compared to its unfunded liabilities, mainly due to contractually guaranteed future pensions for its employees.

In the last dozen years, California state revenues—mainly from taxes—increased about 25 percent. Pension costs for the state's public employees, in contrast, increased by about 2,000 percent. No, that is not a typo. Recall our example of Gary Clift above. When he retired from the Department of Corrections & Rehabilitation, he was eligible to apply for a disability "bonus" that would have added many thousands of dollars to his pension every year. Gary had this option not because he was disabled, but because the state of California says that working for the Department of Corrections is stressful—and so an employee *might* become disabled. Gary didn't put in for the disability bonus, but he was the only manager at the prison where he worked that did not.

IT GETS WORSE

California's problem is more widespread than simply the prisons, however. In the 1960s, about 5 percent of retiring California state workers received so-called public safety pensions. That meant the individuals had been working in a "dangerous" job. Today, about 35 percent of retiring state workers obtain this "public safety" retirement bonus, which was intended originally just for firefighters and police officers. In addition, California is the only state that uses the last year of an employee's salary to determine her or his long-term pension benefits, rather than averaging over the salaries of the last several years of work. Because pay usually rises over time, California's method generates extra pension benefits—and extra liabilities for taxpayers.

But there is more. Every year for decades, the legislature in Sacramento has improved public pension benefits. Consider just one of those passed in 1999. It was supposed to cost the state about $650 million per year by 2010. It actually cost $3.1 billion in 2010 and $3.5 billion in 2011.

Okay, so how bad can it be—a few billion here and a few billion there? Well, some studies have estimated that California has a $500 billion unfunded pension liability problem. This problem cannot go away by itself because the courts have consistently upheld government employee pension benefits as untouchable contracts, except in a few rare situations in which a local government declares bankruptcy. In one recent year alone, over $3 billion of California state spending was diverted to pension costs from other programs. The diversion of state spending to fund pensions seems certain to do nothing but rise in the future. In 2012, California did manage to cut $55 billion out of pension liabilities. But because those cuts chiefly affect *future* workers, it will be decades before the savings are realized.

A Closer Look at the "Garden State"

New Jersey, the self-described "garden state," is looking wilted. It, too, has been running billions of dollars of pension red ink per year. By the latest estimates, the New Jersey employee pension fund is well over $30 billion in the hole. What does this mean for a typical four-member household in New Jersey? Each is on the hook for about $16,000 in tax liabilities, just to make up this underfunding.

How did New Jersey get in this mess? Well, as in California, a big part of the problem started back in the 1990s. The stock market was booming, producing high rates of return on state investments. Under the assumption that these abnormally high returns were the new reality, state legislatures enhanced retirement benefits. Two stock market crashes later, the hoped-for returns haven't materialized, but the promised pensions are still there.

The Total Picture

Throughout the United States, only four states—Florida, New York, Washington, and Wisconsin—have fully funded pension systems. The remaining states are facing different degrees of fiscal disaster. Illinois and Kansas, for example, have enough assets on hand to pay for only 50–60 percent of their pension liabilities.

The PEW Center on the States did an exhaustive study just prior to the 2008 financial meltdown, and concluded that the 50 states had a $1 *trillion* pension funding gap. The states combined had contractually promised $3.35 trillion in pension, health, and other retirement benefits but only had $2.35 trillion on hand to pay for them. Between 2008 and 2012, some 45 states managed to implement some manner of pension reform. But the net savings are likely to be only about $100 billion— leaving $900 billion in unfunded liabilities awaiting state taxpayers. (And, by the way, cities are also in deep trouble. One conservative estimate puts the funding gap for them at nearly $600 billion.)

The Private Sector Has Problems, Too

Don't think that government decision makers at the state and local level have been the only ones to create unfunded pension liabilities. In the private sector, large corporations have found themselves with growing pension funding problems. One major company that has long loved to hide future pension liabilities is General Motors. In an effort to report better earnings, that company routinely used aggressive accounting practices and made pension contributions that were just a fraction of what it really needed to make. Eventually, though, GM's actual pension promises became due. When the company tried to pay for these costs by hiking the price of the cars it manufactured, those cars quickly became uncompetitive. Consumers started buying other brands that were cheaper for the same quality. The result was GM bankruptcy and a federal takeover. Taxpayers own a high percentage of shares in "Government Motors," as it came to be called. Hence, taxpayers are now on the hook for future pension liabilities of the company.

General Motors is not alone. Over 75 percent of the largest 500 corporations in the United States have unfunded pension fund obligations. It is perhaps no surprise that many of these companies have lobbied Congress to let them off the hook from meeting their legal obligations to more fully fund their pension plans.

BANKRUPTCIES ON THE HORIZON?

Returning our examination to the public sector, even though you may not be expecting to retire for decades, your economic well-being is already changing because of retirement commitments that cities and states have already made. To fulfill those unfunded pension liabilities, city and state governments are cutting back on essential services—education, police and prisons, and firefighters. You might think we should not or "cannot" let essential government services be cut back just to pay pension benefits. Right now that is reality, however, all across the country.

Is there a way to reduce unfunded pension liabilities? Yes, but it is ugly. Just ask the residents of Vallejo, California. In 2008, 18 police personnel and firefighters unexpectedly retired early. This city of 120,000 was immediately obligated to pay out several million dollars for their first year of retirement. This is a city that was already forking over $220 million for pensions and health care. Vallejo City government filed for **bankruptcy.**

Under so-called Chapter 9 of our **Bankruptcy Code,** municipal governments can propose their own reorganization plans and void union contracts without having to sell off their assets, such as buildings and investments. The public pension obligations of Vallejo were lumped together with all the rest of its obligations. Everyone from private accounting firms to public pensioners who were owed money had to take a "haircut"—accept less than 100 cents on the dollar owed. So now we see at least one way that cities, indeed, even states, can get out of the jam in which they find themselves. Declaring bankruptcy can allow them to renegotiate future pension benefits to put them more in line with future funding possibilities.

Right now, some cities are defaulting on the loans that they took out in past years. In a recent year, $3 billion in city debt was not paid when it came due. As we have already seen, that is a trivial amount compared to total unfunded pension liabilities. When more municipal governments choose to go bankrupt, as Stockton, California, did in 2012, the rate of municipal bond defaults will increase accordingly. This process will be painful and costly for retirees and bondholders alike. But the simple fact is this: State and local governments have been making promises they cannot realistically keep. Something must give and that means one of three things must happen. State and local spending on other programs must be slashed, taxes have to be hiked dramatically, or pensions need to be cut. Eventually, the easy political promises of the past must collide with the hard economic reality of the future.

Why Isn't the Federal Government in the Same Fix?

As you might have noticed, there has been little discussion of the federal government's retirement system to which all of us contribute—**Social Security.** The reason is that Social Security is a **pay-as-you-go system.** The federal government has *not* taken your Social Security "contributions" and invested them in some special account. Indeed, there is no "account" earning interest now so that it will be there with your name on it when you choose to retire in your sixties. While you may have heard about something called a Social Security trust fund, this fund is just on paper. It's a myth, and a huge liability itself, about which you will learn more in the next chapter.

Discussion Questions

1. If there is no government- or company-provided pension system, how can an individual create a financially safe retirement?

2. Why would a state or local government ever commit more resources for future pension benefits than it could possibly have resources to pay?

3. Many state and local governments have been using an assumed 8 percent rate of return figure when calculating future funding of promised pension benefits. Why do you suppose they used this rather than an assumption of 2 percent, or even 0 percent?

4. Why can't state and local governments simply continue to borrow funds through the bond market to cover not only shortfalls in current tax revenues but also shortfalls in future available funding to pay contractual pension benefits?

5. The economic climate since 2008 has caused many workers to defer their retirements. How will this affect large employers in state and local governments?

6. In the private sector, one in five workers have been promised life-time pensions. In the public sector, four in five workers have life-time pensions. Why does the private sector offer so few lifetime pensions compared to the public sector?

CHAPTER **24**

The Graying of America

America is aging. The 78 million baby boomers who pushed the Beatles and the Rolling Stones into stardom are beginning to retire. In less than twenty years, roughly 20 percent of all Americans will be sixty-five or older. Just as the post–World War II baby boom presented both obstacles and opportunities, so does the graying of America. Let's see why.

THE ORIGINS OF THE "SENIOR BOOM"

Two principal forces are behind America's "senior boom." First, we're living longer. Average life expectancy in 1900 was forty-seven years; today, it is seventy-eight and is likely to reach eighty within the next decade. Second, the birthrate is near record-low levels. Today's mothers are having far fewer children than their mothers or grandmothers had. In short, the old are living longer, and the ranks of the young are growing too slowly to offset this fact. Together, these forces are pushing up the proportion of the population over age sixty-five. Indeed, the number of seniors is growing at twice the rate of the rest of the population. In 1970, the **median age** in the United States—the age that divides the older half of the population from the younger half—was twenty-eight. It is now thirty-seven and rising. Compounding these factors, the average age at retirement is low by historical standards. The result is more retirees relying on fewer workers to help ensure that their senior years are also golden years.

THE COSTS OF THE ELDERLY

Why should a person who is, say, college age be concerned with the age of the rest of the population? Well, old people are expensive. In fact, people over sixty-five now consume over one-third of the federal government's budget. Social Security payments to retirees are the biggest item, now running over $800 billion per year. Medicare, which pays hospital and doctors' bills for the elderly, costs around $600 billion per year and is increasing rapidly. Moreover, roughly one-third of the $350 billion annual budget for Medicaid, which helps pay medical bills for the poor of all ages, goes to people over the age of sixty-five.

Under current law, the elderly will consume 40 percent of all federal spending within less than fifteen years: Medicare's share of the gross domestic product (GDP) will double, as will the number of very old—those over eighty-five and most in need of care. Within about twenty-five years, probably *half* of the federal budget will go to the old. In a nutshell, senior citizens are the beneficiaries of an expensive and rapidly growing share of all federal spending. What are they getting for our dollars?

Today's elderly are already more prosperous than any previous generation. Indeed, the annual discretionary income of Americans over sixty-five averages 30 percent higher than the average discretionary income of all other age groups. Each year, inflation-adjusted Social Security benefits paid to new retirees are higher than the first-year benefits paid to people who retired the year before. In addition, for the past forty years, cost-of-living adjustments have protected Social Security benefits from inflation. The impact of Social Security is evident even at the lower end of the income scale: The poverty rate for people over sixty-five is much lower than for the population as a whole. Retired people today collect Social Security benefits that are two to five times what they and their employers contributed in payroll taxes plus interest earned.

Not surprisingly, medical expenses are a major concern for many elderly. Perhaps reflecting that concern, each person under the age of sixty-five in America currently pays an average of more than $2,000 per year in federal taxes to subsidize medical care for the elderly. Indeed, no other country in the world goes to the lengths that America does to preserve life. Some 30 percent of Medicare's budget goes to patients in their last year of life. Coronary bypass operations, costing over $40,000 apiece, are routinely performed on Americans in their sixties and seventies. For those over sixty-five, Medicare picks up the tab. Even heart transplants are now performed on people in their sixties and paid for by Medicare for those over sixty-five. By contrast, the Japanese offer no organ transplants. Britain's National Health Service limits access to kidney dialysis for people over fifty-five. Yet Medicare subsidizes dialysis for more than one hundred thousand Americans, half of them over age sixty. The cost: well over $5 billion per year. Overall, the elderly receive Medicare benefits worth five to twenty times the payroll taxes (plus interest) they paid for this program.

THE COSTS ARE PAID BY YOU

The responsibility for the huge and growing bills for Social Security and Medicare falls squarely on current and future workers because both programs are financed by payroll taxes. Thirty years ago, these programs were adequately financed with a payroll levy of less than 10 percent of the typical worker's earnings. Today, the tax rate exceeds 15 percent of median wages and is expected to grow rapidly.

By the year 2020, early baby boomers, born in the late 1940s and early 1950s, will have retired. Late baby boomers, born in the early 1960s, will be nearing retirement. Both groups will leave today's college students, and their children, a staggering bill to pay. For Social Security and Medicare to stay as they are, the payroll tax rate may have to rise to 25 percent of wages over the next decade. And a payroll tax rate of 40 percent is not unlikely by the middle of the twenty-first century.

One way to think of the immense bill facing today's college students and their successors is to consider the number of retirees each worker must support. In 1946, the burden of one Social Security recipient was shared by 42 workers. By 1960, nine workers had to foot the bill for each retiree's Social Security benefits. Today, roughly three workers pick up the tab for each retiree's Social Security and Medicare benefits. By 2030, only two workers will be available to pay the Social Security and Medicare benefits due each recipient. Thus, a working couple will have to support not only themselves and their family but also someone outside the family who is receiving Social Security and Medicare benefits.

POLITICAL ECONOMY IN ACTION

Congress and the executive branch have seemed unwilling to face the pitfalls and promises of an aging America. Although the age of retirement for Social Security purposes is legislatively mandated to rise to sixty-seven, the best that politicians in Washington, D.C., appear able to do is appoint commissions to "study" the problems we face. And what changes are our politicians willing to make? We got a sample of this in 2003, with new legislation promising taxpayer-funded prescription drug benefits for senior citizens. Even people in favor of the new program called it the largest expansion in **entitlement programs** in forty years.

Before passage of the law, President Bush claimed it was going to cost $35 billion per year, but within a couple of months, that estimate had been hiked to over $50 billion. In fact, the benefits of the program will be less than claimed, and the costs will be even higher, because more than three-quarters of senior citizens had privately funded prescription drug plans *before* the new law took effect. Many of these private plans disappeared, leaving seniors with fewer choices and sticking younger taxpayers with a larger tax bill.

By now you may be wondering how we managed to commit ourselves to the huge budgetary burden of health and retirement benefits for senior citizens. There are three elements to the story. First, the cause is worthy: After all, who would want to deny the elderly decent medical care and a comfortable retirement? Second, the benefits of the programs are far more concentrated than the costs. A retired couple, for example, collects more than $25,000 per year in Social Security and consumes another $15,000 in subsidized medical benefits. In contrast, the typical working couple pays only about half of this each year in Social Security and Medicare taxes. Hence, the retired couple has a stronger **incentive** to push for benefits than the working couple has to resist them. And finally, senior citizens vote at a far higher rate than members of any other age group, in no small part because they are retired and thus have fewer obligations on their time. They are thus much more likely to make it clear at the ballot box exactly how important their benefits are to them.

THE FUTURE PATH

It is possible for government to responsibly address the crisis in funding programs for senior citizens. Chile, for example, faced a national pension system with even more severe problems than our Social Security system. Its response was to transform the system into one that is rapidly (and automatically, as time passes) converting itself into a completely private pension system. The result has been security for existing retirees, higher potential benefits for future retirees, and lower taxes for all workers. Americans could do exactly what the Chileans have done—if we chose to do so.

In the meantime, if Social Security and Medicare are kept on their current paths and older workers continue to leave the workforce, the future burden on today's college students is likely to be unbearable. If we are to avoid the social tensions and enormous costs of such an outcome, the willingness and ability of older individuals to retain more of their self-sufficiency must be recognized. To do otherwise is to invite a future in which the golden years are but memories of the past.

DISCUSSION QUESTIONS

1. How do the payroll taxes levied on the earnings of workers affect their decisions about how much leisure they consume?

2. When the government taxes younger people to pay benefits to older people, how does this affect the amount of assistance that younger people might voluntarily choose to offer older people?

3. When the government taxes younger people to pay benefits to older people, how does this affect the size of the bequests that older people are likely to leave to their children or grandchildren when they die?

4. In general, people who are more productive earn higher incomes and thus pay higher taxes. How would a change in the immigration laws that favored more highly educated and skilled individuals affect the future tax burden of today's American college students? Would the admission of better-educated immigrants tend to raise or lower the wages of American college graduates? On balance, would an overhaul of the immigration system benefit or harm today's college students?

5. How would a change in immigration laws that allowed *more* legal immigration affect the budget crisis we face with Social Security and Medicare?

6. How does the promise of guaranteed Social Security and Medicare benefits affect an individual's decision to save during the years before retirement age?

Property Rights and the Environment

Introduction

You saw in Part Four that **monopoly** produces outcomes that differ significantly from the outcomes of **competition** and yields gains from trade that fall short of the competitive ideal. In Part Six, you will see that when **externalities** are present—when there are discrepancies between the **private costs** of action and the **social costs** of action—the competitive outcome differs from the competitive ideal. Typically, the problem of externalities is said to be one of *market failure*, but the diagnosis might just as well be termed *government failure*. For markets to work efficiently, **property rights** to **scarce goods** must be clearly defined, cheaply enforceable, and fully transferable, and it is generally the government that is believed to have a **comparative advantage** in ensuring that these conditions are satisfied. If the government fails to define, enforce, or make transferable property rights, the market will generally fail to produce socially efficient outcomes, and it becomes a moot point as to who is at fault. The real point is: What might be done to improve things?

SAVE THAT SPECIES

As we see in Chapter 25, the world's ocean fisheries are in decline. Since 1950, nearly 30 percent of all fisheries have collapsed, and in forty years, *all* of the world's fisheries could disappear. The problem is that in almost all of the world's fisheries, the governmentally established rules of fishing are such that to "own" a fish, someone must catch the fish, that is, kill it. Thus, each harvester knows that if he or she doesn't take the fish now, the future benefits (from growth and reproduction) of leaving the fish in the water will be enjoyed by someone else who later catches the larger fish or its offspring. The fishers thus "race to fish," catching the fish before they have a chance to grow more fully and often before they have had a chance to reproduce. This causes declining fish stocks and, eventually, collapse of the fishery. Mounting evidence shows that so-called "catch share" systems can reverse this process. Under such systems of property rights, a **total allowable catch (TAC)** size is determined, based on biological and other scientific criteria. Then members of the fishing community are assigned shares of the TAC. The shares, often called **individual transferable quotas (ITQs),** can be used, sold, or leased to others. The catch shares give fishermen enforceable, transferable **property rights** in the fish, much as they have such property rights in their boats and gear.

The fishers then have an incentive to protect and maintain the value of the fishery, just as they do to protect and maintain their other property. Not only does this system dramatically improve both the biological and the economic health of fisheries, but it can also be easily modified for use with *any* species. The message of this chapter is thus that saving a species is easy—as long as property rights to the members of the species are clearly established and cheaply enforceable and transferable.

GREENHOUSE ECONOMICS

We turn from the world's oceans to its atmosphere in Chapter 26. Evidence is growing that human action is responsible for rising concentrations of so-called greenhouse gases in the earth's atmosphere, and if left unchecked, this growth may produce costly increases in the average temperature of our planet. Given the nature of the problem—a **negative externality**—private action taken on the individual level will not yield the best outcome for society. Thus, the potential gains from government action, in the form of environmental regulations or taxation, are substantial. The key word here is *potential*, for government action, no matter how well intentioned, does not automatically yield benefits that exceed the **costs.** As we seek solutions to the potential problems associated with greenhouse gases, we must be sure that the consequences of premature action are not worse than those of delaying action until the problem can be examined further. If we forget this message, greenhouse economics may turn into bad economics—and worse policy.

ETHANOL MADNESS

Getting our government to take actions that simultaneously protect our environment and our wealth is sometimes seemingly impossible. We explore the reasons behind this fact in Chapter 27, in which we answer this simple query: If the **biofuel** ethanol doesn't protect the environment or conserve resources, why do we mandate its use as a gasoline additive and (until recently) subsidize its production? Here we find that the principles of **political economy,** explored in Chapters 20–24, can be used to answer this question, too. It is true (as we emphasized in Chapter 4) that a critical function of government is to provide the institutional structure necessary for the creation and retention of our total wealth, broadly construed.

Nevertheless, the essence of much government policymaking has nothing to do with making the economic pie larger. Instead, many government policies are directed at dividing up the pie in new ways, so that one group gets more resources at the expense of some other group. To do this successfully, politicians must be adept at exploiting the **rational ignorance** of voters, concentrating the benefits of policies among a few favored recipients while dispersing the costs of those policies across a large number of disfavored individuals. In the case of ethanol, we see that members of Congress do this in ways that enrich farmers and large ethanol producers at the expense of consumers—and, we should add, at the expense of the environment also.

THE TRASHMAN COMETH

As both population and per capita income rise, consumption rises faster than either, for it responds to the combined impetus of both. With consumption comes the residue of consumption, also known as plain old garbage. Many of us have heard of landfills being closed because of fears of groundwater contamination or of homeless garbage scows wandering the high seas in search of a place to off-load. All of us have been bombarded with public service messages to recycle everything from aluminum cans to newspapers. The United States, it seems, is becoming the garbage capital of the world. This is no doubt true, but it is also true that the United States is the professional football capital of the world—and yet professional football teams seem to have no problem finding cities across the country willing to welcome them with open arms. What is different about garbage?

You are probably inclined to answer that football is enjoyable and garbage is not. True enough, but this is not why garbage sometimes piles up faster than anyone seems willing to dispose of it. Garbage becomes a problem only if it is not priced properly—that is, if the consumers and businesses that produce it are not charged enough for its removal, and the landfills where it is deposited are not paid enough for its disposal. The message of Chapter 28 is that garbage really is no different from the things we consume in the course of producing it. As long as the trashman is paid, he will come, and as long as we have to pay for his services, his burden will be bearable. We will still have garbage, but we will not have a garbage problem.

CHAPTER 25

Save That Species

Codfish off the New England and eastern Canadian coasts were once so abundant, it was said, that a person could walk across the sea on their backs. The fish grew into six-foot-long, 200-pound giants, and generations of families from coastal communities knew they could count on the fish for a prosperous livelihood. Indeed, the northwestern Atlantic became known as the world's premier cod fishery (a **fishery** is an area where it is commercially feasible for fish or other aquatic animals to be harvested). Slowly over time, however, nature's bounty began to disappear. Fishing became more difficult, the number of fish caught each year diminished, and the average size of the fish shrank. In recent years, the problems accelerated. Between 1970 and 2000, the catch dropped more than 75 percent, and the typical fish caught these days weighs but twenty pounds. As a result, the Canadians have closed down their cod fishery, and the American fleet is a ghost of its former self.

FISHERY COLLAPSE IS WIDESPREAD

The cod is not alone in its demise. The world's ocean fisheries are in decline. Since 1950, nearly 30 percent of all fisheries have collapsed, and some scientists project that in forty years, *all* of the world's fisheries could disappear. The problem, it is widely agreed, is a failure of humans to manage fisheries in a way that is consistent with both maximum economic benefit and long-term survival of ocean fish stocks. Of course, this wide agreement just begs the real question: Why have humans been able to manage wheat farms and cattle ranches, but failed so miserably in managing fisheries?

The answer starts here: In almost all of the world's fisheries, the governmentally established rules of fishing are such that to "own" a fish, someone must catch the fish, that is, remove it from the water, at which point it typically dies within minutes. This is unlike the rules for cattle, pigs, chickens, or sheep, of course, under which to own an animal one need only put a brand on it, or surround it with a fence, or enclose it in a building. The peculiar rules imposed by governments on most fisheries lead to a peculiar and destructive set of incentives.

When the decision is made to harvest any living animal, biological issues are important in accurately gauging the true cost of the harvest. In particular, if harvest does *not* take place (i) the animal will continue growing, yielding a larger effective harvest in the future and (ii) it may reproduce, leaving offspring that will also contribute to a larger future yield. For cattle, pigs, and so forth, the harvesters (ranchers and farmers) take both of these facts into account, waiting until growth and reproduction rates have reached the point that it makes sense to harvest the animals now rather than waiting.

But with ocean fish, each harvester knows that if he or she doesn't take the fish now, the future benefits (from growth and reproduction) will be enjoyed by someone else who happens to catch the larger fish or its offspring later on. The fishers respond quite rationally to this incentive. They "race to fish," catching the fish before the fish have a chance to grow more fully and often before they have had a chance to reproduce. This causes declining fish stocks and, eventually, collapse of the fishery.

THE FAILURE OF COMMAND AND CONTROL

Based on a growing body of evidence, however, it has become apparent that a simple change in the way fisheries are managed has the power to stop and even reverse these declines. Traditional management of fisheries by government is referred to as a "command and control" system, because in an effort to control the fishers, the government issues a series of commands about allowable behavior. These management systems limit, for example, the number of fishers, the size of boats they may use, the type of fishing gear, and season length, all in an effort to keep total harvests down. Although such systems historically have held sway around the world, even the best of them suffer from a profound misalignment of **incentives:** The self-interest of the individual harvester is generally inconsistent with actions that would both maximize the value of the fishery and ensure its sustainability. Because individuals don't own any fish until they harvest them, they are motivated to outcompete other harvesters, taking fish that are too small and too young for long-term sustainability. The results are twofold. In the short run, the fishers harvest too many fish, and in the long run, they successfully lobby the government for more lenient rules, adding to the destruction. So far, no government has figured out how to use a command and control system to prevent excessive harvests, reduced stocks, and eventual collapse.

In recent years, the failure of command and control fishery management has become increasingly clear, but the question has been: Is there a viable alternative? Economists have suggested that catch shares assigned to individual harvesters offer such an alternative because property rights systems, of which catch shares are an example, are generally the most effective way to conserve resources.

CATCH SHARE SYSTEMS

Catch share systems combine two features. First, based on biological and other scientific criteria, a **total allowable catch (TAC)** size is determined. Then members of the fishing community (individuals or cooperatives, for example) are assigned shares of the TAC. Typically, the shares are granted to existing fishers in proportion to their historical fishing patterns. The shares, often called **individual transferable quotas (ITQs),** can then be used, sold, or leased to others. No one is permitted to harvest in excess of the amount specified in the harvester's **quota.** The catch shares give fishermen enforceable, transferable **property rights** to the fish, much as they have such property rights to their boats and gear. These owners of rights then have an incentive to protect and maintain the value of the fishery, just as they do to protect and maintain their other property.

Numerous studies of the use of catch shares show that this system can dramatically improve both the biological and the economic health of fisheries. Alaska, British Columbia, Iceland, and New Zealand all represent locations where catch shares, such as ITQs, are regarded as having succeeded. Recent research covering more than 11,000 fisheries around the world reveals that catch shares are effective worldwide. In fact, the outcomes for fisheries with and without catch share systems have been studied systematically, accounting for factors (such as ecosystem characteristics and fish species) that might have played a role in the health and viability of the fish stocks. This research approach amounts to conducting a statistically controlled experiment—and the results are striking.

THE POWER OF INCENTIVES

A conventional measure of collapse for a fishery is a decline in catch to a level that is less than 10 percent of the maximum recorded catch for that fishery. By this criterion, an average of more than fifty fisheries have reached collapse each year since 1950, in a worldwide pattern that seems to be pointing toward the demise of all fisheries. But in fisheries, when a catch share system is implemented, the process of collapse halts—completely. Moreover, in many of the ITQ fisheries, recovery of fish stocks begins soon after implementation, even as fishermen continue to profitably catch fish.

It is now estimated that had ITQs been implemented in all fisheries beginning in 1970, the incidence of collapse would have been cut by two-thirds. Moreover, instead of watching fisheries collapse today, we would be seeing them getting healthier, even as they were supporting harvesters and nourishing consumers. Most importantly, it appears that the power of ITQs to prevent and even reverse fishery collapse applies to species and ecosystems throughout the world.

Can We Save the Whales, Too?

Could a catch share system help protect whaling stocks around the world? In principle, the answer is "yes," although three aspects of whales would make the task more difficult. Consider, for example, blue whales, which are believed to migrate thousands of miles each year. A blue whale, which can weigh almost one hundred tons, is difficult to kill even with the most modern equipment. Nevertheless, intensive hunting gradually reduced the stock from somewhere between 300,000 and one million to, at present, somewhere between 5,000 and 12,000. Since 1965, international treaty has banned all hunting of the blue whale, although sporadic hunting of blues by some nations, such as Brazil, Chile, and Peru, has continued.

The enormous range of the blue whales means that enforcing rules for their capture—and this includes a catch share system—would likely be quite expensive. It is one thing to enforce catch limits over several thousand square miles. It is quite another to enforce them over millions of square miles. The second difficulty with designing a catch share system for blue whales is that because of the long-standing ban on hunting, and the sharp restrictions on hunting before that, little is known about their population, or whether that population is shrinking or growing. Hence, setting the correct TAC would be extremely difficult.

The final tricky issue of designing a catch share program for whales is that they are a "charismatic" species—that is, people seem to get satisfaction out of simply knowing they are out there swimming around. (We doubt, for example, whether you have ever seen a bumper sticker that says "Save the cod.") Thus, whales are said to have "existence value"—some people get great satisfaction just out of knowing that they exist, satisfaction that would be irreparably lost if the whales were hunted to extinction. Clearly, although harvesters and biologists might be quite knowledgeable about growth and reproduction rates of all sorts of fish and ocean-going mammals, they are unlikely to know the value that Uncle Fred or Aunt Jane in Peoria place on the survival of the blue whale species. So people worry that a catch share system for whales might yield an unacceptably low stock of whales. As we'll see in a moment, however, the biologists and harvesters of whales might not have to know anything at all about Uncle Fred or Aunt Jane to make sure that there are plenty of whales to keep them happy and the whales healthy.

Serve the Bison

Ted Turner, the founder of CNN and former owner of the Atlanta Braves baseball team, has thirteen ranches spanning two million acres. Ted also owns 55,000 head of bison spread out over many of these ranches. Simply put, Ted owns more bison than anyone else in the world. His bison holdings are obviously nowhere near as big as the enormous herds that once dominated the American plains. But they are big enough to ensure genetic diversity among the animals, and also to make it a good bet that bison are not going to become extinct at any time in the foreseeable future.[1] There are no doubt many reasons Ted has so many bison hanging around, but of one of them we can be certain: He turns thousands of head into burgers and steaks every year, both for his own chain of restaurants and for many hundreds more restaurants that serve bison on their menus. And although Ted raises the most bison in America, there are plenty of other bison ranchers out there doing much the same thing and for the same reason. In North America alone, bison stocks are about 400,000, with another 100,000 head scattered across the rest of the world.

So, just acting in their own self-interests, Ted and his fellow ranchers are able to keep bison stocks plenty big enough to ensure the survival of the species, and thus big enough to satisfy the desires of Aunt Jane and Uncle Fred that the bison continue to exist. Moreover, Ted's herds are big enough to *simultaneously* satisfy the existence value demands of a million (or even 7 billion) people around the world, all without any of these demanders putting up a penny of their own money (unless they stop by for a burger, of course).

---

1 Note that we don't claim that this or any system can prevent extinction *forever*. Only about 0.02 percent (about one in five thousand) species that have ever existed are currently extant. There is no evidence to date that any species—*Homo sapiens* included—has any claim on immortality.

In effect, this is exactly what is happening in fisheries around the world where catch share systems are at work. The incentives of the harvesters to keep stocks large enough for profitable fishing are *also* sufficient to protect the fish from any threat of extinction. It thus seems likely that catch share systems have the potential to save the whales, too. Indeed, the consistent ability of catch share systems to enable recovery of fish stocks and of the profits from harvesting illustrates a compelling general message: The clear assignment of enforceable property rights remains the most effective way we know to protect other species from the depredations of *Homo sapiens.*

Discussion Questions

1. Has there ever been a problem with the extinction of dogs, cats, or cattle? Why not?

2. Some people argue that the best way to save rare species is to set up private game reserves to which wealthy hunters can travel. How could this help save endangered species?

3. Is government *ownership* of animals needed to protect species from extinction?

4. In the United States, most fishing streams are public property, with access available to all. In Britain, most fishing streams are privately owned, with access restricted to those who are willing to pay for the right to fish. Anglers agree that over the past thirty years, the quality of fishing in the United States has declined, while the quality of fishing in Britain has risen. Can you suggest why?

5. Aquaculture is the business of raising water-dwelling animals, including fish, mollusks (such as oysters), and shell fish (such as shrimp) in enclosed areas. For fish, this means raising them in large net pens. Do you suppose there is a problem with "overfishing" with aquaculture? What is a key difference between aquaculture animals and wild animals that plays a role in your conclusion?

6. Although much credit is given to buffalo hunters for causing the near extinction of bison, there was another factor at work. Cattle are easily herded by men on horseback and readily contained by barbed wired fences. Bison simply break through ordinary barbed wire and kill (by goring) horses used in any attempt to herd them. Explain how these characteristics of bison helped seal their fate on the Great Plains.

CHAPTER 26

Greenhouse Economics

The sky may not be falling, but it is getting warmer—almost surely. The consequences will not be catastrophic, but they will be costly—probably. We can reverse the process but should not spend very much to do so right now—maybe. Such is the state of the debate over the greenhouse effect—the tendency of carbon dioxide (CO_2) and other gases to accumulate in the atmosphere, acting like a blanket that traps radiated heat, thereby increasing the earth's temperature. Before turning to the economics of the problem, let's take a brief look at the physical processes involved.

CO_2 AND CLIMATE

Certain gases in the atmosphere, chiefly water vapor and CO_2, trap heat radiating from the earth's surface. If they did not, the earth's average temperature would be roughly 0°F instead of just over 59°F, and everything would be frozen solid. Human activity helps create some so-called greenhouse gases, including CO_2 (mainly from combustion of fossil fuels) and methane (from landfills, livestock, and fossil fuel production). We have the potential, unmatched in any other species, to profoundly alter our ecosystem.

There seems little doubt that humankind has been producing these gases at a record rate and that they are steadily accumulating in the atmosphere. Airborne concentrations of CO_2, for example, are increasing at the rate of about 0.5 percent per year. Over the past fifty years, the amount of CO_2 in the atmosphere has risen a total of about 25 percent. Laboratory analysis of glacial ice dating back at least 160,000 years indicates that global temperatures and CO_2 levels in the atmosphere do, in fact, tend to move together, suggesting that the impact of today's rising CO_2 levels may be higher global temperatures in the future. Indeed, the

National Academy of Sciences has suggested that by the middle of the twenty-first century, greenhouse gases could be double the levels they were in 1860 and that global temperatures could rise by 2–9°F.[1] The possible consequences of such a temperature increase include:

- A rise in the average sea level, inundating coastal areas, including much of Florida
- The spread of algal blooms capable of deoxygenating major bodies of water, such as Chesapeake Bay
- The conversion of much of the Midwestern wheat and corn belt into a hot, arid dust bowl.

What to Do about CO_2?

When an individual drives a car or heats a house, greenhouse gases are produced. In economic terms, this creates a classic **negative externality.** Most of the **costs** (in this case, those arising from global warming) are borne by individuals *other than* the one making the decision about how many miles to drive. Because the driver enjoys all the benefits of the activity but suffers only a part of the cost, that individual engages in more than the economically efficient amount of the activity. In this sense, the problem of greenhouse gases parallels the problem that occurs when someone smokes a cigarette in an enclosed space or litters the countryside with fast food wrappers. If we are to get individuals to reduce production of greenhouse gases to the efficient rate, we must somehow induce them to act *as though* they bear all the costs of their actions. The two most widely accepted means of doing this are government regulation and taxation, both of which have been proposed to deal with greenhouse gases.

The 1988 Toronto Conference on the Changing Atmosphere, attended by representatives from 48 nations, favored the regulation route. The conference recommended a mandatory cut in CO_2 emissions by 2005 to 80 percent of their 1988 level—a move that would have required a major reduction in worldwide economic output. The 1997 Kyoto conference on climate change, attended by representatives from 160 nations, made more specific but also more modest proposals. Overall, attendees agreed that by 2012, thirty-eight developed nations should cut greenhouse emissions by 5 percent relative to

---

1 This may not sound like much, but it does not take much to alter the world as we know it. The global average temperature at the height of the last ice age eighteen thousand years ago—when Canada and most of Europe were covered with ice—was 51°F, a mere 8°F or so cooler than today.

1990 levels.[2] Developing nations, including China and India, would be exempt from emissions cuts. (The so-called Kyoto Protocol has since expired, with worldwide emissions of CO_2 now *higher* than back in 1997.) On the taxation front, one prominent U.S. politician has proposed a tax of $100 per ton on the carbon emitted by fuels. It is estimated that such a tax would raise the price of coal by $70 per ton and elevate the price of oil by $8 per barrel. These proposals, and others like them, clearly have the potential to reduce the buildup of greenhouse gases but only at substantial costs. It thus makes some sense to ask: What are we likely to get for our money?

Some Facts of Life

Perhaps surprisingly, the answer to this question is not obvious. Consider the raw facts of the matter. On average over the past century, greenhouse gases have been rising, and so has the average global temperature. Yet most of the temperature rise occurred before 1940, whereas most of the increase in greenhouse gases occurred after 1940. In fact, global average temperatures fell about 0.5°F between 1940 and 1970. This cooling actually led a number of prominent scientists during the 1970s to forecast a coming ice age!

Between 1975 and 2000, the upward march of global temperatures resumed, accompanied by rising concentrations of greenhouse gases. At the same time, however, sunspot and other solar activity rose considerably, and the sun became brighter than in a thousand years. Since 2000, global temperatures have stabilized. Whether this is due to the diminished solar activity over this period, or whether the sun has played much role at all in climate changes over the last 45 years, is a matter of contention. Indeed, many scientists believe that temperatures will soon resume their upward march. Let us suppose for the moment that barring a significant reduction in greenhouse gas emissions, more global warming is on the way. What can we expect? It appears that the answer is a "good news, bad news" story.

Good News, Bad News

The bad news is this: The likely rise in sea level by one to three feet over the next 100 years will inundate significant portions of our existing coastline. The expected precipitation decline in key regions will necessitate more widespread use of irrigation. The higher average temperatures will compel more widespread use of air conditioning, along with the

---

2 This agreement has not been adhered to. In fact, emissions among this group of nations are *higher* than they were in 1990.

associated higher consumption of energy to power it. The blazing heat in southern latitudes may make these areas too uncomfortable for all but the most heat-loving souls and will likely lead to a rise in heat-caused deaths.

The good news is that the technology for coping with changes such as these is well known and the costs of coping are surprisingly small (on a scale measured in hundreds of billions of dollars, of course). Moreover, many of the impacts that loom large at the individual level will represent much smaller costs at a societal level. For example, although higher average temperatures could prove disastrous for farmers in southern climes, the extra warmth would be an enormous windfall farther north, where year-round farming might become feasible (and cold-weather-caused deaths will likely fall). Similarly, the loss of shoreline due to rising sea levels would partly just be a migration of coastline inland—current beachfront property owners would suffer, but their inland neighbors would gain.[3]

None of these changes are free, of course, and there remain significant uncertainties about how global warming might affect species other than *Homo sapiens.* It is estimated, for example, that temperate forests can "migrate" only at a rate of about 60 miles per century, not fast enough to match the speed at which warming is expected to occur. Similarly, the anticipated rise in the sea level could wipe out between 30 and 70 percent of today's coastal wetlands. Whether new wetlands would develop along our new coastline and what might happen to species that occupy existing wetlands are questions that have not yet been resolved.

Yet the very uncertainties that surround the possible warming of the planet suggest that policy prescriptions of the sort that have been proposed—such as the cut in worldwide CO_2 emissions agreed to at Kyoto—may be too much, too soon. Caution seems particularly wise because the exclusion of China, India, and other developing nations from any emissions cuts could result in huge costs for developed nations but little or no reduction in worldwide greenhouse gases. Some sense of the damage that can be wrought by ignoring such counsel and rushing into a politically popular response to a complex environmental issue is well illustrated by another atmospheric problem: smog.

Gasoline and Smog

Gasoline is a major source of the hydrocarbons in urban air, but its contribution to smog plummeted because cars now run much cleaner than their predecessors. In the 1970s, cars spewed about nine grams

---

3 There would be a net loss of land area and thus a net economic loss. Nevertheless, the net loss of land would be chiefly in the form of less valuable inland property.

of hydrocarbons per mile. Emissions controls brought this down to about 1.5 grams per mile by 1995. The cost of this reduction is estimated to be approximately $1,000 for each ton of hydrocarbon emissions prevented—a number that many experts believe to be well below the benefits of the cleaner air that resulted. Despite the improvements in air quality, smog remained a problem in many major cities. Additional federal regulations aimed primarily at the nine smoggiest urban areas, including New York, Chicago, and Los Angeles, went into effect in 1995. Meeting these standards meant that gasoline had to be reformulated at a cost of about 6 cents per gallon. This brought the cost of removing each additional ton of hydrocarbons to about $10,000—ten times the per-ton cost of removing the first 95 percent from urban air.

Over the years since 1995, new Environmental Protection Agency (EPA) rules for reformulated gasoline (RFG) have added even more to the cost of gasoline and have had other (presumably unintended) adverse consequences. For example, initially, the RFG standards could be met only with the addition to gasoline of ethanol or methyl tertiary butyl ether (MTBE). Because ethanol was considerably more expensive than MTBE, refiners used MTBE. But after a few years, it appeared that leakage of MTBE from storage tanks was contaminating groundwater and that the substance was highly carcinogenic. Numerous states banned its use on the grounds that whatever it did to improve air quality, its adverse effects elsewhere were likely far more damaging. (The EPA has since allowed refiners more flexibility in meeting the RFG standards.)

Overall, EPA rules on RFG have led to a "patchwork quilt" of regulations across the country: Some dirty-air locations must use one type of gas, while others, with cleaner air, can use different gas. The presence of multiple EPA standards across the country has left supplies of gasoline vulnerable to disruption because fuel often cannot be transshipped from one area to another to meet temporary **shortages.** This fact has contributed substantially to large spikes in the price of gasoline in major Midwestern cities, such as Milwaukee and Chicago, every time there has been even a minor supply disruption. (California, which has its own special rules for gas, can see price spikes of 20–50 cents per gallon when even a single refinery has problems.)

Overall, the costs of EPA-mandated gasoline reformulation are huge, even though the EPA has never shown that RFG is necessary to meet its air quality standards. The benefits of RFG appear to be small compared to the costs, yet we are stuck with this EPA mandate because few politicians want to be accused of being in favor of smog. Thus, a well-intentioned policy that initially seemed quite beneficial has likely ended up doing more harm than good.

THE TAKE AWAY

There is no doubt that atmospheric concentrations of greenhouse gases are rising and that human actions are playing a role. It is probable that as a result, the global average temperature will rise in the coming decades. If temperatures rise significantly, the costs will be large, but the consequences are likely to be manageable. Given the nature of the problem, private action, taken on the individual level, will not yield the optimal outcome for society. Thus, the potential gains from government action, in the form of environmental regulations or taxation, may be substantial. But the key word here is *potential*, because government action, no matter how well intentioned, does not automatically yield benefits that exceed the costs. As we seek solutions to the potential problems associated with greenhouse gases, we must be sure that the consequences of action are not worse than those of first examining the problem further. If we forget this message, greenhouse economics may turn into bad economics—and worse policy.

DISCUSSION QUESTIONS

1. Why will voluntary actions, undertaken at the individual level, be unlikely to bring about significant reductions in greenhouse gases such as CO_2?

2. Does the fact that the CO_2 produced in one nation results in adverse effects on other nations have any bearing on the likelihood that CO_2 emissions will be reduced to the optimal level? Would the problem be easier to solve if all the costs and benefits were concentrated within a single country? Within a single elevator or office?

3. The policy approach to greenhouse gases will almost certainly involve limits on emissions rather than taxes on emissions. Can you suggest why limits rather than taxes are likely to be used?

4. It costs about $100,000 per acre to create wetlands. How reasonable is this number as an estimate of what wetlands are worth?

5. Suppose the United States decides to discourage CO_2 emissions by imposing a tax on CO_2 emissions. How large should the tax be?

6. Human-caused (anthropogenic) emissions of CO_2 are only about 3 percent of *total* CO_2 emissions each year. (Oceans are the biggest emitters.) Why is so much attention directed at anthropogenic emissions of CO_2?

CHAPTER 27

Ethanol Madness

Henry Ford built his first automobile in 1896 to run on pure ethanol. If Congress has its way, the cars of the future will be built the same way. But what made good economic sense in the late nineteenth century doesn't necessarily make economic sense in the early twenty-first century—although it does make for good politics. Indeed, the ethanol story is a classic illustration of how good politics routinely trumps good economics to yield bad policies.

ETHANOL MANDATES AND SUBSIDIES

Ethanol is made in the Midwest just like moonshine whiskey is made in Appalachia. Corn and water are mixed into a mash, enzymes turn starch to sugar, yeast is added, and heat ferments the brew. Once this is distilled, the liquid portion is ethanol and the solids are used as a high-protein animal food. The high-proof ethanol is combustible but yields far less energy per gallon than gasoline does. Despite this inefficiency, federal law requires that ethanol be added to gasoline, in increasing amounts through 2022. This requirement is supposed to conserve resources and improve the environment. It does neither. Instead, it lines the pockets of American corn farmers and ethanol makers, and incidentally enriches some Brazilian sugarcane farmers along the way.

Federal law has encouraged, subsidized, or mandated ethanol as a so-called alternative fuel for more than thirty years. But it was not until 2005 that ethanol really achieved national prominence. The use mandates of the Energy Policy Act, combined with surging gas prices and a hefty federal ethanol subsidy, created a boom in ethanol production. Soon ethanol refineries were springing up all over the Midwest, and imports of ethanol from Brazil reached record-high levels.

THE SUPPOSED VIRTUES OF ETHANOL

Three factors are typically used to justify federal policy that pushes ethanol. First, it is claimed that adding ethanol to gasoline reduces air pollution and so yields environmental benefits. That may have been true fifteen or twenty years ago, but even the Environmental Protection Agency (EPA) acknowledges that ethanol offers no environmental advantages over other modern methods of making reformulated gasoline. Hence, neither the congressional mandate to add ethanol nor subsidy paid until 2012 for its use as a fuel additive can be justified on environmental grounds.

A second argument advanced on behalf of ethanol is that it is "renewable," in that fields on which corn is grown to produce ethanol this year can be replanted with more corn next year. This is true enough, but we are in little danger of running out of "nonrenewable" crude oil any time in the next century. Indeed, proven reserves of oil are at record-high levels and rising. Perhaps more to the point, the production of ethanol uses so much fossil fuel and other resources that under most circumstances, its production actually *wastes* resources overall compared to gasoline. In part, this is because ethanol is about 25 percent less efficient than gasoline as a source of energy. But it is also because the corn used to make ethanol in the United States has a high **opportunity cost.** If it were not being used to make fuel, it would be used to feed humans and livestock. Moreover, because ethanol production is most efficiently conducted on a relatively small scale, it must be transported by truck or rail, which is far more costly than the pipelines used for gasoline.

The third supposed advantage of ethanol is that its use reduces our dependence on imports of oil. In principle, this argument is correct, but its impact is tiny, and the likely consequences are not what you might expect. Total consumption of all **biofuels** in the United States amounts to only 3 percent of gasoline and diesel usage. To replace the oil we import from the Persian Gulf with corn-based ethanol, at least *50 percent* of the nation's total farmland would have to be devoted to corn for fuel. Moreover, any cuts in oil imports will likely *not* come from Persian Gulf sources. Canada and Mexico are two of the three biggest suppliers of crude oil to the United States, and both countries send almost 100 percent of their exports to the U.S. market.

THE POLITICAL ECONOMY
OF ENVIRONMENTAL POLICY

All of this raises an interesting question. If ethanol doesn't protect the environment, conserve resources, or have any compelling foreign policy advantages, why do we mandate its use and, until recently, subsidize its production? The answer lies at the heart of **political economy,** the use of economics to study the causes and consequences of political decision making. It is true that a critical component of what the government does (such as providing for national defense and law enforcement) provides an institutional structure necessary for the creation and retention of our total wealth. Nevertheless, the essence of much government policymaking, especially in the environmental arena these days, has nothing to do with making the size of the economic pie larger than it otherwise would be. Instead, many government policies are directed at dividing up the pie in new ways so that one group gets more resources at the expense of some other group. To do this successfully, politicians must be adept at concentrating the benefits of policies among a few favored recipients while dispersing the costs of those policies across a large number of disfavored individuals.

At first blush, such an approach sounds completely at odds with the essence of democracy. After all, under the principle of "one person, one vote," it seems that benefits should be widely spread (to gain votes from many grateful beneficiaries) and costs should be concentrated (so that only the votes of a few disfavored constituents are lost). The concept of **rational ignorance** explains what is really going on. It is costly for individuals to keep track of exactly how the decisions of their elected representatives affect them. When the consequences of political decisions are large enough to outweigh the **monitoring costs,** voters swiftly and surely express their pleasure or displeasure, both in the voting booth and in their campaign contributions. But when the consequences to each of them individually are small relative to the monitoring costs, people don't bother to keep track of them—they remain "rationally ignorant."

Ethanol Winners and Losers

About one-fifth of all ethanol for fuel is made by one company, Archer Daniels Midland (ADM). Clearly, even small changes in the price of ethanol are important to ADM. The federal mandate that ethanol be added to gasoline increases the profitability of making ethanol, so ADM has strong incentives to ensure that members of Congress are aware of the benefits (to ADM) of the use mandate. Similarly, corn farmers derive most of their income from sales of corn. Federal ethanol policy increases the demand for corn and thus increases its price. Because the resulting benefits are highly concentrated on corn farmers, each has a strong incentive to ensure that his or her members of Congress understand the benefits (to the farmer) of such policy.

Contrast this with the typical taxpayer or consumer of gasoline. It is true that the $20 billion spent on ethanol subsidies from 2004 through 2011 came out of taxpayers' pockets. Nevertheless, this amount was spread thinly across tens of millions of federal taxpayers. Similarly, although the mandated use of ethanol in gasoline is estimated to raise the cost of gas by about 8 cents per gallon, this amounts to no more than $50 per year for the typical driver. Neither taxpayer nor motorist is likely to spend much time complaining to his or her senator.

Thus, farmers and ethanol producers are willing to lobby hard for ethanol mandates and subsidies at the same time that taxpayers and drivers put up little effective resistance to having their pockets picked. It may make for bad economics and lousy environmental policy, but it is classic politics.

DISCUSSION QUESTIONS

1. Brazilian ethanol producers (who make ethanol from sugarcane) have lower production costs than U.S. producers. Until 2012, Congress protected U.S. producers from Brazilian competition by imposing an **import tariff** of nearly 60 cents per gallon on Brazilian ethanol. If Congress really cares about protecting the environment and reducing our reliance on foreign crude oil, why do you suppose we had a large import tariff on ethanol?

2. Ethanol in the European Union (EU) is made from beets. The EU imposes a tariff of about 35 cents per gallon on imports of ethanol into the EU. Explain who wins and who loses due to this tariff. Consider both producers and consumers, and consider not just the EU, but also Brazil, where ethanol is produced much more cheaply than it is in the EU.

3. Why do you suppose the federal government gives special treatment to owners of fertile farmland rather than, say, automobile mechanics?

4. From 2004 through 2011, the federal subsidy on U.S. ethanol production was roughly 50 cents per gallon. Use the theory of rational ignorance to explain why the ethanol subsidy was only about 50 cents per gallon rather than, say, $5 per gallon.

5. The EPA has approved the use of up to 15 percent ethanol in fuel blends. Cars built before 2007 are at risk of considerable engine damage if they run on such "E15" fuel. Who will foot the bill for such damages, if they occur?

6. Why are foreign producers of products so often the subject of special taxes such as the tax on imported ethanol?

CHAPTER 28

The Trashman
Cometh

Is garbage really different? To answer this question, consider a simple hypothetical situation. Suppose a city agreed to provide its residents with all the food they wished to consume, prepared in the manner they specified, and delivered to their homes for a flat, monthly fee that was independent of what or how much they ate. What are the likely consequences of this city food-delivery service? Most likely, people in the city would begin to eat more because the size of their food bill would be independent of the amount they ate. They would also be more likely to consume lobster and filet mignon rather than fish sticks and hamburger because, again, the cost to them would be independent of their menu selections. Soon the city's food budget would be astronomical, and either the monthly fee or taxes would have to be increased.

People from other communities might even begin moving (or at least making extended visits) to the city just to partake of this wonderful service. Within a short time, the city would face a food crisis as it sought to cope with providing an ever-increasing amount of food from a city budget that could no longer handle the financial burden.

If this story sounds silly to you, just change "food delivery" to "garbage pickup." What we have just described is the way most cities in the country have historically operated their municipal garbage-collection services. The result during the 1990s was the appearance of a garbage crisis, with overflowing landfills, homeless garbage barges, and drinking-water wells said to be polluted with the runoff from trash heaps. This seeming crisis—to the extent it existed—was fundamentally no different from the food crisis just described. The problem was not that almost nobody wants garbage or that garbage can have adverse environmental effects or even that we had too much garbage. The problem lay in that (i) we often do not put a price on garbage in the way we put prices on the goods that generate the garbage and (ii) a strange assortment of participants used a few smelly facts to make things seem worse than they were.

AMERICA'S TRASH

First things first. America produces plenty of garbage each year—about 250 million tons of household and commercial solid waste that has to be burned, buried, or recycled. (This works out to about 1,600 pounds per person.) About 29 percent of this is paper. Yard waste (such as grass trimmings) accounts for another 13 percent. Plastic accounts for about 20 percent of the volume of material that has to be disposed of, but because plastic is relatively light, it makes up only about 12 percent of the weight. More than eighty million tons of this trash is recycled.

Landfills are the final resting place for most of our garbage, although incineration is also widely used in some areas, particularly in the Northeast, where land values are high. Both methods began falling out of favor with people who lived near these facilities (or might eventually), as "not in my backyard" attitudes spread across the land. Federal, state, and local regulations also made it more difficult to establish new waste disposal facilities or even to keep old ones operating. The cost to open a modern 100-acre landfill rose to an estimated $70 million or more, and the permit process needed to open a new disposal facility soared to seven years in some states.

Meanwhile, environmental concerns forced the closure of many landfills throughout the country and prevented others from ever beginning operations. By the early 1990s, all but five states were exporting at least some of their garbage to other states. Today, most of the garbage from some densely populated states in the Northeast ends up in other people's backyards: New Jersey ships garbage to six other states, and New York keeps landfill operators busy in nine states. Across the country, some Americans have wondered where all of the garbage is going to go.

A CRISIS THAT WASN'T

Although the failure of America's cities to price garbage appropriately led to an inefficient amount of the stuff, much of the appearance of a garbage crisis has been misleading. Rubbish first hit the headlines in 1987 when a garbage barge named *Mobro*, headed south with New York City trash, couldn't find a home for its load. As it turns out, the barge operator wanted to change his disposal contract after he sailed. When he tried to conduct negotiations over the radio while under way, operators of likely landfills (mistakenly) suspected he might be carrying toxic waste rather than routine trash. When adverse publicity forced the barge back to New York with its load, many people thought it was a lack of landfill space, rather than poor planning by the barge operator, that was the cause. This notion was reinforced by an odd combination of environmental groups, waste management firms, and the Environmental Protection Agency (EPA).

The Environmental Defense Fund wanted to start a major campaign to push recycling, and the *Mobro* episode gave things the necessary push. As one official for the organization noted, "An advertising firm couldn't have designed a better vehicle than a garbage barge." Meanwhile, some farsighted waste management companies had begun loading up on landfill space, taking advantage of new technologies that increased the efficient minimum size of a disposal facility. Looking to get firm contracts for filling this space, the trade group for the disposal industry started pushing the notion that America was running out of dump space. State and local officials who relied on the group's data quickly bought into the new landfills, paying premium prices to do so. The EPA, meanwhile, was studying the garbage problem but without noticing that its own regulations were causing the efficient scale of landfills to quadruple in size. Thus, the EPA merely counted landfills around the country and reported that they were shrinking in number. This was true enough, but what the EPA failed to report was that because landfills were getting bigger much faster than they were closing down, total disposal capacity was *growing* rapidly, not shrinking.

Recycling

For a while, it seemed that recycling was going to take care of what appeared to be a worsening trash problem. In 1987, for example, old newspapers were selling for as much as $100 per ton (in 2013 dollars), and many municipalities felt that the answer to their financial woes and garbage troubles was at hand. Yet as more communities began putting mandatory recycling laws into effect, the prices for recycled trash began to plummet. Over the next five years, 3,500 communities in more than half the states had some form of mandatory curbside recycling. The resulting increase in the supply of used newsprint meant that communities soon had to pay to have the stuff carted away. For glass, the story is much the same. The market value of the used material is routinely below the cost of collecting and sorting it. Numerous states have acted to increase the demand for old newsprint by requiring locally published newspapers to have a minimum content of recycled newsprint. Because of these mandates, the recycling rate for newsprint has doubled over the past twenty years, but the current rate of 70 percent is thought by many experts to be about the practical maximum.

Recycling raises significant issues that were often ignored during the early rush to embrace the concept. For example, the production of 100 tons of deinked fiber from old newsprint produces about 40 tons of sludge that must be disposed of somehow. Although the total volume of material is reduced, the concentrated form of what is left can make it more costly to dispose of properly. Similarly, recycling paper is unlikely to save trees because most virgin newsprint is made from trees planted expressly for that purpose and harvested as a crop. If recycling increases, many of these trees simply will not be planted. In a study done for Resources for the Future, A. Clark Wiseman concluded, "The likely effect of [newsprint recycling] appears to be smaller, rather than larger, forest inventory." Moreover, most virgin newsprint is made in Canada, using clean hydroelectric power. Makers of newsprint in the United States (the primary customers for the recycled stuff) often use higher-polluting energy such as coal. Thus, one potential side effect of recycling is the switch from hydroelectric power to fossil fuels.

Product Bans

Some analysts have argued that we should simply ban certain products. For example, styrofoam cups have gotten a bad name because they take up more space in landfills than paper hot-drink cups and because styrofoam remains in the landfill forever. Yet according to a widely cited study by Martin B. Hocking of the University of Victoria in British Columbia, Canada, the manufacture of a paper cup consumes 36 times as much electricity and generates 580 times as much wastewater as the manufacture of a styrofoam cup. Moreover, as paper degrades underground, it releases methane, a greenhouse gas that may contribute to global climate change.

In a similar vein, consider disposable diapers, which have been trashed by their opponents because a week's worth generates 22.2 pounds of post-use waste, whereas a week's worth of reusable diapers generates only 4 ounces. Because disposable diapers already amount to 2 percent of the nation's solid waste, the edge clearly seems to go to reusable cloth diapers. Yet the use of reusable rather than disposable diapers consumes more than three times as many British thermal units of energy and generates ten times as much water pollution. It would seem that the trade-offs that are present when we talk about "goods" are just as prevalent when we discuss "bads" such as garbage.

GOVERNMENT REGULATION

It also appears that more government regulation of the garbage business is likely to make things worse rather than better, as may be illustrated by the tale of two states, New Jersey and Pennsylvania. A number of years ago, to stop what was described as price gouging by organized crime, New Jersey decided to regulate waste hauling and disposal as a public utility. Once the politicians got involved in the trash business, however, politics very nearly destroyed it. According to Paul Kleindorfer of the University of Pennsylvania, political opposition to passing garbage-disposal costs along to consumers essentially ended investment in landfills. In 1972, there were 331 landfills operating in New Jersey. By 1991, the number had fallen to fifty, because the state-regulated fees payable to landfill operators simply didn't cover the rising costs of operation. More than half of the state's municipal solid waste is now exported to neighboring Pennsylvania, in part because only 13 landfills remain open in New Jersey.

Pennsylvania's situation provides a sharp contrast. The state does not regulate the deals that communities make with landfill and incinerator operators. The market takes care of matters instead. For example, despite the state's hands-off policy, tipping fees (the charges for disposing of garbage in landfills) are below the national average in Pennsylvania, effectively limited by competition among disposal facilities. The market seems to be providing the right **incentives.** In one recent year, there were thirty-one pending applications to open landfills in Pennsylvania but only two in New Jersey, even though New Jersey residents are paying the highest disposal rates in the country to ship garbage as far away as Ohio and Georgia.

THE MARKET SOLUTION

Ultimately, two issues must be solved when it comes to trash. First, what do we do with it once we have it? Second, how do we reduce the amount of it that we have? As hinted at by the Pennsylvania story and illustrated further by developments elsewhere in the country, the market mechanism can answer both questions. In many areas of the country, population densities are high and land is expensive. Hence, a large amount of trash is produced, and it is expensive to dispose of locally. In contrast, there are some areas of the country where there are relatively few people around to produce garbage, where land for disposal facilities is cheap, and where wide open spaces minimize any potential air-pollution hazards associated with incinerators.

The sensible thing to do, it would seem, is to have the states that produce most of the trash ship it to states where it can be most efficiently disposed of—for a price, of course. This is already being done to an extent, but residents of potential recipient states are (not surprisingly) concerned, lest they end up being the garbage capitals of the nation. Yet Wisconsin, which imports more than a million tons of garbage each year, is demonstrating that it is possible to get rid of the trash without trashing the neighborhood. Landfill operators in Wisconsin are now required to send water table monitoring reports to neighbors and to maintain the landfills for forty years after closure. Operators have also guaranteed the value of neighboring homes to gain the permission of nearby residents, and sometimes have purchased homes to quiet neighbors' objections. These features all add to the cost of operating landfills, but as long as prospective customers are willing to pay the price and neighboring residents are satisfied with their protections—and so far these conditions appear to have been met—it would seem tough to argue with the outcome.

Some people might still argue that it does not seem right for one community to be able to dump its trash elsewhere. Yet the flip side is this: Is it right to prevent communities from accepting trash if that is what they want? Consider Gilliam County, Oregon (population 1,645), which wanted Seattle's garbage so badly that it fought Oregon state legislators' attempts to tax out-of-state trash coming into Oregon. Seattle's decision to use the Gilliam County landfill generated $1 million per year for the little community—some 25 percent of its annual budget and enough to finance the operations of the county's largest school.

Garbage by the Bag

Faced with the prospect of paying to dispose of its garbage, Seattle had to confront the problem of reducing the amount of trash its residents were generating. Its solution was to charge householders according to the amount they put out. Seattle began charging $16.55 per month (now $29.35) for weekly pick up of a thirty-two-gallon can. Yard waste that has been separated for composting costs $9.35 per month, and paper, glass, and metal separated for recycling are hauled away at no charge. In the first year that per-can charges were imposed, the total tonnage that had to be buried fell by 22 percent. Voluntary recycling rose from 24 percent of waste to 36 percent—a rate almost triple the national average at the time. The "Seattle stomp" (used to fit more trash into a can) became a regular source of exercise, and the city had trouble exporting enough garbage to fulfill its contract with Gilliam County.

The Seattle experience is paralleled by a similar program in Charlottesville, Virginia. A few years ago, this university town of 40,000 began charging 80 cents per thirty-two-gallon bag or can of residential garbage collected at the curb. The results of the city's new policy suggest that people respond to garbage prices just as they do to all other prices: When an activity becomes more expensive, people engage in less of it. In fact, after controlling for other factors, the introduction of this unit-pricing plan induced people to reduce the volume of garbage presented for collection by 37 percent.

Where did all of the garbage go? Well, some of it didn't go anywhere because many residents began practicing their own version of the Seattle stomp, compacting garbage into fewer bags. Even so, the total weight of Charlottesville's residential garbage dropped by 14 percent in response to unit pricing. Not all of this represented a reduction in garbage production because some residents resorted to "midnight dumping"—tossing their trash into commercial Dumpsters or their neighbors' cans late at night. This sort of behavior is much like the rise in gasoline thefts that occurred in the 1970s when gas prices jumped to the equivalent of over $3 per gallon. But just as locking gas caps ended most gas thefts, there may be a simple way to prevent most midnight dumping. Economists who have studied the Charlottesville program in detail suggest that property taxes or monthly fees could be used to cover the cost of one bag per household each week, with a price per bag applied only to additional bags. According to these estimates, a one-bag allowance would stop all midnight dumping by most one-person households and stop almost half the dumping by a typical three-person household. Moreover, such a scheme would retain most of the environmental benefits of the garbage-pricing program.

The message beginning to emerge across the country, then, is that garbage is no different from the things we consume in the course of producing it. As long as the trashman is paid, he will come, and as long as we must pay for his services, his burden will be bearable.

DISCUSSION QUESTIONS

1. How do deposits on bottles and cans affect the incentives of individuals to recycle these products?

2. Why do many communities mandate recycling? Is it possible to induce people to recycle more without requiring that all residents recycle?

3. How do hefty per-can garbage pickup fees influence the decisions people make about what goods they will consume?

4. A community planning on charging a fee for trash pickup might structure the fee in any of several ways. It might, for example, charge a fixed amount per can, an amount per pound of garbage, or a flat fee per month without regard to amount of garbage. How would each of these affect the amount and type of garbage produced? Which system would lead to an increase in the use of trash compactors? Which would lead to the most garbage?

5. How does interstate trade in trash differ from interstate trade in other products?

6. The population concentrations of most counties in the United States tend to be located in the middle of each county. Where do you think most landfills are located within each county?

PART SEVEN

Globalization and Economic Prosperity

Introduction

Many of the key public issues of our day transcend national borders or affect the entirety of our $16 trillion economy. The rapid developments in information processing, communications, and transportation over the past thirty years are gradually knitting the economies of the world closer together. Political developments, most notably the demise of the Iron Curtain and the dissolution of the Soviet Union, have contributed to this growing **globalization** of world economies, as have reductions in long-standing barriers to international trade. Moreover, over the past decade or so, awareness has been growing that the economic vitality of individual markets is importantly affected by decisions made in Washington, D.C.

THE ECONOMICS OF THE BIG MAC

Almost invariably, when the discussion turns to globalization, people want to know: Who's richer than whom, and how is that changing over time? Because most nations use different currencies, at a minimum we must convert reported income levels into some common currency (such as the dollar in the United States or the euro in many parts of Europe). But these simple conversions fail to account for differences in costs of living in various places. Housing in Europe, for example, is much more costly than housing in the United States.

Although there are complicated ways of adjusting for differences in the cost of living, we see in Chapter 29 that there is also a stunningly simple way—using the McDonalds Big Mac. Because this iconic monster burger is sold almost everywhere, uses virtually identical ingredients

199

and standardized methods of construction, and is built by workers who have the same skills, its local price serves as a benchmark measure of the relative cost of living in each country. Moreover, when we combine the price of the Big Mac with information on the wages paid to McDonalds workers, we can also construct simple measures of relative standards of living and movements in worker productivity over time. So, although nutritionists might complain about the Big Mac, it is in many respects an economist's delight.

GLOBALIZATION AND THE WEALTH OF AMERICA

The passage of the North American Free Trade Agreement (NAFTA) and the creation of the **World Trade Organization (WTO)** have substantially reduced the barriers to trade between the United States and most of the rest of the world. If we take advantage of these lower **trade barriers,** we have the opportunity to make ourselves far better off by specializing in activities in which we have a **comparative advantage** and then trading the fruits of our efforts with other nations. Yet voluntary exchange also often redistributes wealth, in addition to creating it, so there will always be some individuals who oppose free trade. There are many smoke screens behind which the self-interested opposition to globalization is hidden, as we see in Chapter 30. Nevertheless, although **protectionism**—the creation of trade barriers such as **tariffs** and **quotas**—often sounds sensible, it is in fact a surefire way to reduce rather than enhance our wealth. If we ignore the value of free trade, we do so only at our peril.

THE $750,000 STEELWORKER

To illustrate the tremendous damage that can result when protectionism gains the upper hand, Chapter 31 examines what happens when tariffs and quotas are imposed in an effort to "save" U.S. jobs from foreign **competition.** The facts are that in the long run, it is almost impossible to protect U.S. workers from globalization, and efforts to do so not only reduce Americans' overall living standards but also end up costing the jobs of other Americans. The moral is that competition is just as beneficial on the international scene as it is on the domestic front.

CHAPTER 29

The Economics
of the Big Mac

The words "two all-beef patties," "special sauce," "lettuce, cheese, pickles, onions," and "on a sesame-seed bun" are from a 1975 advertising jingle for the Big Mac. The world's favorite monster burger was born in Uniontown, Pennsylvania, created by Jim Delligatti in August 1967. Delligatti's family has operated McDonalds restaurants since the earliest days of the company, and now owns 18 of those restaurants. The family even opened a Big Mac Museum Restaurant near that burger's birthplace. A Big Mac contains twenty nine grams of fat, or a little over one ounce of artery-clogging substances. But we are not here to attack the Big Mac. Rather, we wish to see how economists can use this standardized product to help compare the cost of living and the levels of real incomes around the world.

SOME ARE POOR, SOME ARE RICH, AND MANY ARE IN BETWEEN

It seems obvious that the average western European or American or Canadian earns a higher income than the average resident of countries such as China and India. What is more difficult to estimate is how *much* better off the citizens are in one nation compared to another. If we want to make such an estimate, some obstacles must be overcome. First there is the matter of national currencies. In the United States, for example, we probably want to make income comparisons in dollars. But dollars are not the national currency in Western Europe or in China or India or Japan, so we must somehow convert from one currency to another.

FOREIGN EXCHANGE RATES

Travel within another country requires that payments be made in the currency of that nation. If you go to Europe, in 17 countries, you will buy goods with euros. If you go to India, you will pay in rupees. If you go to Russia, you will buy using rubles.

So, to compare the average Russian's income in rubles with the average American's income in dollars, we must convert the rubles to the equivalent amount of dollars. The data for converting are readily available on a daily basis, because there is a worldwide market in **foreign exchange,** or national currencies. You might find that it takes 30 rubles to buy one dollar. Or you may find that it take 50 rupees to buy one dollar. So, as a first approximation, this means that to compare incomes across the world, simple arithmetic is involved. We convert, via **foreign exchange rate** tables—found on hundreds of Internet sites—other nations' average incomes in their own currencies to what they are in the U.S. currency, dollars.

For example, if the average income in France is 30,000 euros, we multiply the current euro exchange rate by that number. Suppose the exchange rate is such that one euro equals 1.20 dollars, then the average income in France is 30,000 euros times 1.2 dollars per euro, or $36,000.

When we do such calculations, we find that on an exchange-rate basis, the average American is thirty five times richer than the average Indian, almost twenty times richer than the average citizen of China, and six times richer than the average Russian.

Problems with Using Market Exchange Rates

Foreign exchange rates are a function of world **supply and demand** (sound familiar?). But demand and supply of currencies is ultimately derived from (or determined by) the demand and supply of, among other things, **traded goods.** Traded goods (and services) are those that, as the name suggest, are traded across national borders. Some examples of traded goods are wines, automobiles, wheat, and shoes. If all goods were traded and if that trade occurred with no distortions, then exchange rates would permit us to perfectly compare incomes around the world.

But there is a complication: Not all goods and services that we consume are traded goods. **Non-traded goods** include houses, haircuts, house-cleaning services, and landscaping, as well as many others. Non-traded goods and service are not involved in exchange across countries' borders.

The existence of non-traded goods implies that bias will result if we use only exchange rates to make international comparisons. This is because in poorer countries, wages are low and so non-traded goods (made with that low-cost labor) are likely to be the cheapest. That is, in low-income nations we expect to see restaurant meals, beauty salon services, and house cleaning to be much less expensive than those same items in high-income nations. Hence, if we use current exchange rates—based on traded goods—to convert incomes to a common currency, differences in average incomes between low-wage nations and high-wage nations are going to be exaggerated.

Often you will read newspaper stories about a developing country in which the average income, say, is $1,000 a year. That number is derived from current foreign exchange rates. It does not take account of how cheaply residents in that country can buy basic foods and services that are not traded in international markets.

Purchasing Power Parity— A Solution?

Somehow we have to adjust current exchange rates to account for differences in the true cost of living across countries. To do so, we may use a concept known as **purchasing power parity,** which creates a type of adjusted foreign exchange rate.[1] The details of how the World Bank and other organizations calculate various purchasing power parity measures for 180 countries are not important here. Suffice it to say that, in doing so, attempts are made to correct market foreign exchange rates for the relative cost of living in each country. So, on a purchasing power parity basis—taking into account the lower cost of living in India, China, and Russia—average American income is only thirteen times higher than in India, eight and a half times higher than in China, and a little over three times higher than in Russia.

A major problem remains, nonetheless. Purchasing power adjustments are difficult to calculate in each country. The residents of each nation buy different combinations of goods and services or, in the alternative, they buy similar goods and services but with subtle variations in quality. Not only are the calculations difficult, but there are disputes over the best way to do them for each country, leading to doubts about whether the measures *really* account for differences in the cost of living.

It is here that the ubiquitous Big Mac proves its worth.

Big Mac to the Rescue

A typical Big Mac is created using virtually identical ingredients around the world (although substitution occurs where religious or cultural norms rule out beef). Big Macs are produced according to a uniform process

---

1 Obviously, there is no market for anything measured in units of purchasing power parity.

detailed in the McDonalds 600-page manual. As well as being a "standard product," local prices of Big Macs are not distorted by international transportation and distribution costs.

In light of these facts, since 1986, the magazine *The Economist* has developed a Big Mac Index. By using one good only—a Big Mac—*The Economist* has thereby created a means of comparing the cost of living around the world, and also a means of determining how much exchange rates fail to account for non-traded goods.

Keeping in mind that the methods of production and the ingredients are the same in Big Macs everywhere, if we convert international Big Mac prices using exchange rates, we "should" get exactly the same price everywhere. But if, using exchange rates, we calculate that a Big Mac costs $6.80 in Switzerland, but only $4.20 in America, this says that a dollar doesn't go very far in Switzerland. That is, the cost of living in Switzerland is relatively high, most likely because non-traded goods (such as housing) are quite expensive there. Similarly, if we also find that, at current exchange rates, a Big Mac costs the equivalent of $2.40 in China, we have found that the dollar goes a long way there: The cost of living is low in China compared to the United States. Again, this is most likely because non-traded goods made with low-wage labor are quite cheap in China.

The upshot is that if we adjust incomes using the Big Mac index to correct for differences in the cost of living, we can get a much better idea of relative real incomes. In one recent year, for example, using exchange rates, income in Switzerland was about $83,000, compared to about $48,000 in the United States. After correcting with the aid of the Big Mac, however, we find that real income in Switzerland is only about $52,000—still higher than in the United States but not by much.

McWages, Real Wages, and Well-Being

Now consider creating a McWage. Given that the talent necessary to make a Big Mac is about the same everywhere, we can collect information on the wages of Big Mac preparers throughout the world. This will provide us with a comparison of the cost of hiring that uniform quality of labor across countries. If we then take McWages and divide them by the local price of a Big Mac, we can discern how many Big Mac equivalents each worker is paid per hour. This is a simple, albeit one-good specific, measure of the **real wage,** that is, the wage rate adjusted for the cost of living in each nation. And this measure—"Big Macs per hour"—can be constructed without worrying about biases in exchange rates or complicated purchasing power parity calculations.

That is exactly what economists Orley Ashenfelter and Stepan Jurajda have done. They have found that workers in America earn about 2.5 Big Macs per hour (or BMPH), compared to the 3.1 BMPH earned in Japan. In Canada and Western Europe, workers are paid about 2.2 BMPH. Using the same calculations, the authors find that workers in Russia earn about 1.2 BMPH, while Eastern European workers collect about 0.8. Workers in China earn about 0.6 BMPH, while those in India earn only about 0.4. The bottom line is that using the BMPH index, we see that standards of living vary greatly around the world, but not nearly to the extent that is suggested by exchange rates.

TRENDS IN PRODUCTIVITY

A basic tenet of economics is that in competitive labor markets (and that is certainly where McDonalds gets its workers) people are paid based on what they produce. Thus, using the data mentioned above, we can infer that workers in America are only about 10 percent more productive than those in Canada or Western Europe, but they are about four times as productive as those in China.

We can also look at the patterns of change in the BMPH index over time, to give us an idea of how **productivity**, and thus standards of living are evolving around the world. As one example, between 2000 and 2007, McWages in the United States rose by 13 percent, while the price of a Big Mac jumped by 21 percent. That means that real wages *fell* in the United States by about 8 percent over this period. Doing the same calculation for the same period, productivity and thus real wages rose 60 percent in China, and by over 50 percent in India. Clearly, average productivity was rising sharply in these two countries.

During 2007–2011, the most recent period for which data are available, real wages have fallen even more in developed nations such as the United States, Canada, and Western Europe. In most developing nations, real wages have been rising, although much more slowly than before. The good news of this story is thus that developing nations are generally closing the standard of living gap. The bad news is that the world financial crisis and its aftermath have diminished opportunities around the world, a development that is surely worth monitoring in the future.

DISCUSSION QUESTIONS

1. Assume you are going to take a trip to Paris. You buy euros at your local bank or at the airport. Then you start spending them once you are in Paris. Every time you buy something there, you explicitly

or implicitly translate the euro price into dollars. Often, you might say to yourself, "how do Parisians afford such high prices?" What is wrong with this line of reasoning? (*Hint*: In what currency do Parisians earn their income?)

2. Why don't the local prices of restaurant meals, haircuts, and gardening services affect a country's exchange rate?

3. If the same amount of materials and the same methods are used to produce Big Macs in over 120 countries, why are the prices of Big Macs not all the same, expressed in dollars?

4. Is there anything that a Big Mac preparer in a developing country can do to earn a higher real wage rate?

5. Why does McDonalds provide a 600-page manual to the company's franchises in every country? (*Hint*: What are the ways that any franchisor can monitor quality of its franchisees?)

6. In a wealthy country, wages are not only high in the traded-goods and services sector, but they are also high in the non-traded goods and services sector. Why? (*Hint*: Are there two separate labor markets or just one?)

CHAPTER 30

Globalization and the Wealth of America

The past two decades have been a time of great change for international trade and **globalization.** The North American Free Trade Agreement (NAFTA), for example, substantially reduced the **trade barriers** among citizens of Canada, the United States, and Mexico. On a global scale, the Uruguay Round of the General Agreement on Tariffs and Trade (GATT) was ratified by 117 nations, including the United States. Under the terms of this agreement, GATT was replaced by the **World Trade Organization (WTO),** whose membership now numbers over 150, and **tariffs** were cut worldwide. Agricultural **subsidies** were reduced, patent protections were extended, and the WTO established a set of arbitration boards to settle international disputes over trade issues.

Many economists believe that both NAFTA and the agreements reached during the Uruguay Round were victories not only for free trade and globalization but also for the citizens of the participating nations. Nevertheless, many noneconomists, particularly politicians, opposed these agreements, so it is important that we understand what is beneficial about NAFTA, the Uruguay Round, and free trade in general.

GAINS FROM TRADE

Voluntary trade creates new wealth. In voluntary trade, both parties in an exchange gain. They give up something of lesser value in return for something of greater value. In this sense, exchanges are always unequal. But it is this unequal nature of exchange that is the source of the increased **productivity** and higher wealth that occurs whenever trade takes place. When we engage in exchange, what we give up is worth less than what we get—for if this were not true, we would not have traded.

And what is true for us is also true for our trading partner, meaning that both partners end up better off.

Free trade encourages individuals to use their abilities in the most productive manner possible and to exchange the fruits of their efforts. The **gains from trade** lie in one of the most fundamental ideas in economics: A nation gains from doing what it can do best *relative to other nations*, that is, by specializing in endeavors in which it has a **comparative advantage.** Trade encourages individuals and nations to discover ways to specialize so that they can become more productive and enjoy higher incomes. Increased productivity and the subsequent increase in economic growth are exactly what the signatories of the Uruguay Round and NAFTA sought—and are obtaining—by reducing trade barriers.

GLOBALIZATION AND THE OPPOSITION TO IT

Globalization differs from free trade chiefly in the degree of integration across nations. For example, although there is free trade in wine, the wines produced in Australia, California, and France are each created wholly within the geopolitical borders indicated by their labels. Moreover, each remains a distinct economic entity, in that significant relative price changes between, say, French and California wines are observed. In contrast, the market for automobiles has become truly "global." If you purchase a "Japanese" automobile in the United States, assembly of the vehicle may have taken place in Japan, the United States, or even Mexico, and the components of the car may have come from a half-dozen or more different nations. And if you call for customer support for your car, the person answering the phone may be at a call center located in any of a variety of English-speaking nations. Globalization thus means that trade between nations becomes as seamless as trade between states, provinces, or cities within a given nation.

Despite the enormous gains from exchange, globalization is routinely opposed by some people. Many excuses are offered for this opposition, but they all basically come down to one issue: When our borders are fully open to trade with other nations, some individuals and businesses in our nation face more competition. As you saw in Chapter 19, most firms and workers hate competition, and who can blame them? After all, if a firm can keep the competition out, **profits** are sure to rise. And if workers can prevent competition from other sources, they can enjoy higher wages and greater selection among jobs. So the real source of most opposition to globalization is that the opponents to trade dislike the competition that comes with it. There is nothing immoral or unethical about this—but there is nothing altruistic or noble about it, either. It is self-interest, pure and simple.

One aspect of globalization that looms large in the minds of its opponents is the unremitting competitive vigilance that it requires. When world markets are completely integrated, one's competitors may emerge at any time from any place—often from corners of the world that one may least expect. And because competitors may only need to create a Web site to get started and can have their products delivered the next day by air freight, that competition can emerge devastatingly quickly. Thus, when operating in a global economy, firms and their employees must contend with a level of uncertainty that is simply not present when trade patterns are less integrated. Note that this highly competitive atmosphere ultimately benefits all of us, but that doesn't make it any less unnerving for those who must endure its pressures, day after day. Competition is tough, and global competition is toughest of all.

BEGGAR-THY-NEIGHBOR

Because of this, opposition to globalization is nothing new. One of the most famous examples of such opposition led to passage of the Smoot–Hawley Tariff of 1930. This major federal statute was a classic example of **protectionism**—an effort to protect a subset of American producers at the expense of consumers and other producers. It included tariff schedules for more than twenty thousand products, raising taxes on affected imports by an average of 52 percent.

The Smoot–Hawley Tariff encouraged beggar-thy-neighbor policies by the rest of the world. Such policies represent an attempt to improve (a portion of) one's domestic economy at the expense of foreign countries' economies. In this case, tariffs were imposed to discourage **imports** so that domestic import-competing industries would benefit. The beggar-thy-neighbor policy at the heart of Smoot–Hawley was soon adopted by the United Kingdom, France, the Netherlands, and Switzerland. The result was a halt to globalization and a massive reduction in international trade that almost certainly worsened the worldwide depression of the 1930s.

Opponents of globalization sometimes claim that beggar-thy-neighbor policies benefit the United States by protecting import-competing industries. In general, this claim is not correct. It is true that some Americans benefit from such policies, but two large groups of Americans lose. First, there are the purchasers of imports and import-competing goods. They suffer from higher prices and reduced selection of goods and suppliers caused by tariffs and import **quotas.** Second, the decline in imports caused by protectionism also causes a decline in **exports,** thereby harming firms and employees in these industries. This follows directly from one of the most fundamental propositions in international trade: *In the long run, imports are paid for by exports.* This proposition simply states that when one country buys goods and services from the rest of the world (imports), the rest of the world eventually wants goods from that country (exports) in exchange. Given this fundamental proposition, a corollary becomes obvious: *Any restriction on imports leads to a reduction in exports.* Thus, any business for import-competing industries gained as a result of tariffs or quotas means at least as much business lost for exporting industries.

DUMPING

Opponents of globalization raise a variety of objections in their efforts to restrict international trade. For example, it is sometimes said that foreign companies engage in dumping, that is, selling their goods in America below cost. The first question to ask is: below *whose* cost? Clearly, if the foreign firm is selling in America, it must be offering the good for sale at a price that is at or below the cost of American firms, or else it could not induce Americans to buy it. But the ability of individuals or firms to get goods at lower cost is one of the *benefits* of free trade, not one of its negatives.

What about claims that import sales are taking place at prices below the foreign company's costs? This amounts to arguing that the owners of the foreign company are voluntarily giving some of their wealth to us, namely, the difference between their costs and the lower price they charge us. It is possible, though unlikely, that they might wish to do this as a way of getting us to try a product that we would not otherwise purchase. But if so, why would we want to refuse this gift? As a nation, we are richer if we accept it. Moreover, it is a gift that will be offered for only a short while, for there is no point in selling below one's cost unless one hopes soon to raise price profitably above cost!

LABOR AND ENVIRONMENTAL STANDARDS

Another argument sometimes raised against globalization is that the goods are produced abroad using unfair labor practices (such as the use of child labor) or using production processes that do not meet American environmental standards. Such charges are sometimes correct. But we must remember two things. First, although we may find the use of child labor (or perhaps sixty-hour work weeks with no overtime pay) objectionable, such practices were once common in the United States. They used to be prevalent in America for the same reason they are now practiced abroad. The people involved were (or are) too poor to do otherwise. Some families in developing nations cannot survive unless all members of the family contribute. As unfortunate as this is, if we insist on imposing our attitudes—shaped in part by our great wealth—on peoples whose wealth is far lower than ours, we run the risk of making them worse off even as we think we are helping them.

Similar considerations apply to environmental standards. It is well established that individuals' and nations' willingness to pay for environmental quality is very much shaped by their wealth. Environmental quality is a **luxury good.** That is, people who are rich (such as Americans) want to consume much more of it per capita than people who are poor. Insisting that other nations meet environmental standards that we find acceptable is much like insisting that they wear the clothes we wear, use the modes of transportation we prefer, and consume the foods we like.[1] The few people who manage to comply will indeed be living in the style to which we are accustomed, but most people will simply be impoverished by the attempt.

Our point is not that foreign labor or environmental standards are, or should be, irrelevant to Americans. Our point is that achieving high standards of either is costly, and trade restrictions are unlikely to be the most efficient or most effective way to achieve them. Just as important, labor standards and environmental standards are all too often raised as smoke screens to hide the real motive—keeping the competition out.

THE POLITICAL ECONOMY OF TRADE BARRIERS

If it is true that globalization is beneficial and that restrictions on trade are generally harmful, we must surely raise the question, how does legislation such as the Smoot–Hawley Tariff (or any other such restriction) ever get passed? As Mark Twain noted many years ago, the reason the free traders win the arguments and the protectionists win the votes is simple. Foreign competition often clearly affects a narrow and specific import-competing industry such as textiles, shoes, or automobiles, and thus trade restrictions benefit a narrow, well-defined group of economic

---

1 There is one important exception to this argument. In the case of foreign air or water pollution generated near enough to our borders (for example, with Mexico or Canada) to cause harm to Americans, good public policy presumably dictates that we seek to treat such pollution as though it were being generated inside our borders.

agents. For example, restrictions on imports of Japanese automobiles in the 1980s chiefly benefited the Big Three automakers in this country—General Motors, Ford, and Chrysler. Similarly, long-standing quotas on the imports of sugar benefit a handful of large American sugar producers. And when tariffs of up to 30 percent were slapped on many steel imports in 2002, an even smaller number of American steelmakers and their employees benefited. Because of the concentrated benefits that accrue when Congress votes in favor of trade restrictions, sufficient lobbying and campaign funds can be raised in those industries to convince members of Congress to impose those restrictions.

The eventual reduction in exports that must follow is normally spread in small doses throughout all export industries. Thus, no specific group of workers, managers, or shareholders in export industries will feel that it should contribute money to convince Congress to reduce barriers to globalization. Furthermore, although consumers of imports and import-competing goods lose due to trade restrictions, they too are typically a diffuse group of individuals, none of whom will be individually affected much because of any single import restriction. It is the simultaneous existence of concentrated benefits and diffuse costs that led to Mark Twain's conclusion that the protectionists would often win the votes. (Concentrated benefits and dispersed costs are at the heart of Chapters 22 and 27 in explaining some U.S. domestic policies.)

Of course, the protectionists don't win all the votes—after all, roughly one-sixth of the U.S. economy is based on international trade. Despite the opposition to globalization that comes from many quarters, its benefits to the economy as a whole are so great that it is unthinkable that we might do away with international trade altogether. Thus, when we think about developments such as NAFTA and the WTO, it is clear that both economic theory and empirical evidence indicate that Americans are better off because of globalization.

Discussion Questions

1. During the late 1980s and early 1990s, American automobile manufacturers greatly increased the quality of the cars they produced relative to the quality of the cars produced in other nations. What effect do you think this had on American imports of Japanese cars, Japanese imports of American cars, and American exports of goods and services other than automobiles?

2. Over the past twenty years, some Japanese automakers have opened plants in the United States so that they could produce (and sell)

"Japanese" cars here. What effect do you think this had on American imports of Japanese cars, Japanese imports of American cars, and American exports of goods and services other than automobiles?

3. For a number of years, Japanese carmakers voluntarily limited the number of cars they exported to the United States. What effect do you think this had on Japanese imports of American cars and on American exports of goods and services other than automobiles?

4. Until recently, American cars exported to Japan had driver controls on the left side (as in the United States), even though Japanese cars sold in Japan have driver controls on the *right* side, because the Japanese (like the British) drive on the left side of the road. Suppose the Japanese tried to sell their cars in the United States with the driver controls on the right side. What impact would this likely have on their sales in this country? Do you think the unwillingness of American carmakers to put the driver controls on the correct side for exports to Japan had any effect on their sales of cars in that country?

5. The U.S. government subsidizes the export of U.S.-manufactured commercial aircraft. What effect do you think this policy has on American imports of foreign goods and American exports of products other than commercial aircraft? Explain.

6. Who bears the costs and enjoys the benefits of the subsidies mentioned in the previous question?

CHAPTER 31

The $750,000 Steelworker

In even-numbered years, particularly years evenly divisible by 4, politicians are apt to give speeches about the need to protect U.S. jobs from the evils of **globalization.** We are thus encouraged to buy American. If further encouragement is needed, we are told that if we do not voluntarily reduce the amount of imported goods we purchase, the government will impose (or make more onerous) either **tariffs** (taxes) on imported goods or **quotas** (quantity restrictions) that will physically limit **imports.** The objective is to save U.S. jobs.

Unlike black rhinos or blue whales, U.S. jobs are in no danger of becoming extinct. There are an infinite number of potential jobs in the American economy, and there always will be. Some of these jobs are not very pleasant, and many others do not pay very well, but there will always be employment of some sort as long as there is **scarcity.** Thus, when steelworkers making $72,000 per year say that imports of foreign steel should be reduced to save their jobs, what they really mean is this: They wants to be protected from **competition** so they can continue their present employment at the same or higher salary rather than move to a different employment that has less desirable working conditions or pays a lower salary. There is nothing wrong with the steelworkers' goal (better working conditions and higher pay), but it has nothing to do with saving jobs.

THE NATURE OF TRADE

In any discussion of the consequences of restrictions on international trade, it is essential to remember two facts. First, *we pay for imports with exports*. It is true that in the short run, we can sell off assets or borrow from abroad if we happen to import more goods and services than we export. But we have only a finite amount of assets to sell, and foreigners do not want to wait forever before we pay our bills. Ultimately, our accounts can be settled only if we provide (export) goods and services to the trading partners from whom we purchase (import) goods and services. Trade, after all, involves *quid pro quo* (literally, something for something). The second point to remember is that *voluntary trade is mutually beneficial to the trading partners.* If we restrict international trade, we reduce those benefits, both for our trading partners and for ourselves. One way these reduced benefits are manifested is in the form of curtailed employment opportunities for workers. In a nutshell, even though tariffs and quotas enhance job opportunities in import-competing industries, they also cost us jobs in export industries; the net effect seems to be *reduced* employment overall.

What is true for the United States is also true for other countries: They will buy our goods only if they can market theirs, because they too must export goods to pay for their imports. Thus, any U.S. restrictions on imports—via tariffs, quotas, or other means—ultimately cause a reduction in our exports, because other countries will be unable to pay for our goods. Hence, import restrictions must inevitably decrease the size of our export sector. So imposing trade restrictions to save jobs in import-competing industries has the effect of costing jobs in export industries.

PROTECTION FOR AUTOMOBILES

Import restrictions also impose costs on U.S. consumers. By reducing competition from abroad, quotas, tariffs, and other trade restraints push up the prices of foreign goods and enable U.S. producers to hike their own prices. One of the best-documented examples of this is the automobile industry.

Due in part to the enhanced quality of imported cars, sales of domestically produced automobiles fell from nine million units in 1978 to an average of six million units per year between 1980 and 1982. **Profits** for U.S. automobile manufacturers plummeted as well, turning into substantial losses for some of them. American automakers and autoworkers' unions demanded protection from import competition. They were joined in their cries by politicians from automobile-producing states. The result was a voluntary agreement by Japanese car companies (the most important competitors of U.S. firms) that restricted U.S. sales of Japanese cars to 1.68 million units per year. This agreement—which amounted to a quota even though it never officially bore that name—began in April 1981 and continued into the 1990s in various forms.

Robert W. Crandall, an economist with the Brookings Institution, has estimated how much this voluntary trade restriction cost U.S. consumers in terms of higher car prices. According to his estimates, the reduced supply of Japanese cars pushed their prices up by $2,000 apiece, measured in 2013 dollars. The higher price of Japanese imports in turn enabled domestic producers to hike their prices an average of $800 per car. The total tab in the first full year of the program was over $8 billion. Crandall also estimated the number of jobs in automobile-related industries that were preserved by the voluntary import restrictions at about 26,000. Dividing $8 billion by twenty-six thousand jobs yields a cost to consumers of about $300,000 *per year* for every job preserved in the automobile industry. U.S. consumers could have saved over $5 billion on their car purchases each year if instead of implicitly agreeing to import restrictions, they had simply given $100,000 to every autoworker whose job was preserved by the voluntary import restraints.

PROTECTION FOR OTHER INDUSTRIES

The same types of calculations have been made for other industries. Tariffs in the apparel industry were increased between 1977 and 1981, preserving the jobs of about 116,000 U.S. apparel workers at a cost of $50,000 per job each year. At about the same time, the producers of Citizens' Band radios also managed to get tariffs raised. Approximately six hundred workers in the industry kept their jobs as a result, at an annual cost to consumers of over $90,000 per job.

The cost of **protectionism** has been even higher in other industries. Jobs preserved in the glassware industry due to trade restrictions cost $200,000 apiece each year. In the maritime industry, the yearly cost of trade protection is $290,000 per job. In the steel industry, the cost of preserving a job has been estimated at an astounding $750,000 per year. If free trade were permitted, each worker moving to employment elsewhere could be given a cash payment of half that amount each year, and consumers would still save a lot of money.

TOTAL EMPLOYMENT FALLS

Even so, this is not the full story. None of these studies estimating the cost to consumers of preserving jobs in import-competing industries have attempted to estimate the ultimate impact of import restrictions on the flow of exports, the number of jobs lost in the export sector, and thus the total number of jobs gained or lost.

When imports to the United States are restricted, our trading partners will necessarily buy less of what we produce. The resulting decline in export sales means fewer jobs in exporting industries. And the total reduction in trade leads to fewer jobs for workers such as stevedores (who load and unload ships) and truck drivers (who carry goods to and from ports). On both counts—the overall cut in trade and the accompanying decline in exports—protectionism leads to job losses that might not be immediately obvious.

Several years ago, Congress tried to pass a domestic-content bill for automobiles. In effect, the legislation would have required that cars sold in the United States have a minimum percentage of their components manufactured and assembled in this country. Proponents of the legislation argued that it would protect 300,000 jobs in the U.S. automobile manufacturing and auto parts supply industries. Yet the legislation's supporters failed to recognize the negative impact of the bill on trade in general and on U.S. export industries. A U.S. Department of Labor study did recognize these impacts, estimating that the domestic-content legislation would actually cost more jobs in trade-related and export industries than it protected in import-competing businesses. Congress ultimately decided not to impose a domestic-content requirement for cars sold in the United States.

More recently, when President Bush decided in 2002 to impose tariffs of up to 30 percent on steel imports, the adverse effects on the economy were substantial and soon apparent. To take but one example, prior to the tariffs, the Port of New Orleans relied on steel imports for more than 40 percent of its revenues, in part because once steel coming into the port is offloaded, the ships are cleaned and refilled with U.S. grain for export. By reducing imports, the tariffs slashed economic activity at the port and also reduced U.S. grain exports. Businesses and farms all up and down the Mississippi River were adversely affected. More broadly, the higher costs of imported steel produced a decline in employment in U.S. industries that use steel as an input. Indeed, one study estimated that due to the tariffs, about 200,000 people lost their jobs in 2002 in these industries alone—a number that exceeded the total number of people actually employed by the steel manufacturing firms protected by the tariff.

The Impossibility of Real Protection

In principle, trade restrictions are imposed to provide economic help to specific industries and to increase employment in those industries. Ironically, the long-term effects may be just the opposite. Researchers at the **World Trade Organization (WTO)** examined employment in three industries that have been heavily protected throughout the world: textiles, clothing, and iron and steel. Despite stringent trade protection for these industries, employment *declined* during the period of protection, in some cases dramatically. In textiles, employment fell 22 percent in the United States and 46 percent in the European Union. The clothing industry had employment losses ranging from 18 percent in the United States to 56 percent in Sweden. Declines in employment in the iron and steel industry ranged anywhere from 10 percent in Canada to 54 percent in the United States. In short, restrictions on free trade are no guarantee against job losses, even in the industries supposedly being protected.

The evidence seems clear: The cost of protecting jobs in the short run is huge. In the long run, it appears that jobs cannot be protected, especially if one considers all aspects of protectionism. Free trade is a tough platform on which to run for office. But it is the one that yields the most general benefits if implemented. Of course, this does not mean that politicians will embrace it, and so we end up "saving" jobs at a cost of up to $750,000 each.

DISCUSSION QUESTIONS

1. Who gains and who loses from import restrictions?

2. What motivates politicians to impose trade restrictions?

3. If it would be cheaper to give each steelworker $375,000 per year in cash than impose restrictions on imports of steel, why do we have the import restrictions rather than the cash payments?

4. Most U.S. imports and exports travel through our seaports at some point. How do you predict that members of Congress from coastal states would vote on proposals to restrict international trade? What other information would you want to know when making such a prediction?

5. When you go shopping for a new computer, is your real objective to "import" a computer into your apartment, or is it to "export" cash from your wallet? What does this tell you about the true object of international trade—is it imports or exports?

6. Some U.S. policy is designed to subsidize exports and thus increase employment in export industries. What effect does such policy have on our imports of foreign goods and thus on employment in industries that compete with imports?

Glossary

absolute advantage: the ability to produce more of a good, without regard for the costs of forgone output of other goods

acreage-restriction program: a federal government limit on the number of acres that a farmer can plant with a particular crop

adverse selection: a process in which "undesirable" (high-cost or high-risk) participants tend to dominate one side of the market, causing adverse effects for the other side; often results from asymmetric information

amenities: desirable or useful features of a person, good, or location

assets: all tangible and intangible items to which an individual or institution holds a legal claim of ownership

asymmetric information: circumstance in which participants on one side of a market have more information than participants on the other side of the market; often results in adverse selection

bank run: the simultaneous attempt by many of a bank's depositors to convert checkable and savings deposits into currency because of a perceived fear for the bank's solvency

bankruptcy: a legal status that permits an individual or firm to escape responsibility for many or all of debts

biofuels: fuels made from once-living organisms or their by-products

capital stock: the collection of productive assets that can be combined with other inputs, such as labor, to produce goods and services

cartel: a group of independent businesses, often on an international scale, that agree to restrict trade, to their mutual benefit

civil law system: a legal system in which statutes passed by legislatures and executive decrees, rather than judicial decisions based on precedent, form the basis for most legal rules

closed access: an element of the property right to a good, ensuring that the owner can effectively exclude other people from using the good

common law system: a legal system in which judicial decisions based on precedent, rather than executive decrees or statutes passed by legislatures, form the basis for most legal rules

common property resource: a good jointly owned by a group of individuals who cannot (for legal or physical reasons) divide the good into pieces and dispose of them separately

congestion: overuse of a resource to the point that one's person use impedes use by other individuals

comparative advantage: the ability to produce a good at a lower opportunity cost than others; the principle of comparative advantage implies that individuals, firms, and nations will specialize in producing goods for which they have the lowest opportunity cost compared to other entities

compensating differential: additional pay given to workers employed in particularly hazardous or unpleasant jobs

competition: rivalry among buyers or sellers of outputs or among buyers or sellers of inputs

complement: a good having the property that a change in its price will cause the demand for another good to change in the opposite direction

constant-dollar price: price corrected for changes in the purchasing power of the dollar, taking inflation and deflation into account

constant-quality price: the price of a good adjusted upward or downward to reflect the higher- or lower-than-average quality of that good

consume: the act of enjoying or using up a service or good

consumer price index: a measure of the dollar cost of a typical bundle of consumer goods relative to the cost of that bundle in a base year

cost: the highest-valued (best) forgone alternative; the most valuable option that is sacrificed when a choice is made

deferred interest: interest charges added to the principal of a loan when that interest is not paid as originally scheduled

demand: the willingness and ability to purchase goods

demand curve: a graphic representation of demand—a negatively sloped line showing the inverse relationship between the price and the quantity demanded

direct foreign investment: resources provided to individuals and firms in a nation by individuals or firms located in other countries, often taking the form of foreign subsidiary or branch operations of a parent company

discount rate: the time value of money, typically expressed as a percentage per year

disposable income: the maximum amount of spending that consumers can undertake after they have paid direct taxes, such as income taxes

dynamic analysis: an assessment of the economic impact of a policy that takes into account the induced responses to that policy

Earned Income Tax Credit: a tax policy that offers payments from the government to people who earn relatively low wages

earnings premium: the excess in the pay for one employment compared to another

economic good: any good or service that is scarce

economic growth: sustained increases over time in real per capita income

economic profits: profits in excess of competitive profits, which are the minimum necessary to keep resources employed in an industry

elastic demand: characteristic of a demand curve in which a given percentage change in price will result in a larger inverse percentage change in quantity demanded; total revenues and price are inversely related in the elastic portion of the demand curve

elasticity: a measure of the responsiveness of one variable to a change in another variable; it is the ratio of two percentage changes

elasticity of demand: responsiveness of the quantity of a commodity demanded to a change in its price per unit

elasticity of supply: responsiveness of the quantity of a commodity supplied to a change in its price per unit

entitlement program: a government program that guarantees a certain level of benefits to persons who meet the requirements set by law

equilibrium price: price that clears the market when there is no excess quantity demanded or supplied; the price at which the demand curve intersects the supply curve; also called market-clearing price

exports: sales of goods or services to a foreign country

externalities: benefits or costs of an economic activity that spill over to a third party; pollution is a negative spillover or externality

fixed exchange rates: a system of legally fixed prices (rates) at which two or more national currencies trade (exchange) for one another

foreign exchange: national currencies

foreign exchange rate: the relative price at which two national currencies trade

fracking: the informal name given to the hydraulic fracturing process, in which water, sand, and small amounts of chemicals are injected deep underground to break rock apart so that natural gas or oil can be extracted from the rock

free good: any good or service available in larger quantities than desired at a zero price

full cost: the combined measure of all of the things that must be given up to undertake an activity; includes both the money price (other goods that must be sacrificed) and the value of the time that must be sacrificed

gains from trade: the extent to which individuals, firms, or nations benefit by engaging in exchange

globalization: the integration of national economies into an international economy as a result of lower trade barriers and reduced transportation, and communication costs

green energy: source of energy that can be harnessed with little pollution

human capital: the accumulated training, education, and knowledge of workers

illiquid: not readily convertible to cash

import tariff: a tax applied specifically to imports of goods or services from another nation

imports: purchases of goods or services from a foreign country

in-kind transfers: grants of goods and services rather than cash to recipients who meet certain criteria; examples include Medicare, Medicaid, subsidized housing, food stamps, and school lunches

incentives: perceived consequences of actions or decisions; they may be positive or negative, monetary or nonmonetary

income elasticity of demand: a measure of the responsiveness of demand to changes in income, calculated as the percentage change in demand for a good divided by the percentage change in consumer income

income mobility: the tendency of individuals to move around in the income distribution over time

increase in supply: a rise in the amount supplied at each price of the good; a shift to the right of the market supply curve

inelastic: relatively unresponsive

inelastic demand: characteristic of a demand curve in which a given change in price will result in a less than proportionate inverse change in the quantity demanded; total revenue and price are directly related in the inelastic region of the demand curve

inflation: a rise in the dollar cost of achieving a given level of satisfaction, often measured in terms of the dollar cost of a particular standard bundle of goods

insolvent: in a financial condition in which the value of one's assets is less than the value of one's liabilities

institutions: the basic rules, customs, and practices of society

intellectual property: creative ideas and expressions of the human mind that have commercial value and receive the legal protection of a property right, as through the issuance of a patent, copyright, or trademark

interest: the charge for the privilege of borrowing money, typically expressed as an annual percentage rate

investment: the acquisition or addition to a property for the purpose of generating additional future services or goods

labor force participation rate: the sum of all people who are working or are available for and looking for work, divided by the population; both numerator and denominator are generally restricted to persons aged 16 and above

law of demand: law stating that quantity demanded and price are inversely related—more is bought at a lower price and less at a higher price (other things being equal)

law of supply: law stating that a direct relationship exists between price and quantity supplied (other things being equal)

lien: a legal claim against the owner of a resource

liabilities: amounts owed; monetary claims against an individual or an institution

luxury good: a good for which the income elasticity of demand is greater than 1, meaning that people spend an increasing proportion of their income on the good as they get richer

marginal analysis: analysis of what happens when small changes take place relative to the status quo

marginal benefits: additional benefits associated with one more unit of a good or action; the change in total benefits due to the addition of one more unit of production

marginal costs: changes in total costs due to a change in one unit of production

market-clearing price: *see* equilibrium price

market share: the proportion of total sales in an industry accounted for by a specific firm or group of firms in that industry

market supply: total quantities of a good offered for sale by suppliers at various prices

median age: age that exactly separates the younger half of the population from the older half

minimum wage: the lowest hourly wage that firms may legally pay their workers

models, or theories: simplified representations of the real world used to make predictions or to better understand the real world

monitoring costs: costs that must be incurred to observe the behavior of a politician or other agent to whom responsibilities have been delegated

monopolistic competition: the situation that exists when producers and sellers offer for sale similar products with slight variations in features or quality; although the products are priced above their average minimum cost, competition among firms reduces long-run economic profits to zero

monopoly: a single supplier; a firm that faces a downward-sloping demand curve for its output and therefore can choose the price at which it will sell the good; an example of a price searcher

monopoly power: the ability of a company to charge a price for its product that is in excess of the marginal cost of producing the product

monopsonist: a firm operating as a monopsony

monopsony: a single buyer; a firm that faces an upward-sloping supply curve for its input and therefore can choose the price at which it will buy the good; an example of a price searcher

moral hazard: the tendency of an entity insulated from risk to behave differently than it would behave if it were fully exposed to the risk

natural resource endowments: the collection of naturally occurring minerals (such as oil and iron ore) and living things (such as forests and fish stocks) that can be used to produce goods and services

negative externality: a cost associated with an economic activity that is paid by third parties; pollution is a negative externality because, for example, someone other than the driver of an automobile bears part of the cost of the car's exhaust emissions

negative tax: a payment from the government made to supplement the incomes of people who earn low wages

nominal prices: the costs of goods, expressed in terms of a nation's currency, such as the dollar

nonprice competition: offering additional services or higher product quality to attract business instead of cutting prices to do so

non-traded goods: those items and services traded only within a country and not across its national borders

oligopoly: a firm that is one of very few sellers (or buyers) in a market; in such a situation, each firm reacts to changes in the prices and quantities of its rivals

open access: an element of the property to a good that prevents the owner from excluding people from using the good; in effect, anyone who wishes to use the good is legally free to do so

opportunity cost: the highest-valued alternative that must be sacrificed to attain something or to satisfy a want

outsourcing: the practice of having workers located in foreign lands perform tasks (typically services) that have traditionally been performed by domestic workers

per capita income: average income per person

perfectly elastic: characterized by an infinite value for the ratio of the percentage change in quantity over the percentage change in price; visually, a perfectly inelastic curve appears horizontal

perfectly inelastic: characterized by a zero value for the ratio of the percentage change in quantity over the percentage change in price; visually, a perfectly inelastic curve appears vertical

physical capital: nonhuman productive resources

political economy: the study of the causes and consequences of political decision-making

price discrimination: selling at prices that do not reflect differences in marginal costs; different prices with the same marginal costs, for example, or the same prices with different marginal costs

price elasticity of demand: the percentage change in quantity demanded divided by the percentage change in price; *see also* elasticity of demand

price elasticity of supply: the percentage change in quantity supplied divided by the percentage change in price; *see also* elasticity of supply

price searcher: a firm that must search for the profit-maximizing price because it faces a downward-sloping demand curve (if it is a seller) or an upward-sloping supply curve (if it is a buyer); often used as a synonym for monopoly or monopsony

price-support program: a government program that mandates minimum prices for crops

price taker: any economic agent that takes the market price as given; often used as a synonym for a firm operating in a market characterized by pure competition

private costs: costs incurred by the relevant decision maker

product differentiation: distinguishing products by brand name, color, and other minor attributes

productivity: output produced per unit of input

profit: income generated by selling something for a higher price than was paid for it; in production, the income generated is the difference between total revenues received from consumers who purchase the goods and the total cost of producing those goods

property and contract rights: legal rules governing the use and exchange of property, and enforceable agreements between people or businesses

property rights: set of rules specifying how a good may be used and exchanged

protectionism: the imposition of rules designed to protect certain individuals or firms from competition, usually competition from imported goods

proven reserves: estimated quantities of oil and gas that geological and engineering data demonstrate with reasonable certainty to be recoverable in future years from known reservoirs under existing economic and operating conditions

purchasing power: ability or means to acquire goods and services

purchasing power parity: the principle that, in long-run equilibrium, all goods traded internationally must trade at the same price, adjusted for exchange rates

pure competition: a market structure in which participants individually have no influence over market prices; all act as price takers

quantity demanded: the amount of a good or service chosen at a particular price for that item

quota: a limit on the amount of a good or an activity; often used in international trade to limit the amount of some foreign good that may be imported into a country

rate of return: the net benefit, in percentage terms, of engaging in an activity; for example, if the investment of $1.00 yields a gross return of $1.20, the net benefit is $0.20 and the rate of return is $0.20/$1.00 = 20 percent

rational ignorance: a state in which knowledge is incomplete because obtaining perfect information is too costly

real, or inflation-adjusted, cost: the cost of an item adjusted for changes in the overall price level

real per capita income: gross domestic product (GDP) corrected for inflation and divided by population

real price: a price that is adjusted for inflation and is expressed in terms of some base year

real wage: a wage that is adjusted for inflation and is expressed in terms of some base year

real property: land, those structures and equipment firmly attached thereto, and all resources under the land

relative prices: the costs of goods, expressed in terms of other goods or in terms of a basic bundle of goods

rent control: a system in which the government tells building owners how much they can charge for rent

resource: any input used in the production of desired goods and services

revealed preferences: the likes and dislikes of consumers, as demonstrated by the choices they make in the marketplace

rule of law: the principle that relations between individuals, businesses, and the government are governed by clearly enumerated rules that apply to everyone in society

scarce: not free; something must be sacrificed to obtain

scarce good: any good that commands a positive price

scarcity: state of nature in which resources are limited even though wants are unlimited; scarcity means that nature does not freely provide as much of everything as people want

shortage: situation in which an excess quantity is demanded or an insufficient quantity is supplied; the difference between the quantity demanded and the quantity supplied at a specific price below the market-clearing price

social cost: the full cost that society bears when a resource-using action occurs; for example, the social cost of driving a car is equal to all private costs plus any additional cost that other members of society bear (such as air pollution and traffic congestion)

Social Security: an entitlement program operated by the federal government in which taxes are levied on workers to enable payment of pensions to retirees

solvent: in a financial condition in which the value of one's assets is greater than the value of one's liabilities

static analysis: any assessment of the economic impact of a policy that does not fully take into account the induced responses to that policy

stock: the quantity of something at a particular point in time; an inventory of goods is a stock, as is a bank account at a point in time; stocks are defined independent of time, although they are assessed at a point in time

subsidies: government payments for the production of specific goods, generally designed to raise the profits of the firms receiving the subsidies and often intended to increase the output of the subsidized goods

subsidization: the act of providing subsidies

substitute: a good having the property that a change in its price will cause the *demand* for another good to change in the same direction

supply: the willingness and ability to sell goods

supply curve: a graphic representation of supply, which slopes upward (has a positive slope), reflecting the positive relationship between price and quantity supplied

supply schedule: a set of prices and the quantity supplied at each price; a schedule showing the rate of planned production at each relative price for a specified time period

support price: the minimum price that farmers are guaranteed to receive for their crop, as set by the federal government; if the market price falls below the support price, the government purchases enough of the crop to bring the market price up to the support price

surplus: excess quantity supplied or an insufficient quantity demanded; the difference between the quantity supplied and the quantity demanded at a price above the market-clearing price; as applied to the government budget, an excess of tax receipts over expenditures

target price: the minimum price that farmers are guaranteed to receive for their crop, as set by the federal government; if the market price falls below the target price, farmers receive a payment equal to the difference between the two (multiplied by their production of the crop)

tariff: a tax levied on imports

tax credit: an offset against current or future income taxes

tax rate: proportion of the value of the taxed item that is collected in taxes

tax revenue: total dollar value of taxes collected

technological change: a change in the set of feasible production possibilities, typically the result of the productive implementation of new knowledge

trade barriers: any rules having the effect of reducing the amount of international exchange; tariffs and quotas are trade barriers

traded goods: those exchanged across national borders

trade-off: term relating to opportunity cost. To get a desired economic good, it is necessary to trade-off (give up) some other desired economic good in a situation of scarcity; a trade-off involves making a sacrifice to obtain something

transaction costs: costs of conducting exchanges of goods

Type I error: an error of commission, such as might arise when an unsafe drug is mistakenly permitted to be sold

Type II error: an error of omission, such as might arise if a beneficial drug is mistakenly prevented from reaching the market

unemployment rate: the percentage of the labor force that is looking for and able to work, but is not currently working

user fees: charges imposed for the use of a good or service; often applied to the charges applied by governments for the use of government-owned resources, ranging from roads to parks

voucher: a document that authorizes a person to receive a specified dollar amount of services at no charge

want: the amount of a good or service that would be chosen if the price of that good or service were zero

white-collar jobs: employment in which workers rely chiefly on their intellect and knowledge rather than their physical skills

willingness to pay: the maximum price someone would voluntarily pay for a good or service

World Trade Organization (WTO): an association of more than 145 nations that helps reduce trade barriers among its members and settles international trade disputes among them

zone pricing: setting different retail prices in different geographic areas, depending on the characteristics of customers in those areas; a practice of major oil companies

Selected References

Chapter 1 Death by Bureaucrat

Kazman, Sam. "Deadly Overcaution: FDA's Drug Approval Process." *Journal of Regulation and Social Cost* 1, no. 1 (1990): 35–54.

Peltzman, Sam. "An Evaluation of Consumer Protection Legislation: The 1962 Drug Amendments." *Journal of Political Economy* 81, no. 1 (1973): 1049–1091.

Walker, Steven. "S.O.S. to the FDA." *Wall Street Journal Online*, August 26, 2003. (online.wsj.com/article/SB106185410295150100-search.html)

Chapter 2 Supersize It

Finkelstein, Eric A et al., "Obesity and Severe Obesity Forecasts through 2030." *American Journal of Preventive Medicine* 42, no. 6 (June 2012): 563–560.

Kuchler, Fran, and Elise Golan. "Is There a Role for Government in Reducing Overweight and Obesity?" *Choices* (Fall 2004): 41–45.

Loureiro, Mauro. "Obesity: Economic Dimensions of a "Super Size" Problem." *Choices* (Fall 2004): 35–39.

Ogden, Cynthia L. et al., "Prevalence of Overweight and Obesity in the United States, 1999–2004." *Journal of the American Medical Association* 295, no. 13 (April 2006): 1549–1555.

Philpson, Tomas, Carolanne Dai, Lorens Helmshen, and J. N. Variyam. *The Economics of Obesity: A Report of the Workshop Held at USDA's Economic Research Service.* E-FAN-04-004, Economic Research Service. Washington, D.C.: USDA, 2004.

Chapter 3 Flying the Friendly Skies?

Mitchell Mark L. and Michael T. Maloney, "Crisis in the Cockpit? The Role of Market Forces in Promoting Air Travel Safety." *Journal of Law and Economics* 32, no. 2 (1989): 139–184.

www.airsafe.com. Statistics on airline safety. www1.faa.gov. Official Web site of the Federal Aviation Administration.

Chapter 4 The Mystery of Wealth

Acemoglu, Daron, and James Robinson. *Why Nations Fail.* New York: Crown. 2012.

Easterly William and Ross Levine. "Tropics, Germs, and Crops: How Endowments Influence Economic Development." *Journal of Monetary Economics* 50, no. 1 (2003): 3–39.

Mahoney Paul G. "The Common Law and Economic Growth: Hayek Might Be Right." *Journal of Legal Studies* 30, no. 3 (2001): 503–525.

Chapter 5   Surf Gangs

Acheson James M. *The Lobster Gangs of Maine*. Hanover, NH: University Press of New England, 1988.
Demsetz Harold. "Towards a Theory of Property Rights." *American Economic Review*, 57, no. 2 (May 1967): 347–357.
Kaffine Daniel T. "Quality and the Commons: The Surf Gangs of California." *Journal of Law and Economics* 52, no. 4 (October 2009): 727–743.

Chapter 6   Sex, Booze, and Drugs

Becker Gary, Kevin M. Murphy, and Michael Grossman. "The Market for Illegal Goods: The Case of Drugs." *Journal of Political Economy* 114, no. 1 (2006): 38–60.
Benjamin Daniel K. and Roger LeRoy Miller. *Undoing Drugs: Beyond Legalization*. New York: Basic Books, 1993.
Hardy, Quentin. "Inside Dope." *Forbes*, November 10, 2003, pp. 146–154.
Miron Jeffrey A. and Jeffrey Zwiebel. "Alcohol Consumption during Prohibition." *American Economic Review* 81, no. 2 (1991): 242–247.

Chapter 7   All Fracked Up

Hitzman Murray W. *et al.*, *Induced Seismic Potential in Energy Technologies*. Washington DC: National Academy of Sciences, 2012.
Moniz Ernest J. *et al.*, *The Future of Natural Gas*. Boston, MA: Massachusetts Institute of Technology, 2012.
Whitney Gene, Carl E. Behrens and Carol Glover. *U.S. Fossil Fuel: Terminology, Reporting, and Summary*. Washington DC: Congressional Research Service, November 10, 2010.

Chapter 8   Kidneys for Sale

Adler Jerry. "Are Kidneys a Commodity?" *Newsweek*, May 26, 2008.
Harrington David E. and Edward A. Sayre. "Paying for Bodies, But Not for Organs." *Regulation*, Winter 2006–2007, pp. 14–19.
Meckler Laura. "A Shortage of Available Kidneys Inspires a Radical Idea: Organ Sales." *Wall Street Journal*, November 16, 2007.
"The Gap between Supply and Demand." *Economist*, October 9, 2008.

Chapter 9   Are We Running Out of Water?

Anderson Terry L., Brandon Scarborough and Lawrence R. Watson. *Tapping Water Markets*. New York: Routledge, 2012.
Casselman Ben. "Desperate Sprinklers." *Wall Street Journal*, July 20, 2007.
Libecap Gary. *Owens Valley Revisited: A Reassessment of the West's First Great Water Transfer*. Stanford, CA: Stanford University Press, 2007.
Olmstead Sheila M. and Robert N. Stavins. "Comparing Price and Nonprice Approaches to Urban Water Conservation." *Water Resources Research* 45, 2009: W04301.

Santos Fernanda. "Inch by Inch, Great Lakes Shrink, and Cargo Carriers Face Losses." *New York Times*, October 22, 2007.

Yardley Jim. "Beneath Booming Cities, China's Future Is Drying Up." *New York Times*, September 28, 2007.

CHAPTER 10   Bankrupt Landlords, from Sea to Shining Sea

Downs Anthony. *Residential Rent Controls: An Evaluation*. Washington, D.C.: Urban Land Institute, 1988.

Glaeser Edward L. and Erzo F. P. Luttmer. "The Misallocation of Housing under Rent Control." *American Economic Review* 93, no. 4 (2003): 1027–1046.

housingnyc.com/html/guidelines/guidelines.html. Official Web site of the New York City Rent Guidelines Board.

smgov.net/Summary_of_Regulations.aspx. Official Web site of the City of Santa Monica Rent Control Board.

CHAPTER 11   (Why) Are Women Paid Less?

Becker Elizabeth and Cotton M. Lindsay. "The Limits of the Wage Impact of Discrimination." *Managerial and Decision Economics* 26 (2005): 513–525.

Becker Gary. *The Economics of Discrimination*. Chicago: University of Chicago Press, 1957.

Heckman James J. "Detecting Discrimination." *Journal of Economic Perspectives* 12, no. 1 (1998): 101–116.

CHAPTER 12   Over $1 Trillion in College Debt, and Rising

Avery Christopher and Sarah Turner. "Student Loans: Do College Students Borrow Too Much—Earn Not Enough?" *Journal of Economic Perspectives* 26, no. 1 (Winter 2012): 165–192.

Casselman Ben. "The Cost of Dropping Out." *Wall Street Journal*. November 22, 2012.

Hoxby Caroline M., ed., *College Choices: The Economics of Where to Go, When to Go, and How to Pay for It*, Chicago, IL, University of Chicago Press, 2004.

Rosen Andrew S. 2011 *"Change.edu: Rebooting for the New Talent Economy."* Kaplan Publishing, New York.

CHAPTER 13   The Effects of the Minimum Wage

Baker Michael, Dwayne Benjamin and Shuchita Stanger. "The Highs and Lows of the Minimum Wage Effects: A Time-Series Cross-Section Study of the Canadian Law." *Journal of Labor Economics* 17, no. 2 (1999): 318–350.

Card David and Alan Krueger. "Minimum Wages and Employment: A Case Study of the Fast-Food Industry in New Jersey and Pennsylvania." *American Economic Review* 84, no. 3 (1994): 772–793.

Neumark David and William Wascher. "Minimum Wages and Employment: A Case Study of the Fast-Food Industry in New Jersey and Pennsylvania: Comment." *American Economic Review* 90, no. 5 (2000): 1362–1396.

Rottenberg Simon (ed.). *The Economics of Legal Minimum Wages.* Washington, D.C.: American Enterprise Institute, 1981.

CHAPTER 14   Immigration, Superstars, and Poverty

Borjas George. *Heaven's Door: Immigration Policy and the American Economy.* Princeton, NJ: Princeton University Press, 2001.

Rosen Sherwin. "The Economics of Superstars." *American Economic Review* 71, no. 5 (1981): 845–858.

U.S. Bureau of the Census. "The Effects of Government Taxes and Transfers on Income and Poverty, 2005." March 2007. (http://www.census.gov/prod/2007pubs/p60-232.pdf)

CHAPTER 15   The (Dis)Incentives of Higher Taxes

Feenberg Daniel R. and James M. Poterba. "The Alternative Minimum Tax and Effective Marginal Tax Rates." *National Tax Journal* 57, no. 2 (2004): 407–427.

Harberger Arnold. *Taxation and Welfare.* New York: Little, Brown and Company, 1974.

Mitchell, Daniel J. "What Can the United States Learn from the Nordic Model?" *Cato Institute Policy Analysis*, November 5, 2007.

CHAPTER 16   Patent Trolls and Seed Monopolies

Benjamin Daniel K. and Roger C. Kormendi. "The Interrelationship between the Markets for New and Used Durable Goods." *Journal of Law and Economics* 17, no. 2 (October 1974): 381–402.

Neuman William. "Rapid Rise in Seed Prices Draws U.S. Scrutiny." *New York Times*, March 11, 2010.

Pollack Andrew. "Study Says Overuse Threatens Gains from Modified Crops." *New York Times*, April 15, 2010.

Varchaver Nicholas. "Who's Afraid of Nathan Myhrvold?" *CNNMoney.com*, June 26, 2006. (Accessed October 31, 2010)

CHAPTER 17   Contracts, Combinations, and Conspiracies

Kanfer, Steven. *The Last Empire: DeBeers, Diamonds, and the World.* New York: Farrar, Straus & Giroux, 1993.

www.eia.doe.gov. Official Web site of the Energy Information Administration.

Zimbalist Andrew. *Unpaid Professionals: Commercialism and Conflict in Big-Time College Sports.* Princeton, NJ: Princeton University Press, 2001.

Chapter 18   Coffee, Tea, or Tuition-Free?

Chevalier Judith and Austan Goolsbee. "Measuring Prices and Price Competition Online: Amazon.com versus BarnesandNoble.com." *Quantitative Marketing and Economics* 1, no. 2 (2003): 203–222.

McCartney Scott. "How Airlines Spend Your Airfare." *Wall Street Journal*. June 6, 2012. (http://online.wsj.com/article/SB100014240527023032966045774505811 396602106.html)

Odlyzko Andrew. *Privacy, Economics, and Price Discrimination on the Internet.* St. Paul: University of Minnesota, Digital Technology Center, 2003.

"They're Watching You." *Economist*, October 18, 2003, p. 77.

Chapter 19   Keeping the Competition Out

Lipton Eric. "Finding the Intersection of Supply and Demand." *New York Times*, November 23, 2003, p. 31.

McCartney Scott. "How Airlines Spend Your Airfare." *Wall Street Journal*. June 6, 2012. (online.wsj.com/article/SB10001424052702303296604577450581396602106.html)

www.schallerconsult.com/taxi/topics.htm. Facts on the New York City taxicab and taxi medallion markets.

Chapter 20   The Green Energy Deception

Conca James. "The Direct Costs of Energy: Why Solar Will Continue to Lag Hydro and Nukes." *Forbes*, July 8, 2012. (www.forbes.com/sites/jamesconca/2012/07/08/the-direct-costs-of-energy-hydronuclear-best-solar-still-lagging/)

Lantz Eric, Ryan Wisser and Maureen Hand. IES Wind Task 26: The Past and Future of Wind Energy." National Renewable Energy Laboratory, Golden, CO, May 2012.

Lipton Eric and Clifford Krause. "A Gold Rush of Subsidies in the Search for Clean Energy." *New York Times*, November 11, 2011.

Ridley Matt. *The Rational Optimist*. HarperCollins, New York, 2010.

Romer Christina D. "Do Manufacturers Need Special Treatment?" *New York Times*, February 4, 2012.

Congressional Budget's Office "Effects of Federal Tax Credits for the Purchase of Electric Vehicles," www.cbo.gov/publication/43576

Chapter 21   Save a Turtle, Kill a Person

Balazs George H. "Impact of Ocean Debris on Marine Turtles: Entanglement and Ingestion." *Proceedings of the Workshop on the Fate and Impact of Marine Debris*, 27-29 November 1984. Richard S. Shomura and Howard O. Yoshida (Editors), Southwest Fisheries Center, Honolulu Laboratory, National Marine Fisheries Service, NOAA, Honolulu.

Klick Jonathan and Joshua D. Wright. "Grocery Bags and Foodborne Illness." Property and Environment Research Center (PERC) Working Paper, September 23, 2012.

Johnson Harold. "Too Good to Be True: Sea Mammals, Plastic Pollution and a Modern Chimera." *Scientific American Online*, October 13, 2011. (blogs. scientificamerican.com/guest-blog/2011/10/13/too-good-to-be-true-sea-mammals-plastic-pollution-and-a-modern-chimera)

CHAPTER 22   Raising Less Corn and More Hell

Becker Elizabeth. "U.S. Corn Subsidies Said to Damage Mexico: Study Finds Farmers Lose Livelihoods." *New York Times*, August 27, 2003, p. C4.

Edwards Chris and Dan DeHaven. *Save the Farms—End the Subsidies*. Washington, D.C.: Cato Institute, 2002.

Fackler Martin. "Japanese Farmers Losing Clout." *Wall Street Journal*, February 20, 2004, p. A10.

CHAPTER 23   The Pension Crisis

Brainard Keith. *Public Fund Survey Summary of Findings for FY2009*. National Association of State Retirement Administrators, October 2010.

Fitch Stephan. "Guilt-Edged Pensions." *Forbes*, February 16, 2009, pp. 79–84.

Malanga Steve. "How States Hide Their Budget Deficits." *Wall Street Journal*, August 23, 2010.

Maher Kris, Bobby White and Valerie Bauerlein. "Hard Times Spread for Cities." *Wall Street Journal*. August 10, 2012.

"Review and Outlook: The Union Pension Bomb". *Wall Street Journal*. May 16, 2012.

The Pew Center of the States. *The Trillion Dollar Gap: Unfunded State Retirement Systems and the Roads to Reform*. Washington, D.C.: The Pew Charitable Trust, February 2010.

CHAPTER 24   The Graying of America

Council of Economic Advisers. "Restoring Solvency to Social Security." *Economic Report of the President*. Washington, D.C.: Government Printing Office, 2004, Ch. 6.

Miron Jeffrey A. and David N. Weil. "The Genesis and Evolution of Social Security." In *The Defining Moment: The Great Depression and the American Economy in the Twentieth Century*, eds. Michael D. Bordo, Claudia Goldin and Eugene N. White. Chicago: University of Chicago Press, 1998, pp. 297–322.

CHAPTER 25   Save That Species

Anderson Terry L. and Peter J. Hill. *The Not So Wild, Wild West: Property Rights on the Frontier*. Stanford: Stanford University Press, 2004.

Coase Ronald. "The Problem of Social Cost." *Journal of Law and Economics* 3 (1960): 1–44.

Costello Christopher, Steven D. Gaines and John Lyman. "Can Catch Shares Prevent Fisheries Collapse?" *Science* 321, no. 5826 (September 2008): 1678–1681.

Gates C. Cormack, Curtis H. Freese, Peter J. P. Gogan and Mandy Kotzman. *American Bison: Status Survey and Conservation Guidelines*. International Union for Conservation of Nature: Gland, Switzerland, 2010

Grafton R. Quentin, Dale Squires and Kevin J. Fox. "Private Property and Economic Efficiency: A Study of A Common-Pool Resource." *Journal of Law & Economics* 43, no. 2 (2000): 679–713.

Lueck Dean and Jeffrey A. Michael. "Preemptive Habitat Destruction under the Endangered Species Act." *Journal of Law & Economics* 46, no. 1 (2003): 27–60.

CHAPTER 26   Greenhouse Economics

Bradsher Keith. "China's Boom Adds to Global Warming Problem." *New York Times*, October 22, 2003, p. A1.

Castles Ian and David Henderson. "The IPCC Emission Scenarios: An Economic–Statistical Critique." *Energy and Environment* 14, nos. 2, 3 (2003): 159–185.

Lomborg Bjorn. *The Skeptical Environmentalist*. New York: Cambridge University Press, 2001.

Sohngen Brent and Robert Mendelsohn. "Valuing the Impact of Large-Scale Ecological Change in a Market: The Effect of Climate Change on U.S. Timber." *American Economic Review* 89, no. 4 (1999): 686–710.

CHAPTER 27   Ethanol Madness

Barrionuevo Alexei. "Boom in Ethanol Reshapes Economy of Heart-land." *New York Times*, June 25, 2006, p. 1.

Environmental Protection Agency. *Regulatory Announcement: Removal of Reformulated Gasoline Oxygen Content Requirement and Revision of Commingling Prohibition to Address Non-Oxygenated Reformulated Gasoline*. Document no. EPA420-F-06–020. Washington, D.C.: Environmental Protection Agency, February 2006.

Tokgoz Simla. "Policy and Competitiveness of U.S. and Brazilian Ethanol." *Iowa Ag Review Online*, Spring 2006. (www.card.iastate.edu/iowa_ag_review/ spring_06/article3.aspx)

www.eia.doe.gov. Official Web site of the Energy Information Administration.

CHAPTER 28   The Trashman Cometh

Benjamin Daniel K. *Recycling Myths Revisited*. no. PS-47. Bozeman, MT: Property and Environment Research Center, 2010.

Fullerton Don and Thomas C. Kinnaman. "Household Responses to Pricing Garbage by the Bag." *American Economic Review* 88, no. 2 (1996): 971–984.

Hocking Martin B. "Paper versus Polystyrene: A Complex Choice." *Science* 251, no. 4993 (February 1991): 504–505.

Hocking Martin B. "Disposable Cups Have Eco-Merit." *Nature* 369, no. 107 (May 1994): 107.

Porter Richard C. *The Economics of Waste*. Washington, DC: Resources for the Future, 2002.

Rathje William and Cullen Murphy. *Rubbish: The Archeology of Garbage.* New York: HarperCollins, 1992.

CHAPTER 29   The Economics of the Big Mac

Ashenfelter, Orley, "Comparing Real Wages," NBER Working Paper No. 18006, April, 2012 (www.nber.org/papers/w18006)

Ashenfelter Orley and Stepan Jurajda, "Cross-Country Comparisons of Wage Rates: The McWage Index," Industrial Relations Section, Princeton University, Princeton, NJ, August 2009.

Clementi Fabio et al., "A Big Mac Test of Price Dynamics and Dispersion of Across Euro Area," *Economic Bulletin*, Vol. 30, Issue 3, August 2010, pp. 2037–2053.

CHAPTER 30   Globalization and the Wealth of America

Eichengreen Barry. "The Political Economy of the Smoot–Hawley Tariff." *Research in Economic History* 12, no. 1 (1989): 1–43.

Federal Reserve Bank of Dallas. *The Fruits of Free Trade.* Annual Report. Dallas, TX: Federal Reserve Bank, 2002.

Irwin, Douglas A. "From Smoot–Hawley to Reciprocal Trade Agreements: Changing the Course of U.S. Trade Policy in the 1930s." In *The Defining Moment: The Great Depression and the American Economy in the Twentieth Century*, eds. Michael D. Bordo, Claudia Goldin and Eugene N. White. Chicago: University of Chicago Press, 1998, pp. 325–352.

CHAPTER 31   The $750,000 Steelworker

Berry Steven, James Levinsohn and Ariel Pakes. "Voluntary Export Restraints on Automobiles: Evaluating a Trade Policy." *American Economic Review* 89, no. 3 (1999): 400–430.

Crandall Robert W. "The Effects of U.S. Trade Protection for Autos and Steel." *Brookings Papers on Economic Activity*, no. 1 (1987): 271–288.

INDEX